IMAGES
of America

WALLAND

On the Cover: This mill, known through much of the 1900s as Peery's Mill and later as Little River Mill, was located on Little River at the Melrose Station, between the Hubbard and Walland stations of the Southern Railway. In the acts of 1801, Little River was declared navigable to Tuckaleechee (in Townsend) by the Tennessee General Assembly. In 1842, Samuel Henry obtained a permit to build a mill. Later, Scales Amerine took over the 1842 permit of Samuel Henry. Bud Hitch bought the mill in 1906. In 1911, Hitch formed a partnership with Ira W. Peery and William Wynn Peery. The trade name of Peery Brothers was soon established and remained in business for 40 years, producing flour and corn meal. In 1953, Fred Frost bought the mill. His widow sold it in 1972 to Lynn Maples of Knoxville, who in turn sold it to George Edgeman. Edgeman sold it to Richard Fuller, and Fuller's estate sold it to Dick Evey, who was the owner when it burned in 1986. This photograph was taken in August 20, 1886, by William Cox Cochran, who visited this area in 1886 and identified it as Neubern's Mills and Dam, Little River below Gap. It had been owned by John G. Newbert, so the spelling of the name may have been changed. (Courtesy of the Great Smoky Mountains Regional Project, the University of Tennessee Libraries, Knoxville, Tennessee, William Cox Cochran Collection.)

IMAGES
of America

WALLAND

Missy Tipton Green
and Paulette Ledbetter

ARCADIA
PUBLISHING

ISBN 978-1-4671-2689-2

Published by Arcadia Publishing
Charleston, South Carolina

Printed in the United States of America

Library of Congress Control Number: 2017946346

For all general information, please contact Arcadia Publishing:
Telephone 843-853-2070
Fax 843-853-0044
E-mail sales@arcadiapublishing.com
For customer service and orders:
Toll-Free 1-888-313-2665

Visit us on the Internet at www.arcadiapublishing.com

This book is dedicated to the memory of Inez McCauley Adams for her willingness to give all of her time and energy to something that was important to her.

Contents

Acknowledgments

During all of the years of researching and digging around in history, we have found that without our many friends and family donating to our cause, we could have never completed any of our journeys of producing history books. We do these books to preserve history that we are afraid will be lost if it is not documented. History is defined as the study of the human past as it is described in the written documents left by human beings. As collectors of the past, we recognize that the rock-solid base can sometimes be the same as quicksand, that bits of our story are yet untold, and that what has been told comes tainted by the conditions of what we are today. The results are often displayed in historical documentation such as books. This book has been really close to our hearts. Missy's maternal family is the Everetts, Paulette's paternal family is the Lawsons, and Paulette's husband David's family is the Ledbetters. Many photographs of the late Inez McCauley Adams collection were donated by her husband, Earl Adams Jr. Inez and Earl have never been selfish with their knowledge or their collection of photographs. Earl has given much time to answer questions when we did not understand something. Many thanks to Gladys Oliver Burns, Beverly and the late Benny Dalton, Todd Teffeteller, Bobbie Walker King, Linda Christopher Baker, Wayne Everett, Sam and Barbara Sloan, Joan Vansickle Sloan and Bill Sloan, Jack and Vonnie Walker, Velda Flynn Powell, Jerry Murphy, Carolyn Gamble Sloan, Mike White, Carol Hatcher Ellis, Mable Compton Whitehead, Marie Hatcher McClanahan, Rita Martin Buchanan, Gail Tipton Stumpf, Hilda Gourley Long, John Edmondson, Bertie West, Lura West Myers, Evelyn West Parrott, Terry Myers Bivens, Evelyn Dalton, Doris Ridings, Jeremy Stephens, Donna Carver Sloan, Pat Proffitt Coppenger, Rodney Myers, Carolyn Lane, Mary Headrick, Allen Ledbetter, Jeanne Braun Whitehead, Sandy David Butler, Janie Coleman, Eddie Vittetoe, and Bill Huskey. Without all of these individuals giving stories, pictures, or information, this book could not have been completed. We hope that this will preserve the history of the Walland–Miller's Cove area of Blount County so that people can understand what life was like in this area. Last but not least, we thank our families for putting up with all of the stress that went into compiling this project.

INTRODUCTION

The community of Walland was known in earlier days as Murphy's Cove and Miller's Cove. This community is situated in a gap of the Chilhowee Mountains, formed by the flow of Little River. In the early pioneer days, it was called Murphy's Cove. About 1800, it became Miller's Cove due to brothers Alexander and Andrew Miller settling there.

Two forts protected this valley in the early days of settlement. James Henry's Fort or Station commanded the passage through the gap and the passage up Little River. Gambles Fort, built in 1790 by Josias Gamble, was near the present Coulter's Bridge.

Miller's Cove settlers made their living from the land, much of which had been acquired from land grants. Churches in the area began to be established around 1810, with the Miller's Cove Baptist Church the first permanent Baptist church in Blount County. In 1820, the Methodist denomination was established in Miller's Cove with both churches using the same building.

During the Civil War, Union sympathizers erected a flagpole at the gap of Chilhowee Mountain in the Miller's Cove area. A rally when the flag was raised was attended by about 1,500 men. At the same time in nearby Maryville, Tennessee, a unit of the Confederate cavalry was commissioned to disarm the people of the area. Before the unit left for nearby Tuckaleechee Cove, a local judge told the commanding Captain White that they would find the Stars and Stripes floating from a tall pole on the left side of the road just as they emerged from the narrow pass between two mountain peaks as they approached up Little River through Chilhowee Gap. The judge asked the captain not to disturb the flag: "This belongs to the mountain men; they placed it there; it belongs to them; if you leave it undisturbed you will be kindly treated on your trip; if you disturb it you will have to get out of those mountains." As they approached, the captain told them to lower their guns and made a speech. He said that this was the flag they were born under and under which many of their fathers had fought and many of them died. While they were now fighting under a different flag, it was still the flag of their fathers and should be honored for its history and for the memory of the blood poured out so freely by their brave ancestors in its defense. Instead of doing it any injury, he proposed that they salute it.

Following Captain White's leadership, they rode single file around the flagpole, lifted their hats and reverently bowed their heads. Forming twos, they moved on. They were unaware of any onlookers, but news of their saluting the flag had already reached Tuckaleechee Cove, their destination. Their honoring the flag saved them from a bloody reception but instead led them to a most kind and hospitable treatment.

The name of the community was changed to Walland when the Schlosser Leather Company came to Miller's Cove. The names of two officials, Walton and England, were combined to make as "Walland." Before the beginning of the 20th century, the first industry was established in Miller's Cove. George Amerine had a forge on Hesses Creek run by water power. The mine providing his iron ore was in West Miller's Cove on top of Chilhowee Mountain. In 1901, the Schlosser Tannery came to the Miller's Cove area and built the village that came to be known as

Walland. A famous resort hotel known as Chilhowee Inn was also built, as was a dam across Little River with a powerhouse. Walland was a thriving community boasting two railroads, industry, electricity in every home, the hotel, and a popular swimming beach. A covered bridge was built across Little River to the Schlosser Leather Company. The bridge was made of timber from the local farm of J.V. Martin.

The first nine-month school in Blount County was in Walland. When the tannery first started, the school term was six months. Tannery officials talked to Blount County School Board about extending the school term to nine months with Schlosser Leather Company paying for the extra three months. The Walland Post Office was opened in 1902, with earlier post offices at Miller's, Seaton, and Waters.

On January 7, 1931, with a blanket of snow on the valley, the tannery whistle began to blow, and it sounded as if the tannery was yelling for help. When the community woke up, it saw a red glow that covered the entire valley. Then it saw that the red glow was its livelihood, education, pride, and future for many going up in smoke.

One

West Miller's Cove

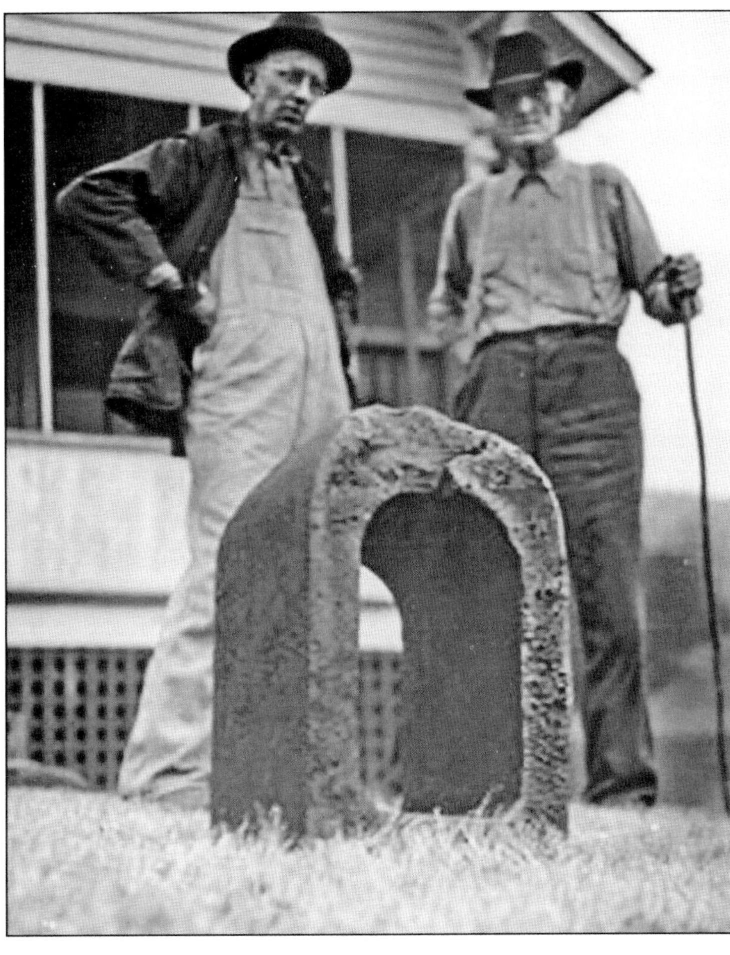

Prof. Henry R. Duncan (left) of the University of Tennessee is pictured with Abe Ogle (right) of West Miller's Cove and a bloomery forge hammer. In 1845, George Amerine built one of the largest and most productive forges in Blount County, Tennessee. It was located on Hess Creek in Miller's Cove. (Courtesy of the University of Tennessee, Knoxville Library, Albert "Dutch" Roth Digital Photograph Collection, Roth 0078, Great Smoky Mountain Regional Project.)

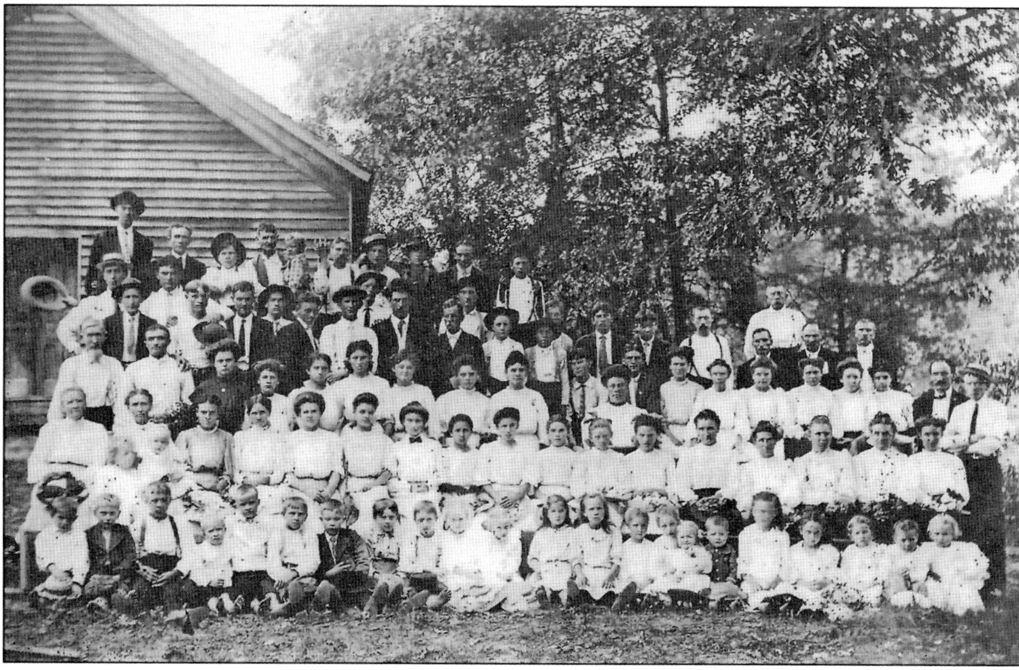

As early settlers came to Miller's Cove, establishing a church was one of their first priorities. This was about the time Blount County was being formed. A Baptist church was formed in nearby Tuckaleechee Cove in 1803, and in 1809 it divided into two congregations for the convenience of its members. Miller's Cove Baptist Church may be regarded as the oldest Baptist church in Blount County. Pictured are members of Miller's Cove Baptist Church. (Courtesy of Earl Adams Jr., Inez McCauley Adams Collection.)

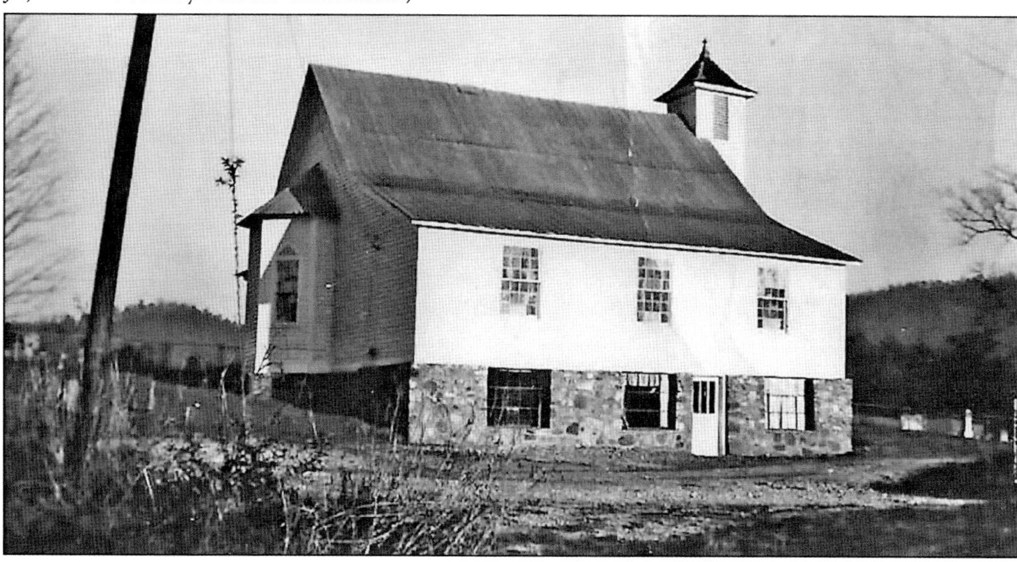

Vance Walker donated land for the first church about 1810, and land for the second church was donated by Alvin Walker about 1905. Miller's Cove Missionary Baptist Church was built in 1906 because the old log building was decaying. The Primitive Baptist and Missionary Baptist churches were built in very close proximity to each other bordering Miller's Cove Cemetery. (Courtesy of Earl Adams Jr., Inez McCauley Adams Collection.)

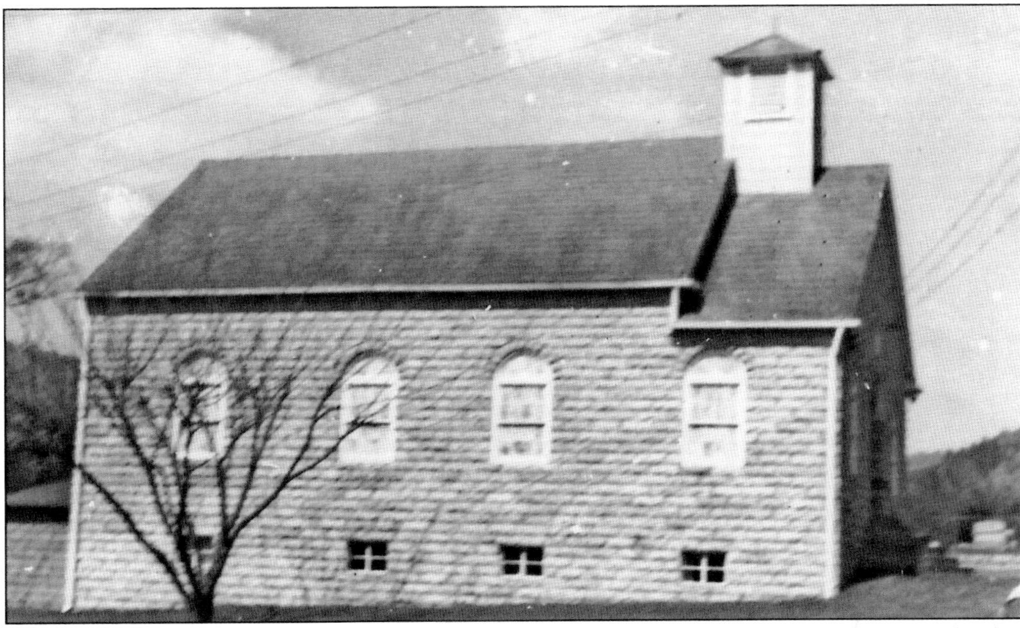

Tragedy came to the members of both of the Baptist churches in March 6, 1949. A fire had started in the Primitive Baptist church and soon spread to the Missionary Baptist church. The bell was the last thing to fall; all the sound was gone from it. The Missionary Baptist church was rebuilt in the same location of the earlier church. (Courtesy of Earl Adams Jr., Inez McCauley Adams Collection.)

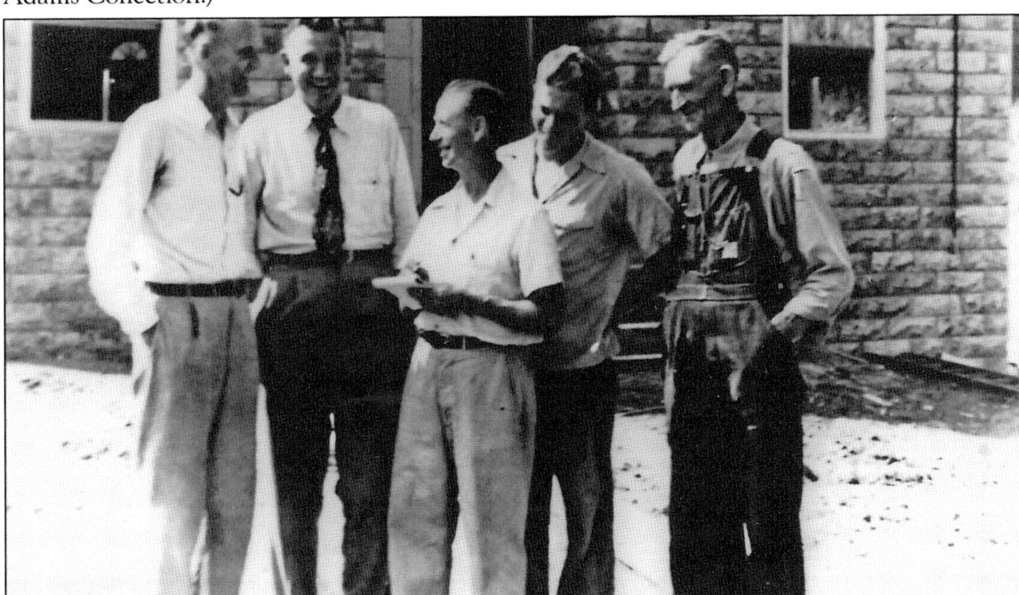

Builders of the new Miller's Cove Missionary Baptist Church include, from left to right, Leason Hearon, Rev. Elmer Hurst, Lawrence Whitehead, R.M. Everett, and his grandfather Manse Everett. Many members of the church as well as the community volunteered their time and work into completing the church building. The building was completed in October 1949 and was ready for services. (Courtesy of Earl Adams Jr., Inez McCauley Adams Collection.)

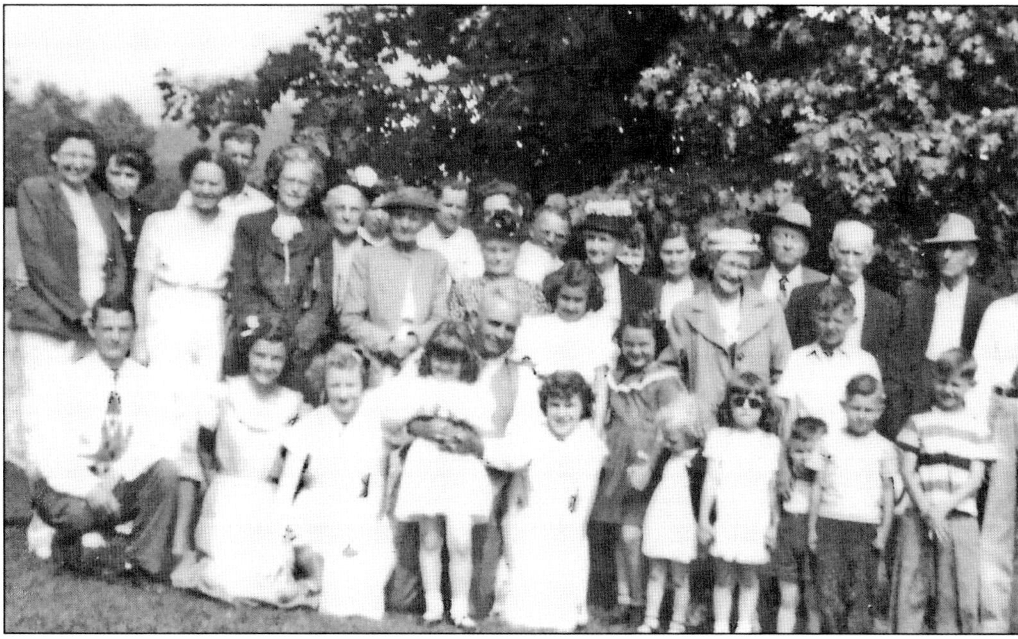

Members of the Miller's Cove Missionary Baptist Church are pictured. Many members can trace their families back to the early church. Many members of both the Primitive Baptist and Missionary Baptist churches are laid to rest in the nearby cemetery. (Courtesy of Earl Adams Jr., Inez McCauley Adams Collection.)

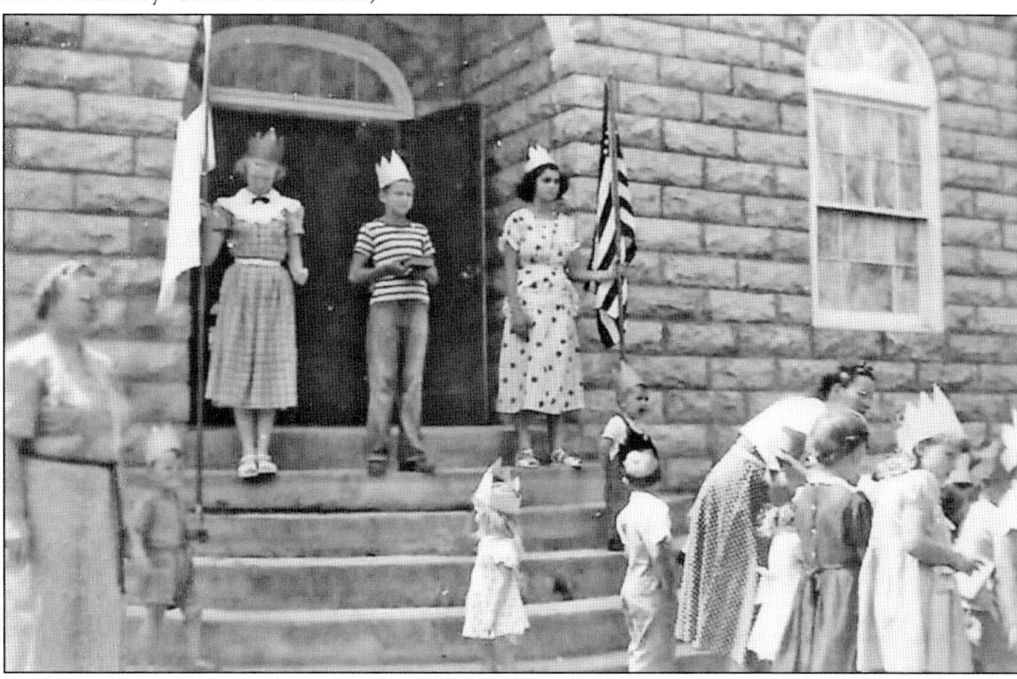

Vacation Bible School (VBS) was something that the community children looked forward to attending every year. This would take place in the summer months when school was not in session. VBS was a way for the church to teach local children about religion and to enjoy fellowship with one another. (Courtesy of Earl Adams Jr., Inez McCauley Adams Collection.)

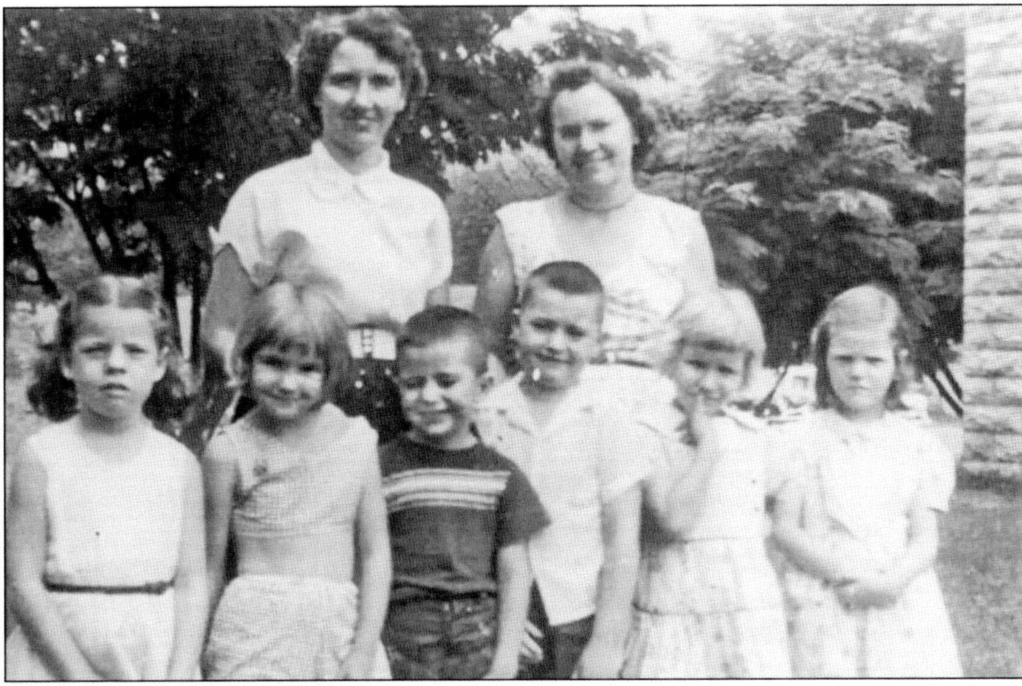

Many hours of Bible school was spent teaching the students to memorize and recite the books of the Bible. This was something that would benefit them for the many years ahead of them. Friday during Vacation Bible School at Miller's Cove Missionary Baptist was a very special treat for everyone. A watermelon split would be held in the backyard of the church. Pictured from left to right are (first row) Trudy Hurst, Donna Lawson, Mike White, Jerry Whitehead, Christina Hatcher, and Jody Murphy; (second row) teachers Aileene Emert and Suzie Flynn. (Courtesy of Earl Adams Jr., Inez McCauley Adams Collection.)

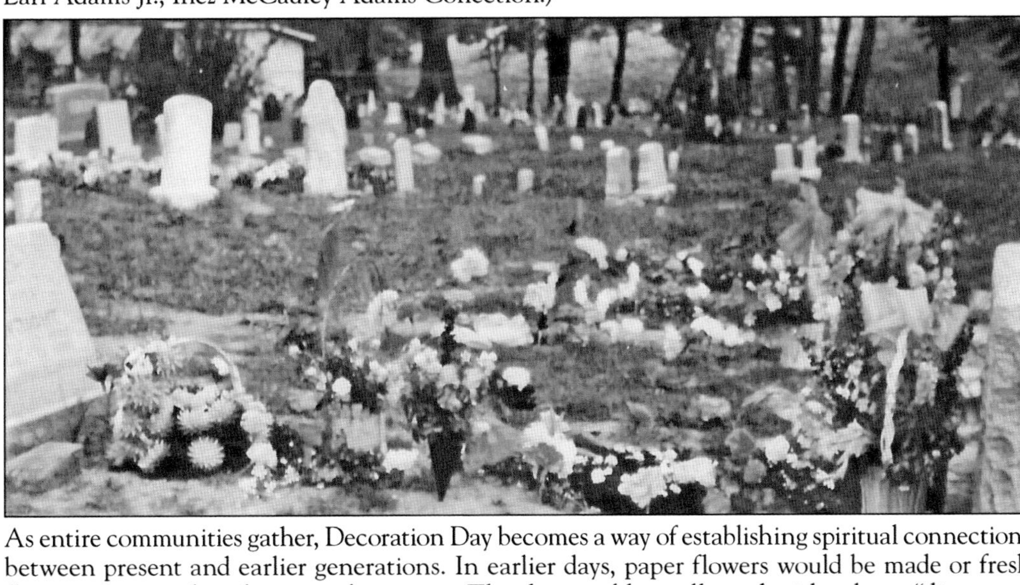

As entire communities gather, Decoration Day becomes a way of establishing spiritual connections between present and earlier generations. In earlier days, paper flowers would be made or fresh flowers were used to decorate the graves. The day would usually end with a large "dinner on the ground." (Courtesy of *Blackberry Farm: The Beginning* by John Edmondson and the Harris-Edmondson family archives.)

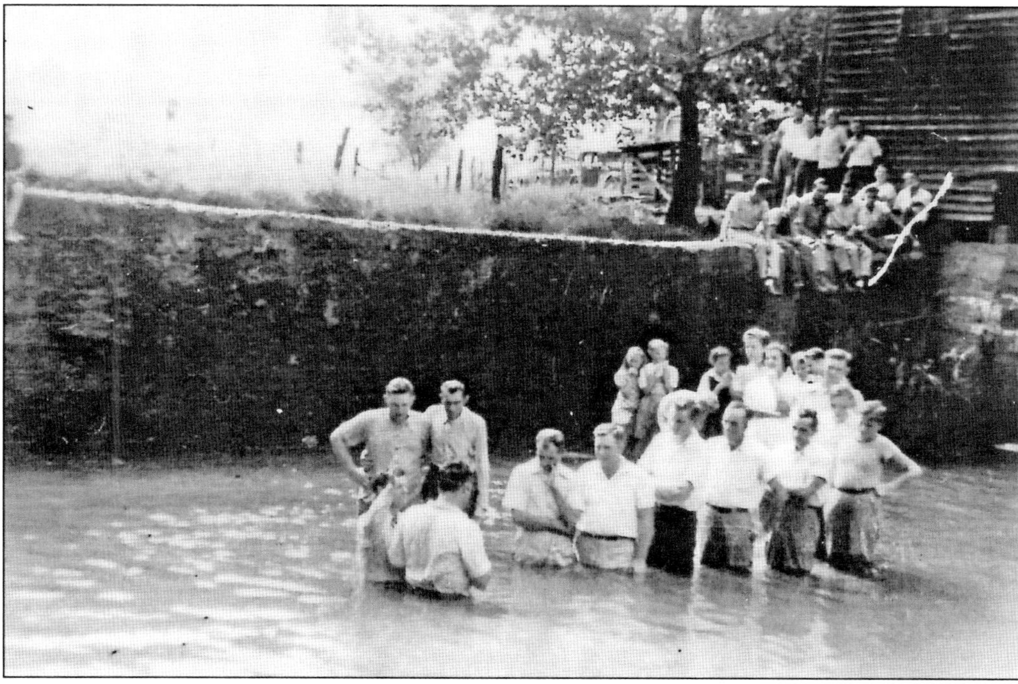

Matthew 28: 19–20 states, "Go ye, therefore, and teach all nations, baptizing them in the name of the Father, and of the Son, and of the Holy Spirit. Teaching them to observe all things whatsoever I have commanded you; and, lo, I am with you always, even unto the end of the age." This photograph shows a baptism at the Martin Mill dam. (Courtesy of Earl Adams Jr., Inez McCauley Adams Collection.)

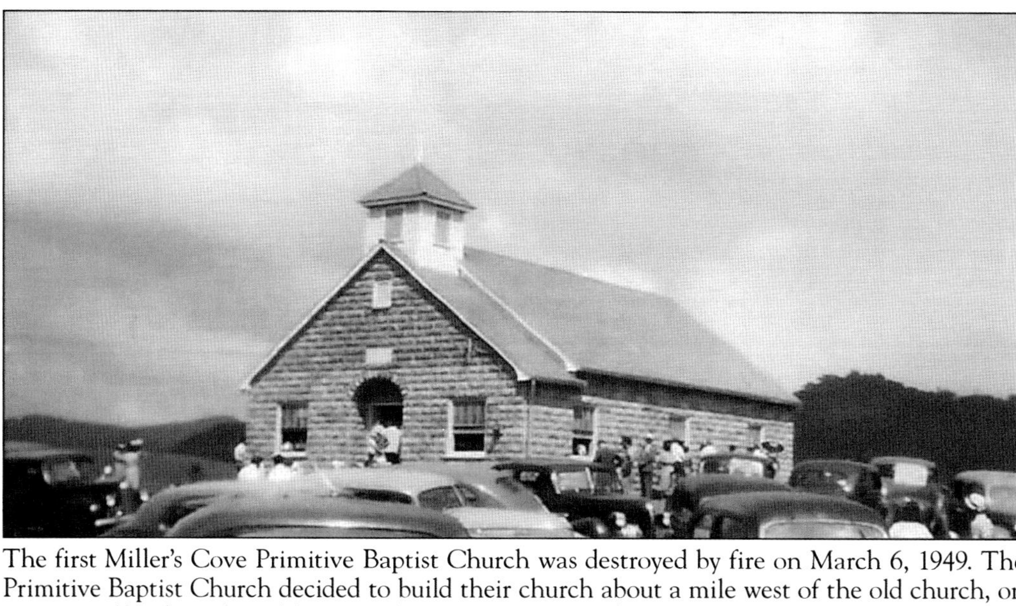

The first Miller's Cove Primitive Baptist Church was destroyed by fire on March 6, 1949. The Primitive Baptist Church decided to build their church about a mile west of the old church, on one acre of land purchased from Brother John Everett for $200. (Courtesy of Earl Adams Jr., Inez McCauley Adams Collection.)

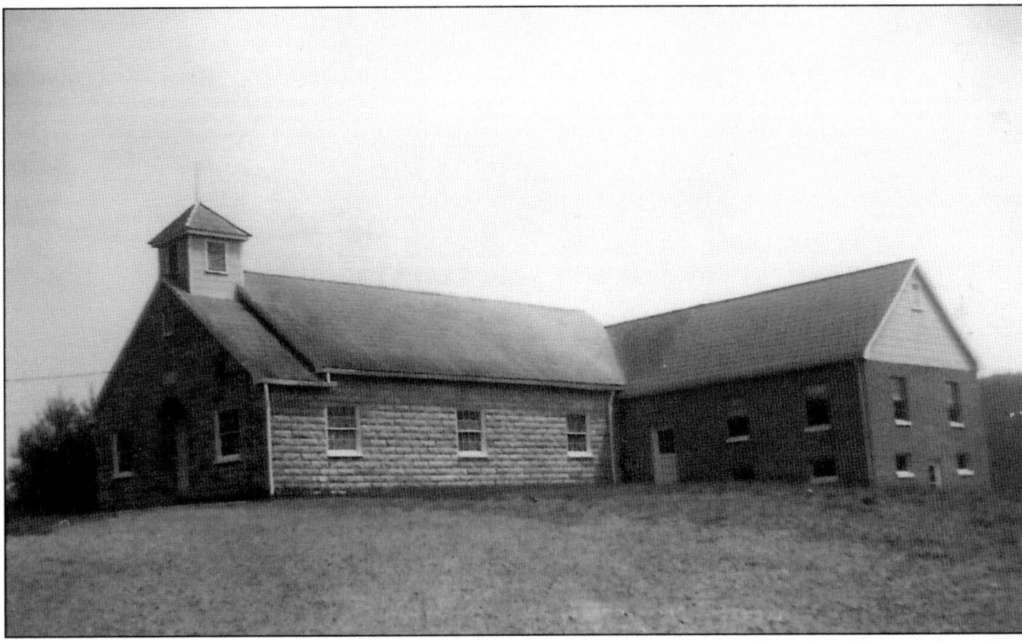

The new Miller's Cove Primitive Baptist Church was 32 feet wide and 50 feet long and made of stone-faced concrete blocks and wood. Many members of the church and the community donated materials and spent many hours together in the construction of the church. (Courtesy of Hilda Gourley Long.)

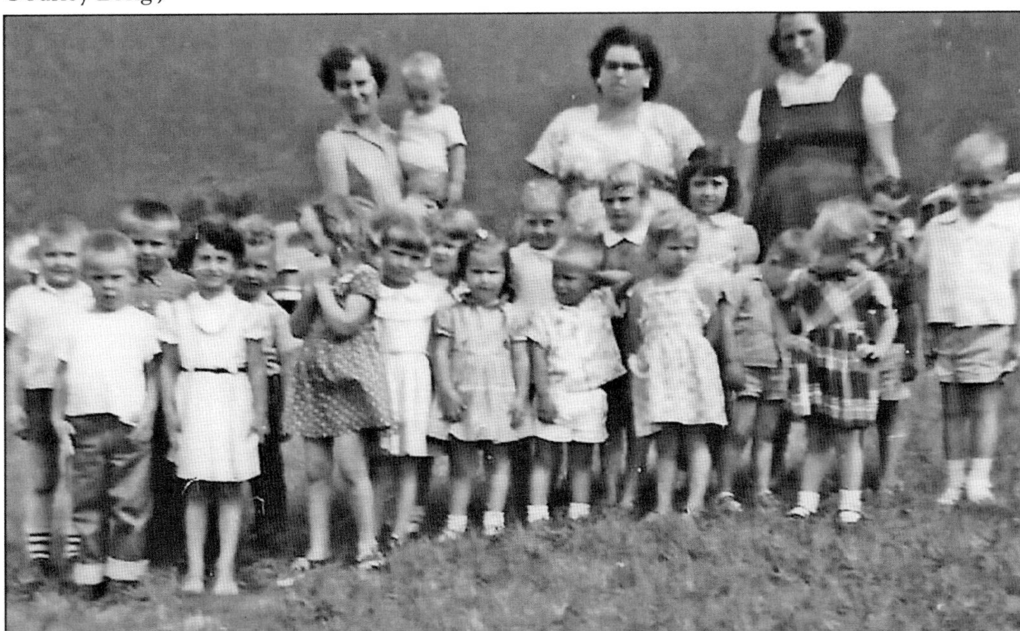

A 1958 Bible school class is pictured at Miller's Cove Primitive Baptist Church. All children enjoyed the opportunity to learn Bible stories and to recite the books of the Bible. Bible school was also a great outreach event to teach the children about Jesus and an opportunity to share the gospel. (Courtesy of Hilda Gourley Long.)

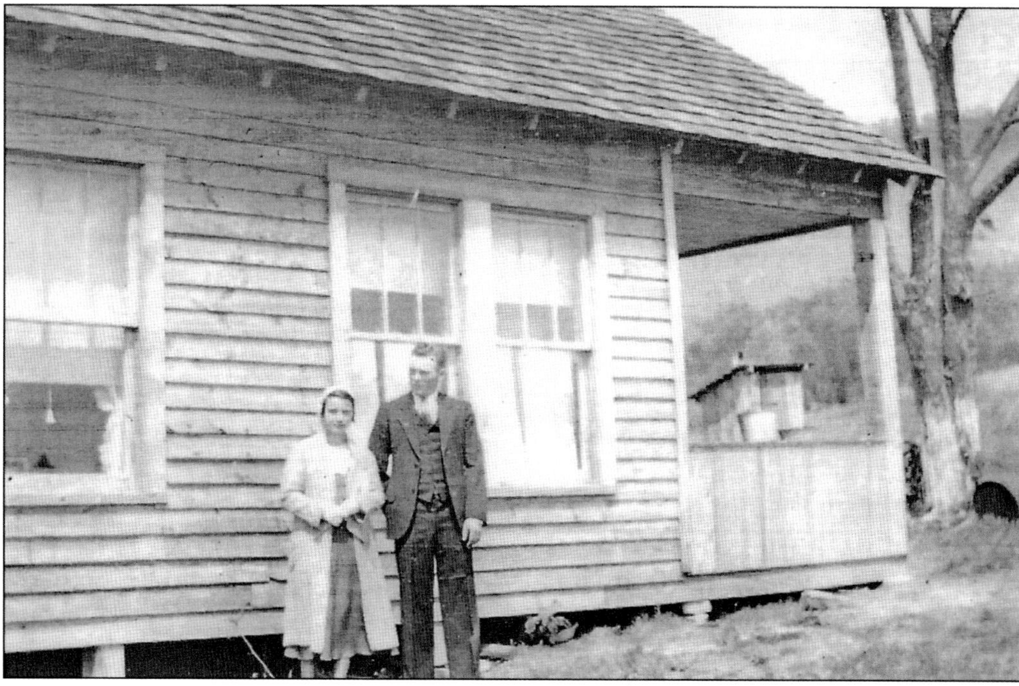

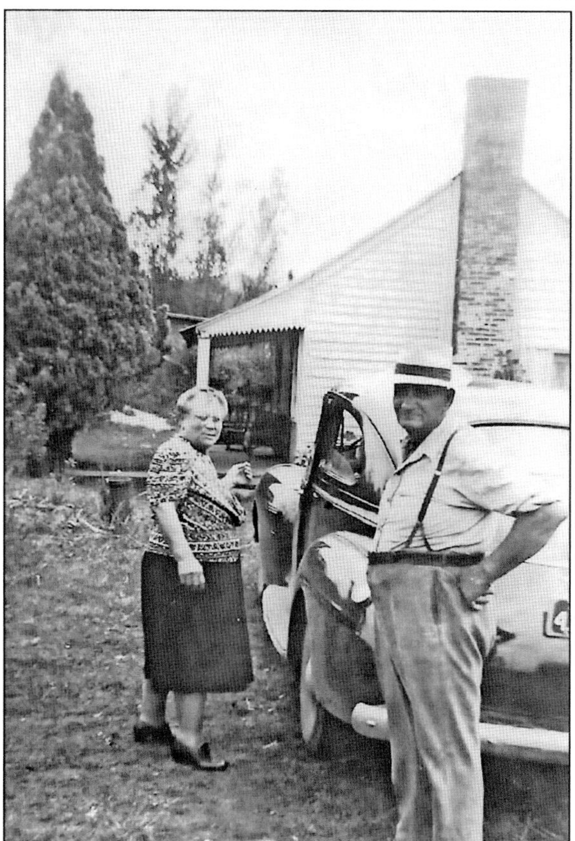

Edna Headrick Martin and Doyle Lonze Martin are pictured in front of the house Doyle built for them in West Miller's Cove. Edna's parents were Lucy Caughron Headrick and Charles Edward Headrick. Doyle was the son of James Vance Martin and Margaret Ann Walker Martin. (Courtesy of Rita Martin Buchanan.)

Lucy Caughron Headrick and Charles Edward Headrick return home from church or some other event. Charles was born on May 18, 1889, to William Wright Headrick and Sara Ann Williams Headrick. Lucy was born on August 18, 1882, to Robert Willis McClain Caughron and Elizabeth J. Gamble Caughron of West Miller's Cove on March 10, 1857. Lucy and Charles were married on September 10, 1909. (Courtesy of Rita Martin Buchanan.)

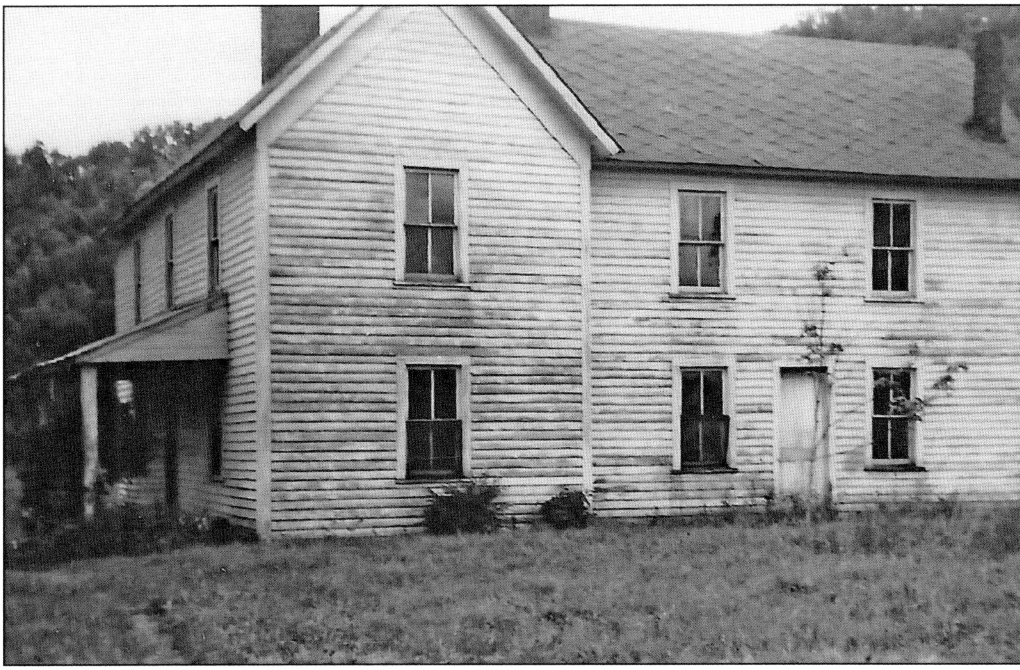

The home of James Robert Headrick and Anna Vedith Headrick was in West Miller's Cove at the intersection of Miller's Cove Road and Mill Loop Road. (Courtesy of Janie Coleman.)

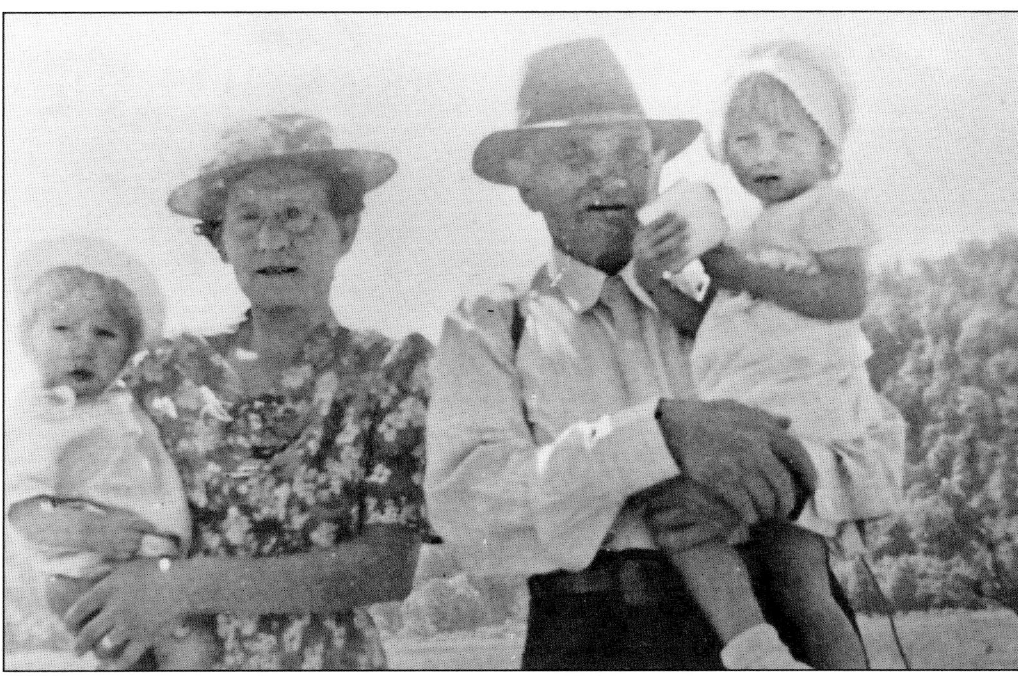

From left to right are Johnny, Vedith, James "Jim" Robert, and Rachel Headrick. James Robert was born on February 20, 1876, to William Wright Headrick and Sarah Ann Williams Headrick. Vedith was born on October 12, 1862, to William Lafayette "Fate" Everett and Della Lane Everett of Rocky Branch. (Courtesy of Mary Headrick.)

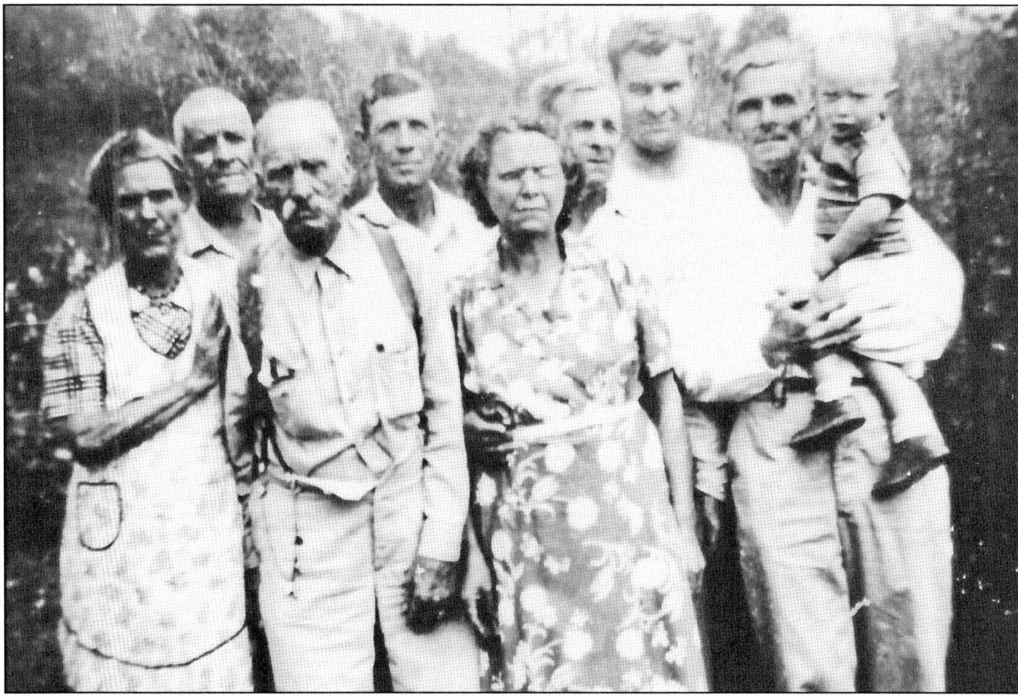

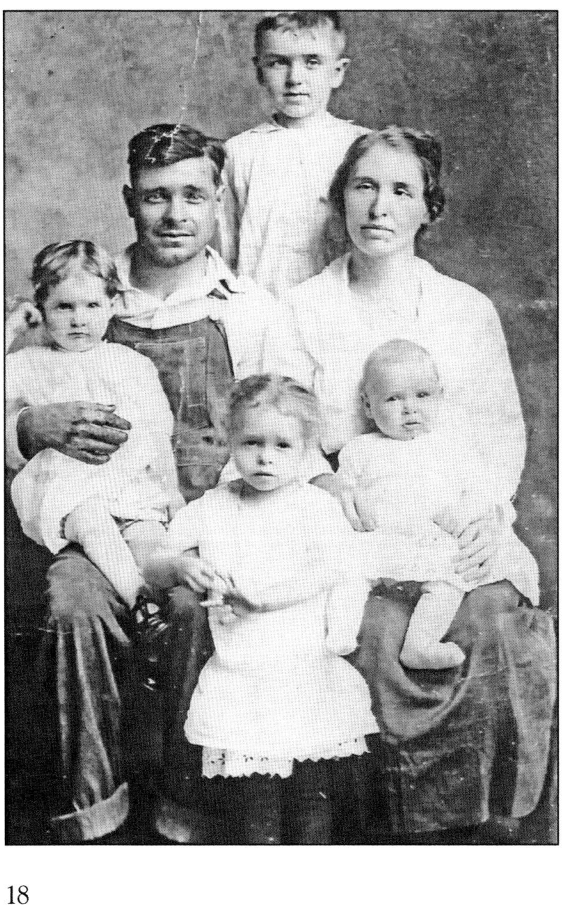

The family of Micajah "Cage" Rogers Murphy and Rebecca Jane "Becky" Hatcher Murphy is, from left to right (first row) Mary, Micajah "Cage," and Laura Murphy; (second row) John, Jim, Mack, Carl, and Henry Murphy holding a child. (Courtesy of Jerry Murphy.)

Harrison Mack Murphy and Eliza Wilcox Murphy are pictured with their children. Harrison Mack was born in Blount County to Micajah "Cage" Murphy and Rebecca Jane Hatcher Murphy. Eliza was born on October 27, 1896, to Caleb Wilcox and Mary Ann Burchfield Wilcox of Cades Cove, Tennessee. Harrison Mack and Eliza were married on November 11, 1915, and then moved to the Miller's Cove area. (Courtesy of Missy Tipton Green.)

George Eugene Garland is pictured with his team of mules at his home place in West Miller's Cove. George was born to Henry Hampton Garland and Floye Sellers Garland on March 30, 1932, in Blount County. (Courtesy of Earl Adams Jr., Inez McCauley Adams Collection.)

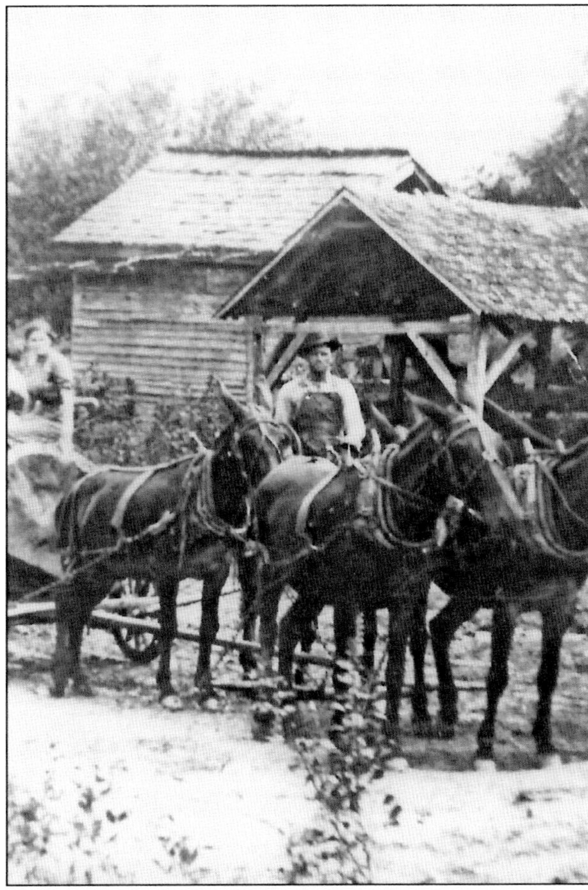

Family and friends pose for a photograph on the front porch of Joseph "Joe" Garland's home on Hess Creek in West Miller's Cove. Joe was born on May 8, 1892, in Miller's Cove. The Garland family soon moved to Cades Cove, and Joe married Jennie Belle Lane on November 4, 1916. She was daughter of Daniel Webster Lane and Cansada Barnes. (Courtesy of Earl Adams Jr., Inez McCauley Adams Collection.)

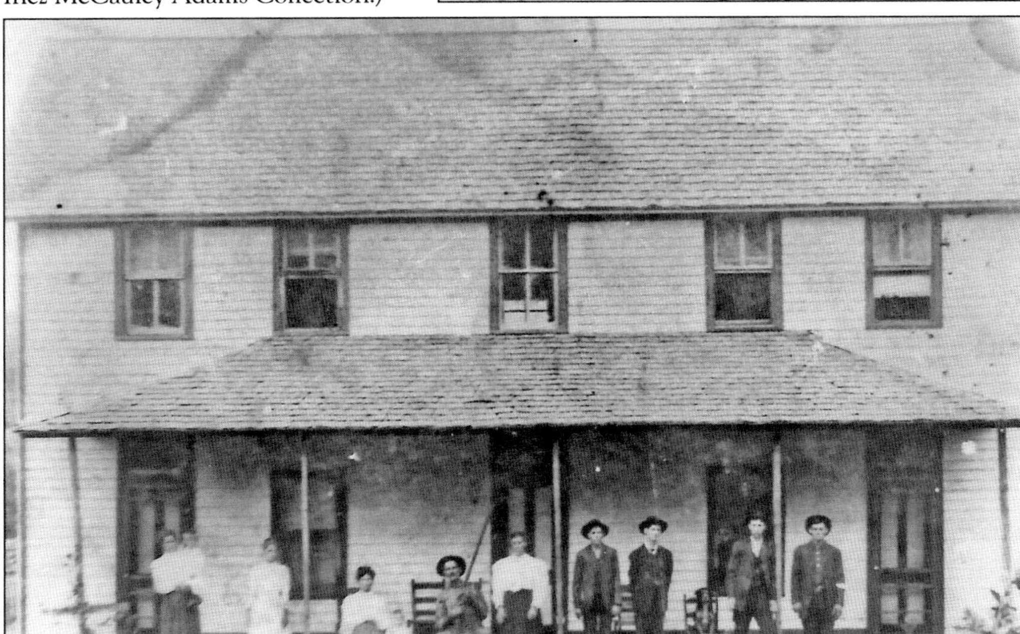

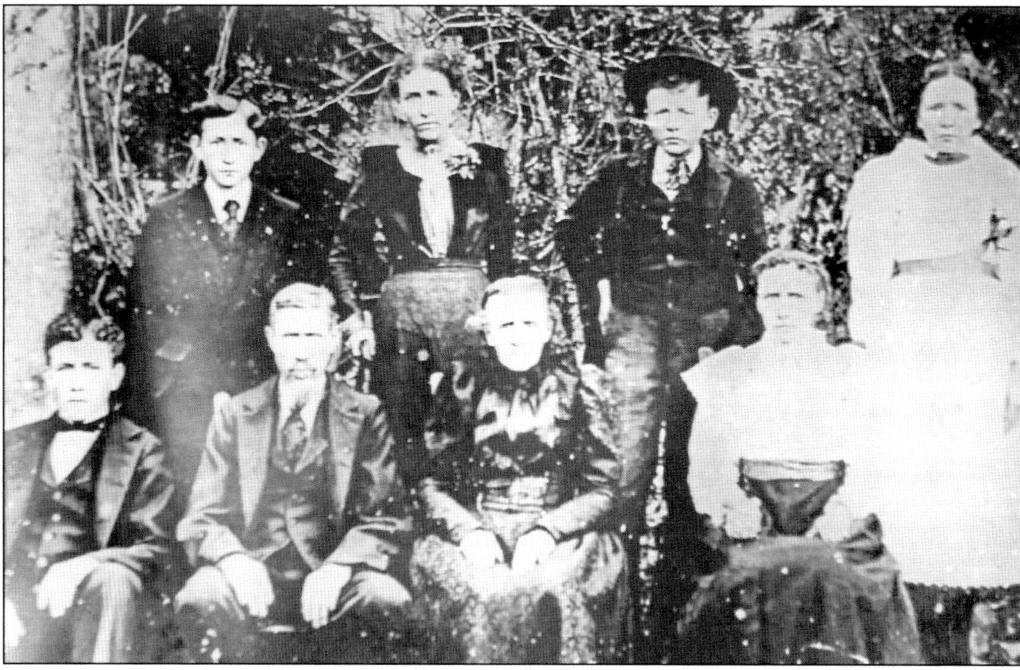

Levi Patterson Caughron's family is, from left to right, (first row) Jim Caughron, Levi Patterson Caughron, Eliza Elliott Caughron, and Betty Caughron; (second row) Bill Caughron, Martha "Mattie" Caughron, George Caughron, and Mary Caughron. Levi Patterson was the son of Samuel Drinkwater Caughron and Amelia Dunn Caughron, early settlers of Miller's Cove. (Courtesy of Earl Adams Jr., Inez McCauley Adams Collection.)

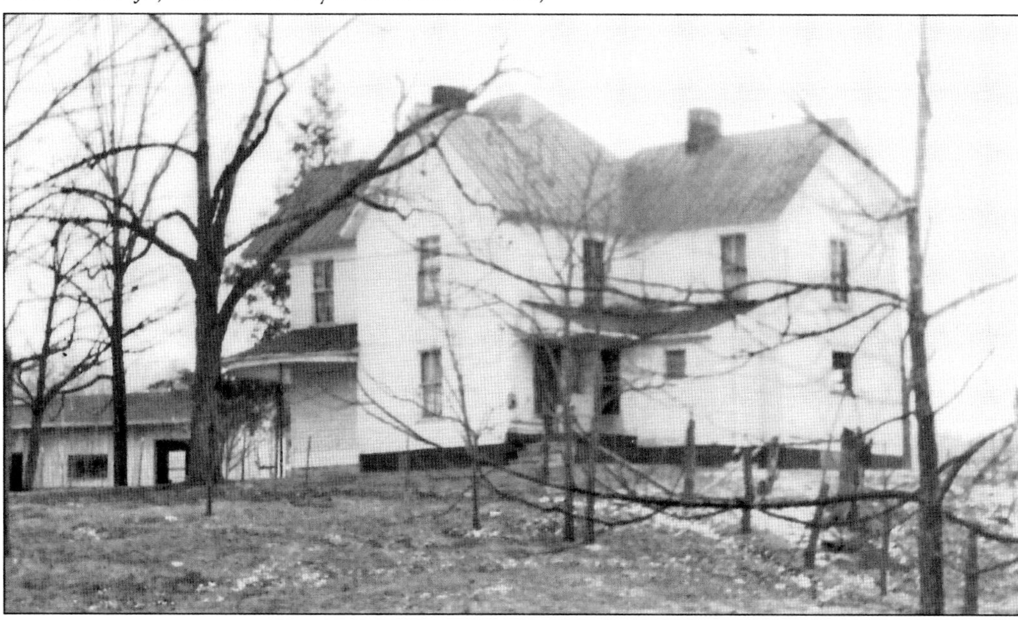

John Hurst Caughron built his house on Caughron land across the road from the Miller's Cove Primitive Baptist Church. John married Ann Tipton, and they raised their family in West Miller's Cove. The Fate Lail family lived in this house after the Caughrons were gone. (Courtesy of Earl Adams Jr., Inez McCauley Adams Collection.)

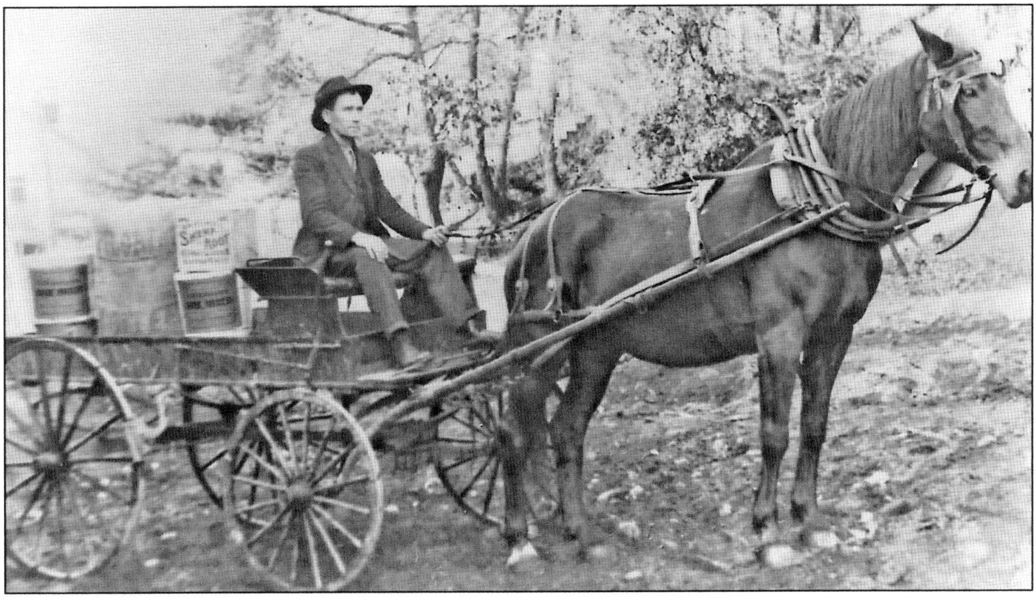

James "Jim" Alexander Caughron of Miller's Cove operated a store in the area and would deliver goods to his customers. Jim was born to Levi Patterson Caughron and Eliza Elliott Caughron on November 30, 1877, in Miller's Cove. (Courtesy of Blount County Library, J.J. "Beef" Myers Collection.)

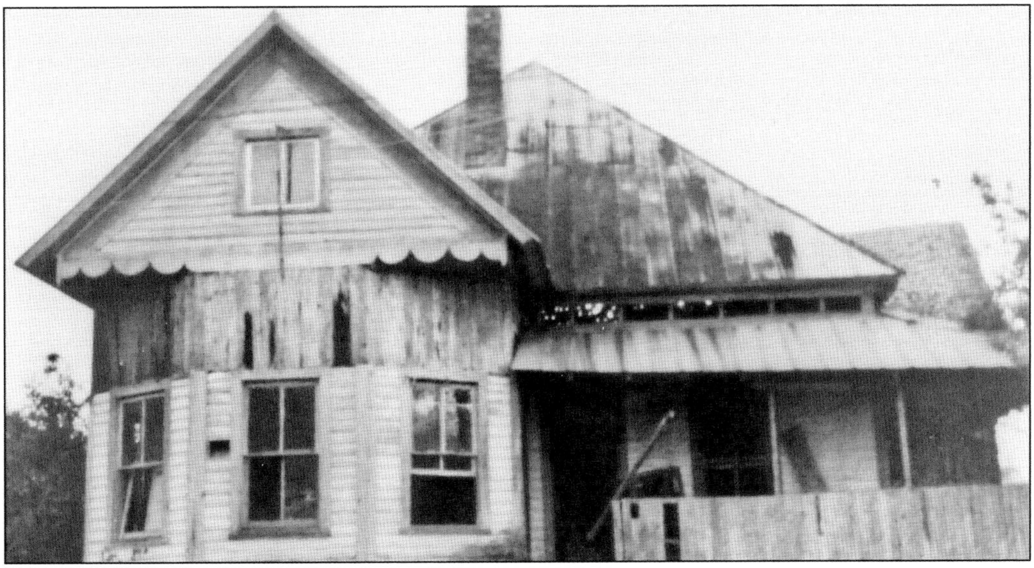

Daniel Greenberry "Green" Caughron built a log barn and house around 1908 on Caughron Property, which was located in the area behind the Miller's Cove Primitive Baptist Church. Known as "Green," he lived in this log house with his wife, Laura Gamble Caughron, and their three sons, John, Samuel Houston Drinkwater, and Clark Commodore. When John was about 12 years old, he was thrown from a horse and passed away. Years later, his wife, Laura, acquired blood poison and passed away in 1908. He then married Clementine Amanda LeQuire, and at this time "Green" built this home closer to the main travel route into Miller's Cove. Green and Clementine had three children: Virgie, Myrtle, and Joseph. Green was the son of Samuel Drinkwater Caughron and Amelia Dunn Caughron. In later years, the Charles Gourley family lived in this house. (Courtesy of Earl Adams Jr., Inez McCauley Adams Collection.)

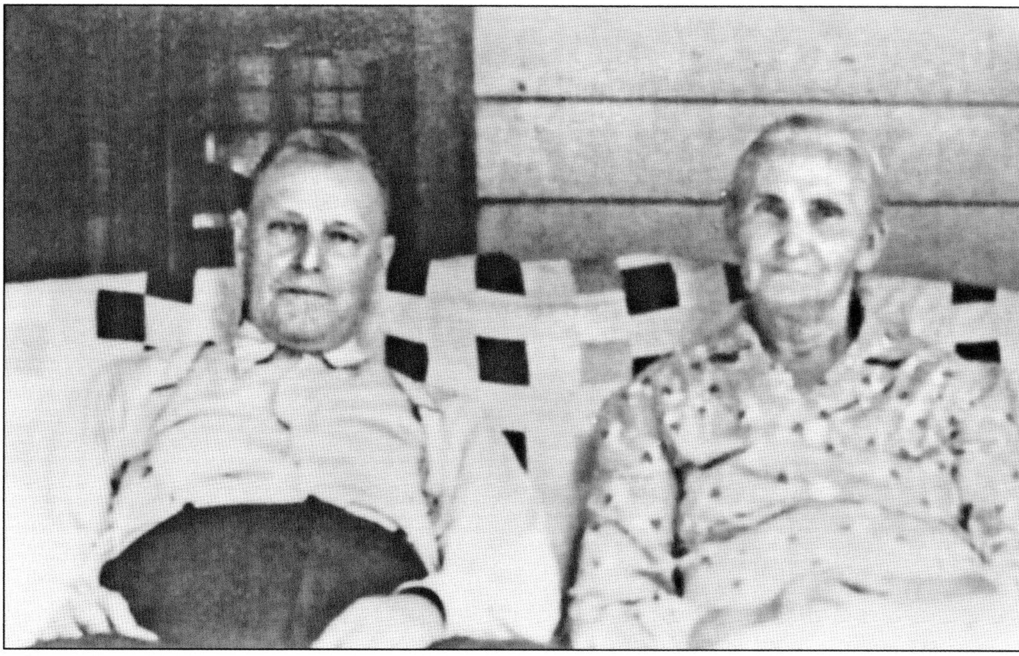

John Robert McNeilly and Rhoda Ellen Webb McNeilly made their home in the West Miller's Cove area. John and Rhoda were married on January 7, 1890; the 1900 census shows them living in Civil District 18, which is Miller's Cove. The 1910, 1920, and 1930 censuses show the same. (Courtesy of Earl Adams Jr., Inez McCauley Adams Collection.)

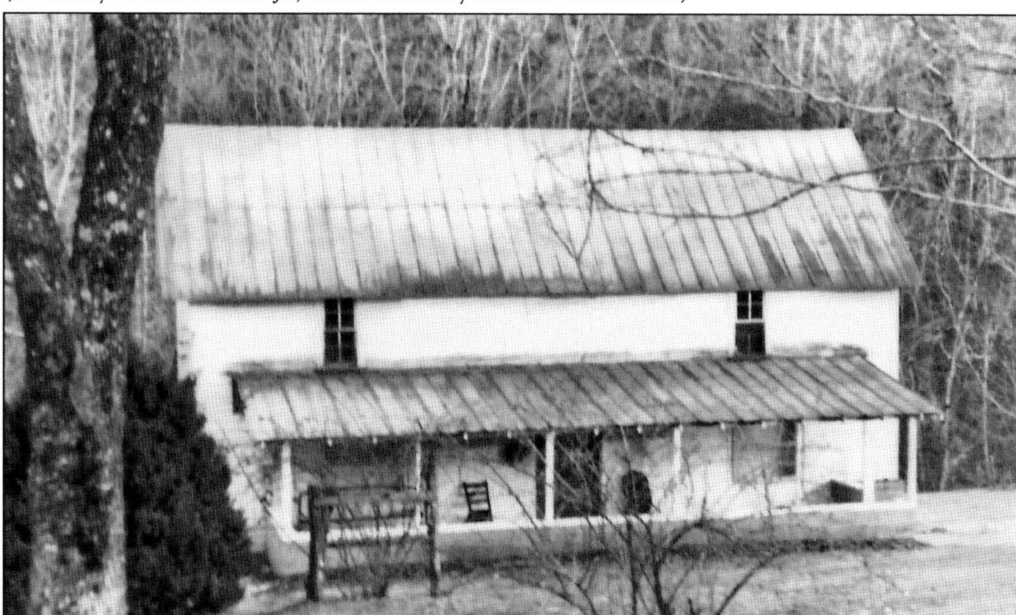

John and Rhoda McNeilly lived on Hesse Creek in West Miller's Cove. John McNeilly was born on May 22, 1869, in North Carolina to John Thomas McNeilly and Rachel Minerva Cook McNeilly. Rhoda was born on January 8, 1875, in Blount County to D.C. Webb and Mary M. Webb, who lived in Civil District 18 in 1880 and 1890. (Courtesy of Earl Adams Jr., Inez McCauley Adams Collection.)

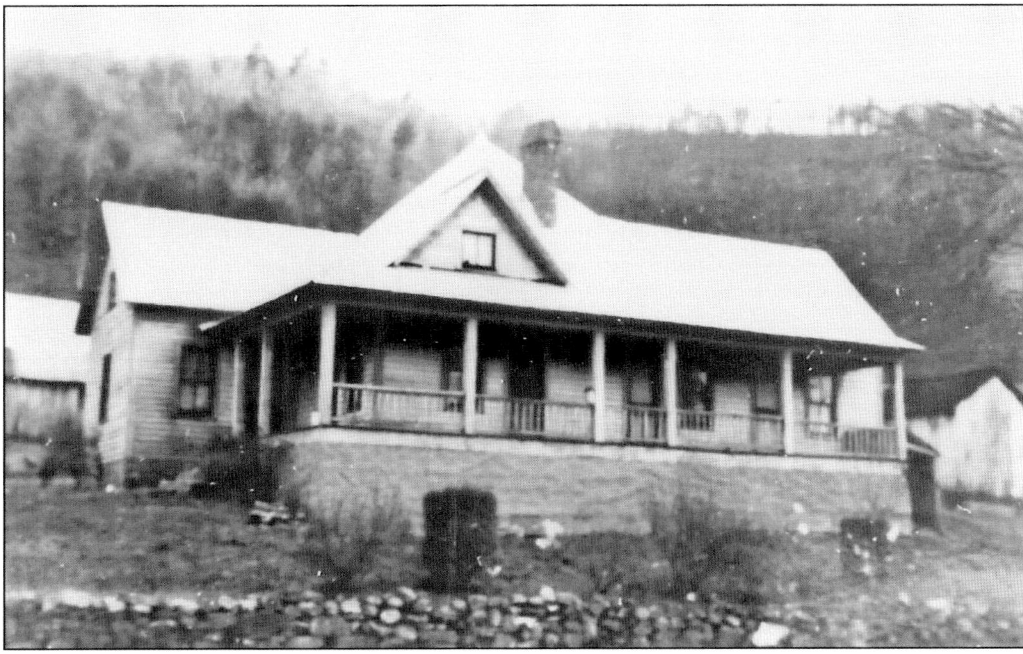

The Daniel Calvin "Cal" Ledbetter and Annie Rebecca Shields Ledbetter home is pictured in West Miller's Cove. The Ledbetters had moved from Cades Cove in 1924 into a house on Dick's Creek. In 1928, they moved into this house, which was built by George Caughron. (Courtesy of David and Paulette Ledbetter.)

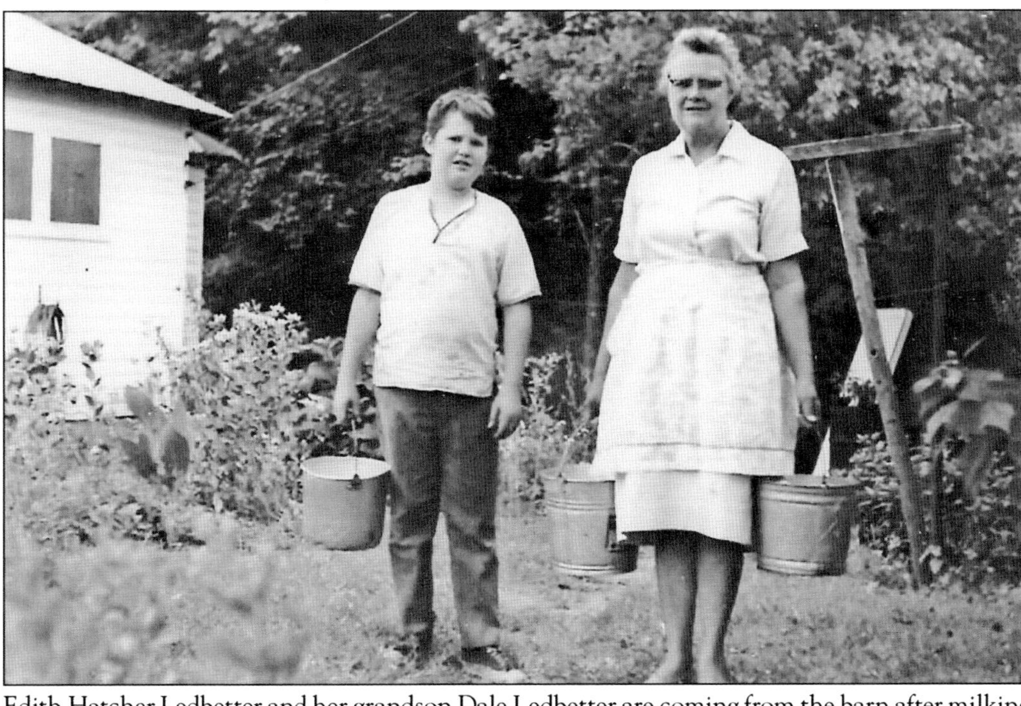

Edith Hatcher Ledbetter and her grandson Dale Ledbetter are coming from the barn after milking the cows. Edith was the daughter of Richard and Cordie Hatcher and married Ervin Ledbetter. (Courtesy of David and Paulette Ledbetter.)

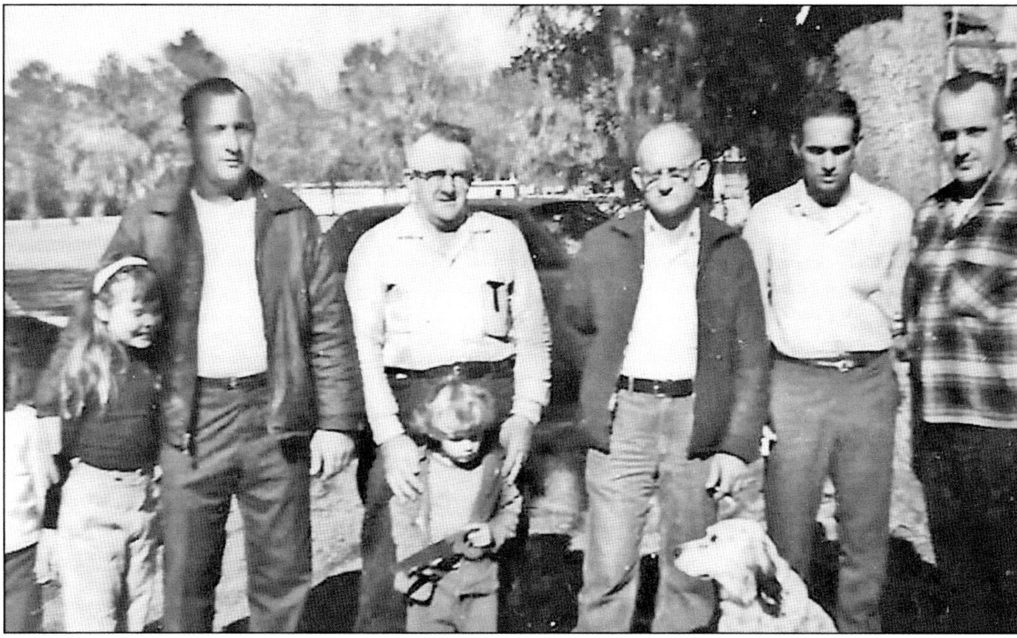

Sons and granddaughters of Daniel Ledbetter and Annie Shields Ledbetter are, from left to right, (first row) granddaughters Kay and Becky Ledbetter with the family pet; (second row) Toye Ledbetter, Ervin Ledbetter, Ernest Ledbetter, Ray Ledbetter (son of Ernest), and Paul Ledbetter. (Courtesy of David and Paulette Ledbetter.)

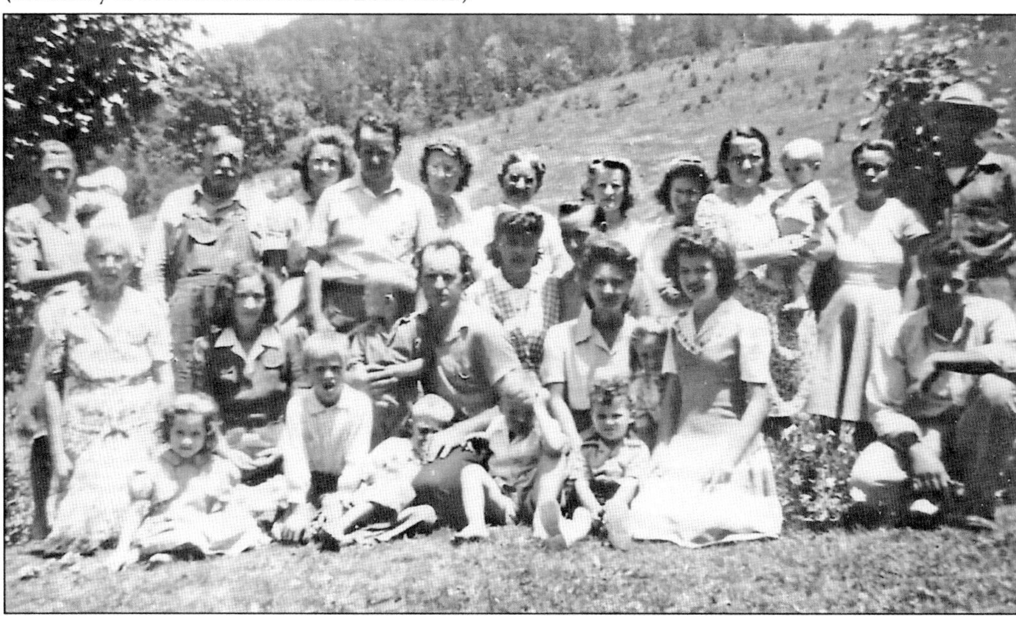

Pictured are family and friends of Daniel Calvin Ledbetter and Leannah Rebecca "Annie" Shields Ledbetter. Daniel was the son of Matthew "Bud" Ledbetter and Mary Ann Sands of White Oak Sinks. Annie was the daughter of Dave Shields and Phoebe Jane Walker Shields. Annie and Daniel eloped in October 1905 and were secretly married on horseback by Rev. R.D. Burchfield on a trail in the Cades Cove area. They moved to the Meadows area off Schoolhouse Gap Road. (Courtesy of David and Paulette Ledbetter.)

David Lee Ledbetter at about three years of age would run off from his house, which was next door to his grandparents' house, and hide from his mom under a chicken coop. When his mom finally found him, he told her a spider had bitten him so he would not get into trouble. His grandmother saved him from a whipping, stating he couldn't help that the spider bit him. David was born on November 4, 1948, to Toye Calvin Ledbetter and Ruth Yearout Ledbetter. (Courtesy of David and Paulette Ledbetter.)

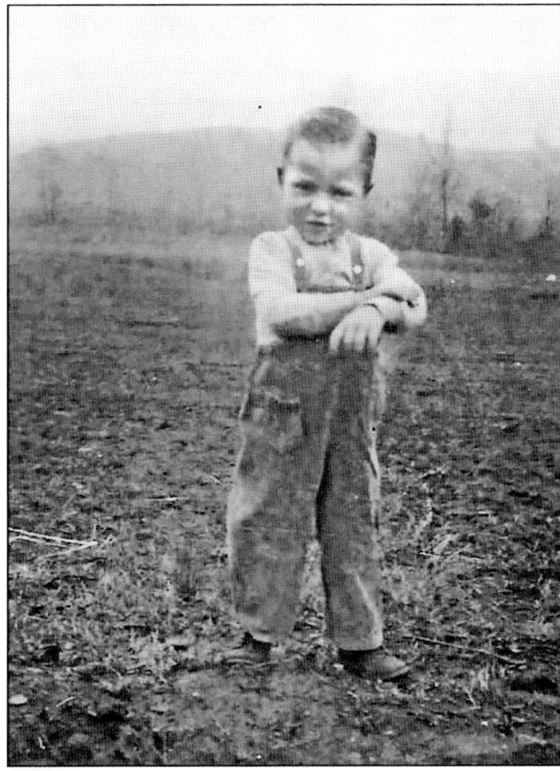

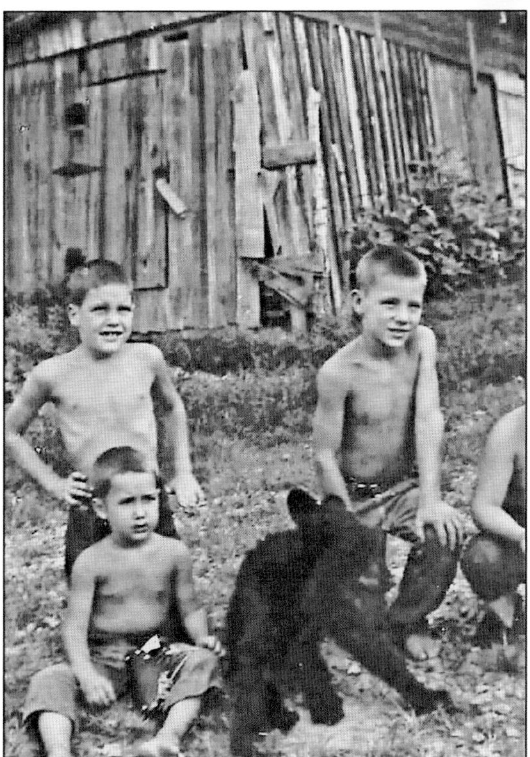

Ronnie Whitehead, David Ledbetter, and Arnold Whitehead (sitting) pose with a bear that was killed by dogs. These boys were good friends and did many things together—swinging in trees, building cabins in the woods, and playing Cowboys and Indians. Ronnie and David would carry measuring sticks for their fathers, Robert Lee Whitehead and Toye Ledbetter, when they cut timber in the Dunn Hollow in East Miller's Cove. (Courtesy of David and Paulette Ledbetter.)

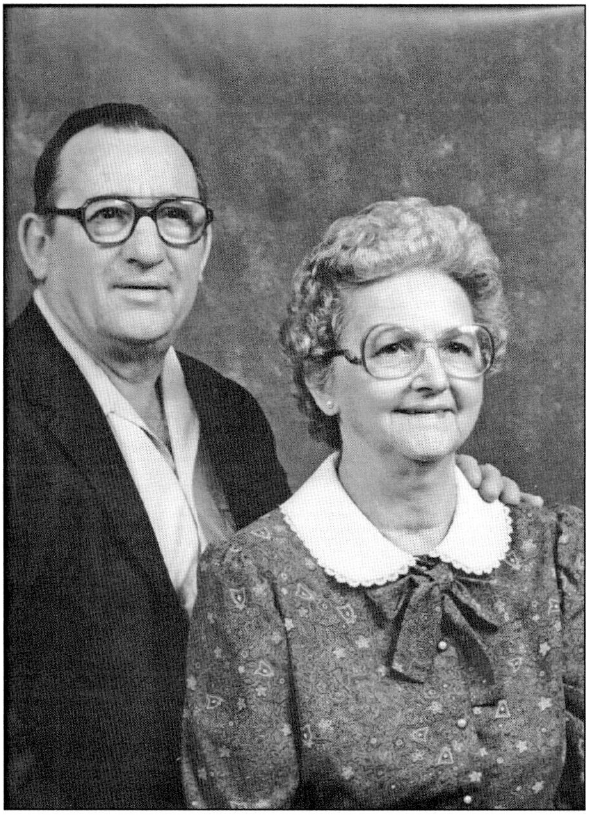

Toye Calvin Ledbetter and Ruth Yearout Ledbetter raised their family in West Miller's Cove. Toye was born on January 25, 1925, to Daniel Calvin Ledbetter and Annie Rebecca Shields Ledbetter, who had moved into the Walland area from nearby Cades Cove. Ruth was born on February 28, 1928, to Frank Yearout and Bethel Trinkle Yearout of the Pea Ridge area. (Courtesy of David and Paulette Ledbetter.)

Mayme Headrick, daughter of John D. Headrick and Mary Farr Headrick, married Hoyle Taylor. Their residence is pictured below. Hoyle was born July 16, 1917, in Cades Cove, Tennessee, to Elder George Taylor and Ruth Hassell Oliver Taylor. The US Census of 1920 listed the Taylor family as living in Civil District 18, Miller's Cove. The original log house was still part of the John D. Headrick house located on Hess' Creek. (Courtesy of Earl Adams Jr., Inez McCauley Adams Collection.)

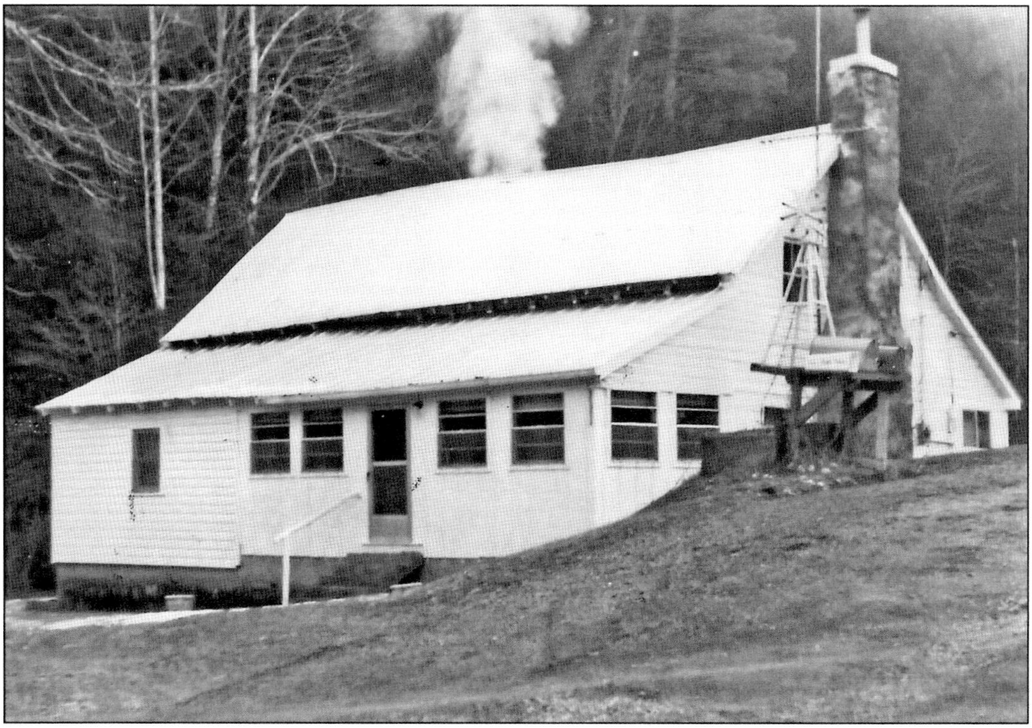

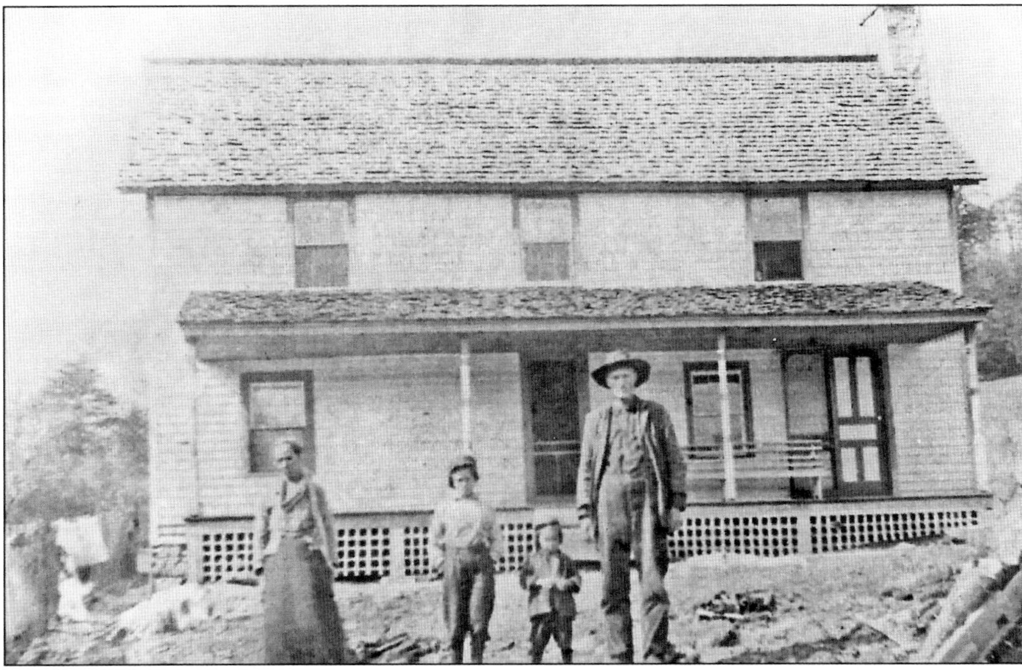

From left to right are Alice, John, Charley, and Abe Ogle at their home place in West Miller's Cove. The house was constructed by Abe and family members. The yard is nothing but dirt. (Courtesy of Hilda Gourley Long.)

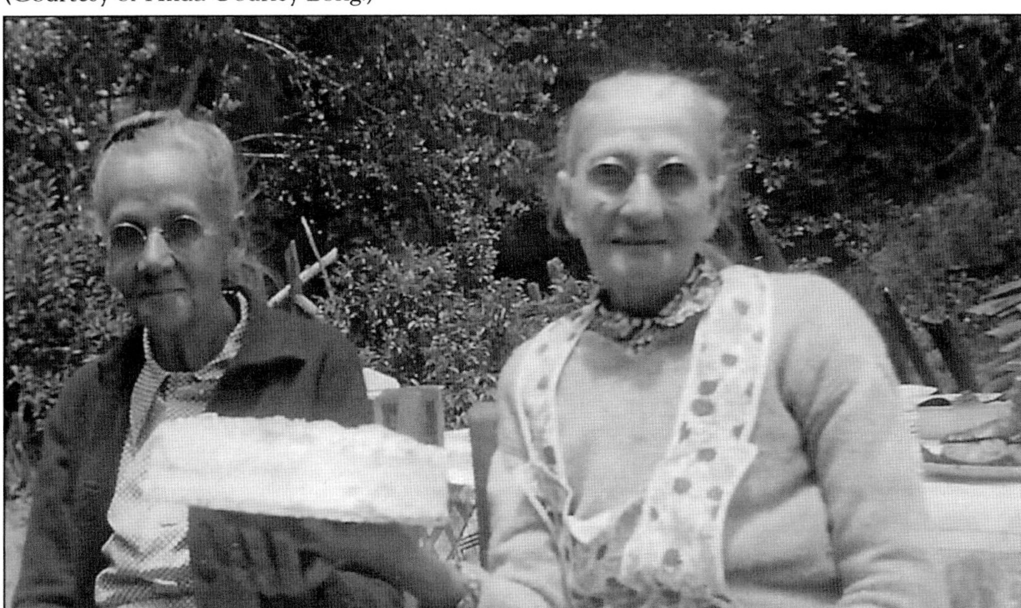

Alice Settlemire Ogle (left), the daughter of David and Catherine Settlemire, married Abe Ogle on September 3, 1890, in Blount County. The Settlemire family had come to Miller's Cove from North Carolina, which both David and Catherine listed as their birthplace in the 1880 Tennessee Census. With Alice is her sister Sarah Jane Settlemire Flynn, who was married to Joseph Winfield Scott Flynn. (Courtesy of Hilda Gourley Long.)

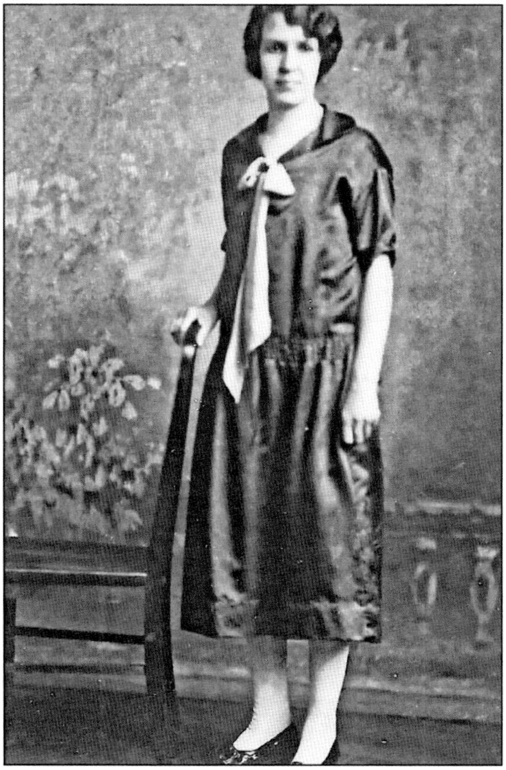

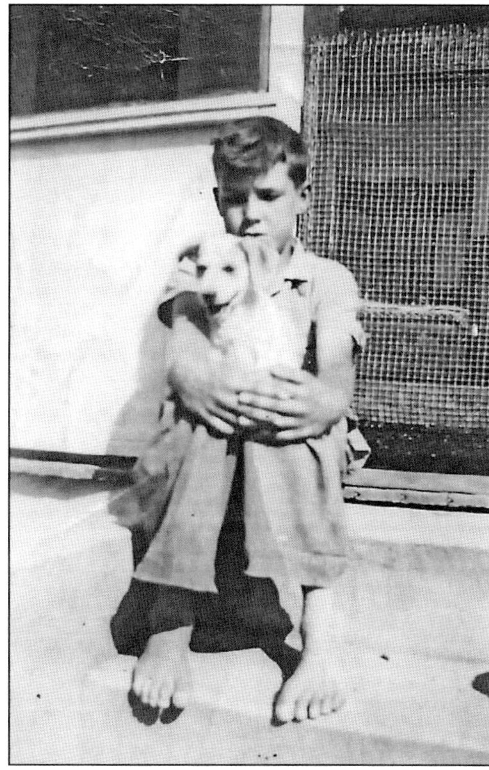

Eliza Alice Ogle (above left), the daughter of Abe Ogle and Alice Settlemire Ogle of West Miller's Cove, was born on April 16, 1899. Eliza always grew a large garden and worked it herself to keep food on the table for her children, Marvin and Ronald. Ronald Ogle (above right) is doing what little boys do best: playing with his dog. (Both, courtesy of Gail Tipton Stumpf.)

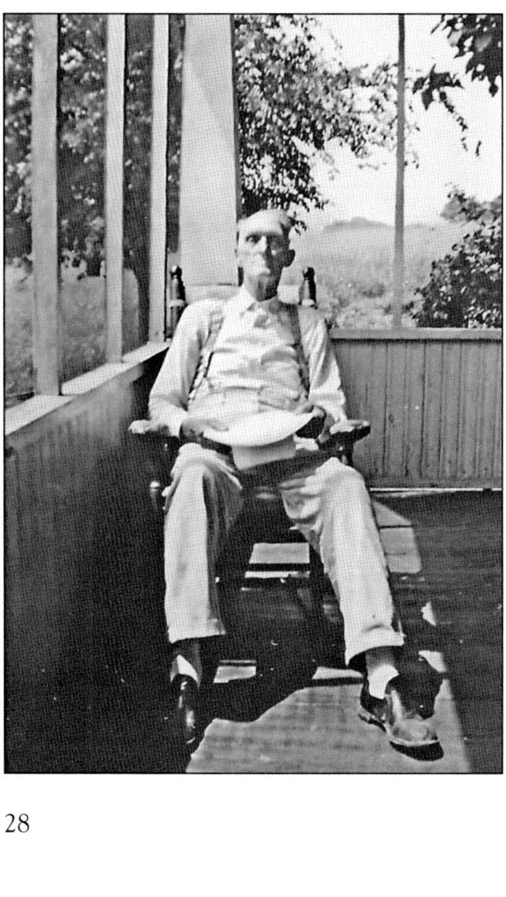

Abe Ogle relaxes in his rocking chair on his front porch. At the break of dawn, the Ogle household came to life. After the noonday meal, Abe is taking it easy before heading back out to do his daily work. (Courtesy of Gail Tipton Stumpf.)

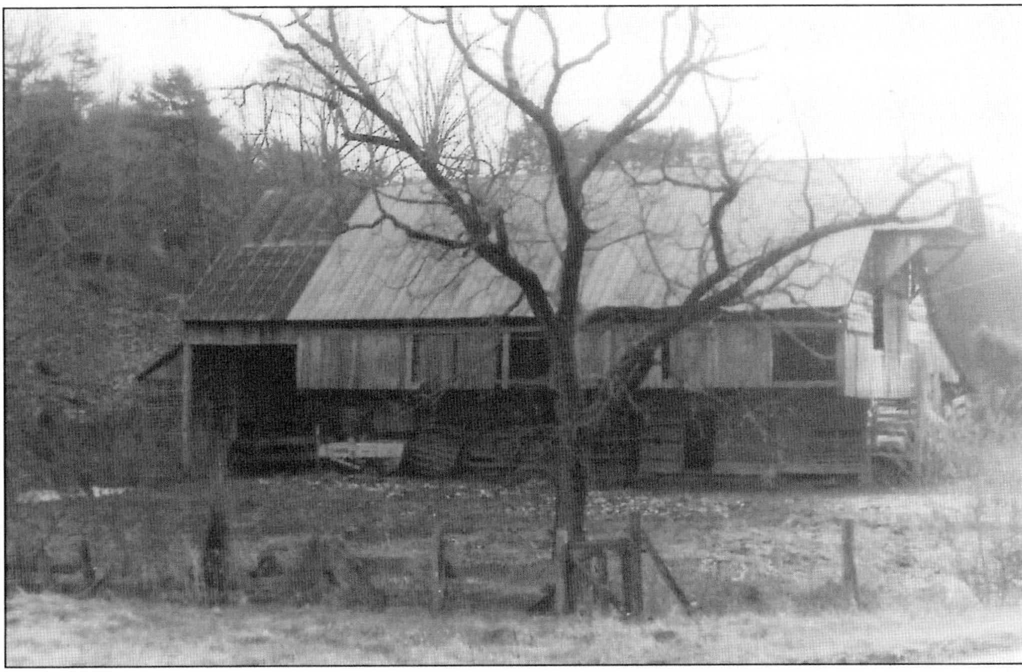

"Abe" Ogle, like other farmers, probably built his barn before he built his house. Barns were the main structure of the farm, and Abe had built a cantilever barn. Cantilever barns were constructed for self-sufficient farms where accommodations for seed corn, feed, livestock, and equipment were the basic needs. (Courtesy of Earl Adams Jr., Inez McCauley Adams Collection.)

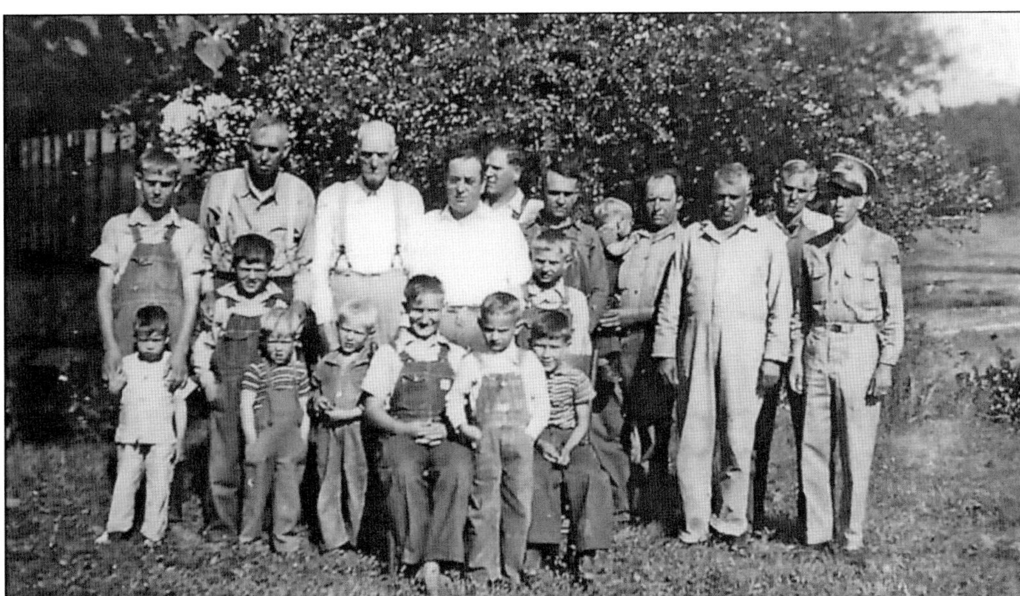

The Abe Ogle family has gathered in West Miller's Cove. The little boys all have on overalls and are barefoot, as all little boys were in those times. Families would take advantage any occasion to get together to enjoy themselves and reminisce about days gone by. (Courtesy of Hilda Gourley Long.)

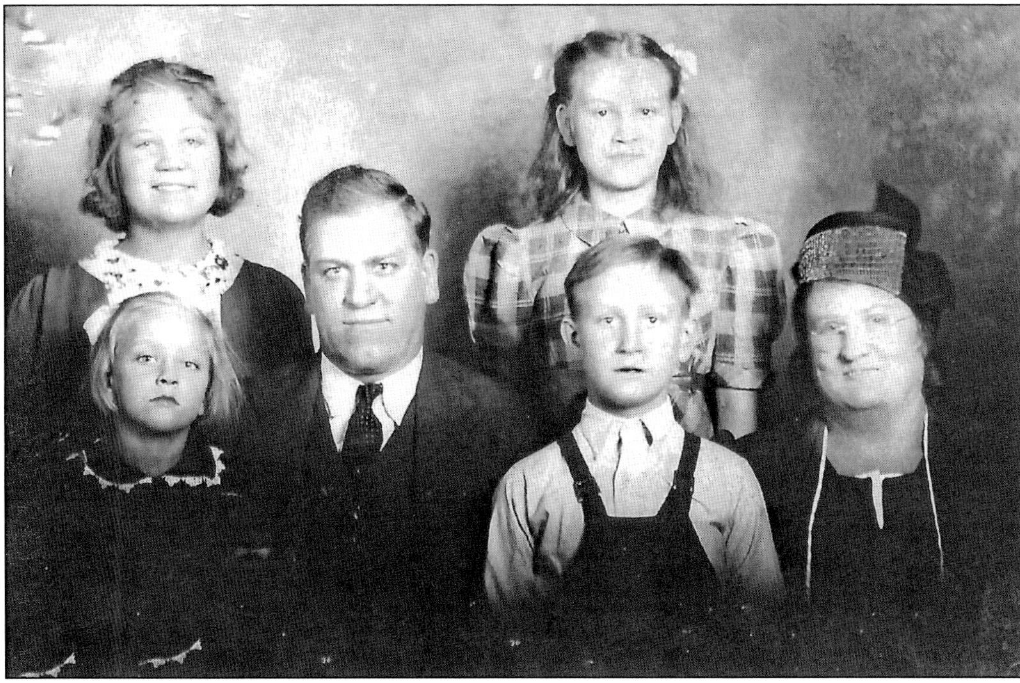

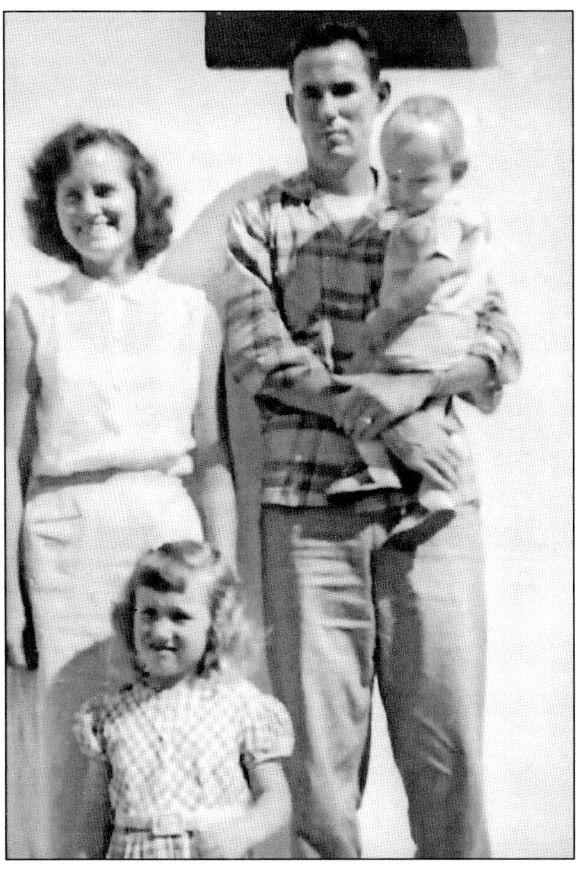

The Charley Ogle and Leona Hatcher Ogle family is, from left to right, (first row) Dean, Charley, Ralph, and Leona; (second row) Sue and June. The Ogle family lived in the house that Charley's father built across the road from the Missionary Baptist Church in West Miller's Cove. Charley was born on August 5, 1906 to Abe and Alice Settlemire Ogle; he married Rose Leona Hatcher on May 5, 1928.

June Ogle Gourley and Leon M. Gourley are pictured with their children, Hilda and Jimmy. June was the daughter of Charley and Leona Hatcher Ogle. Leon was the son James Harrison Gourley and Lura Myrtle Gregory. (Courtesy of Hilda Gourley Long.)

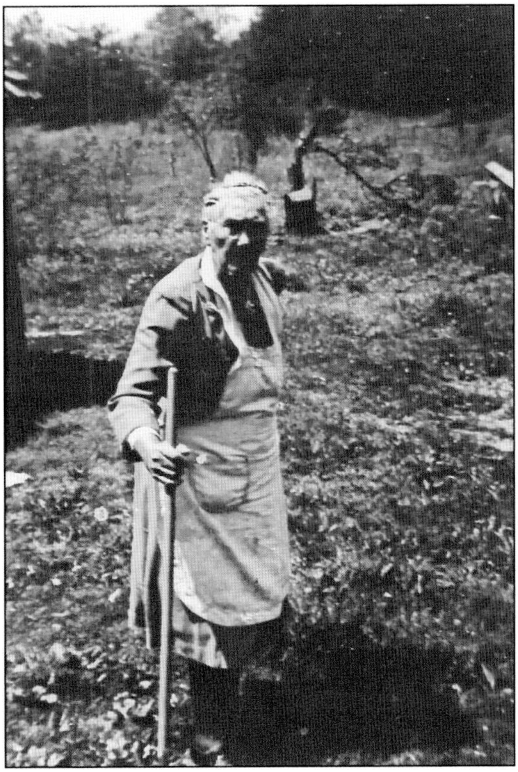

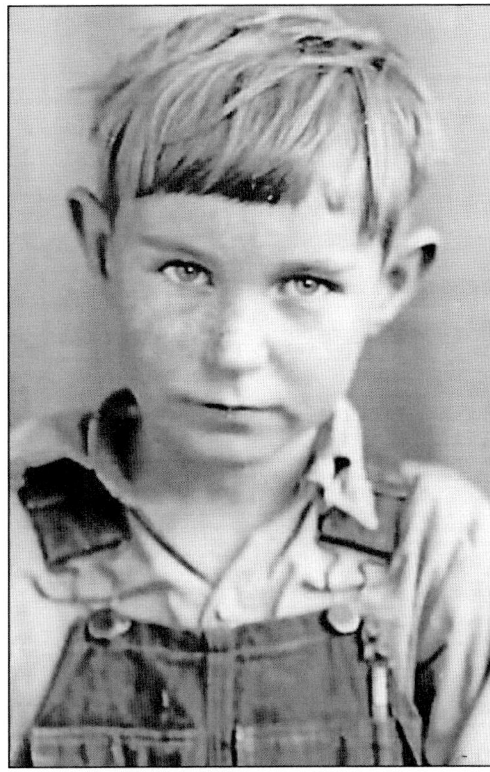

Dolly Eva Smith Gourley (above, left) was the wife of Charles Mack Gourley. Dolly and Charles's son, James Harrison Gourley, is responsible for keeping the family name in West Miller's Cove. Leon M. Gourley (above, right) was born on November 19, 1928, in Cades Cove to James Harrison Gourley and Lura Myrtle Gregory Gourley. (Both, courtesy of Hilda Gourley Long.)

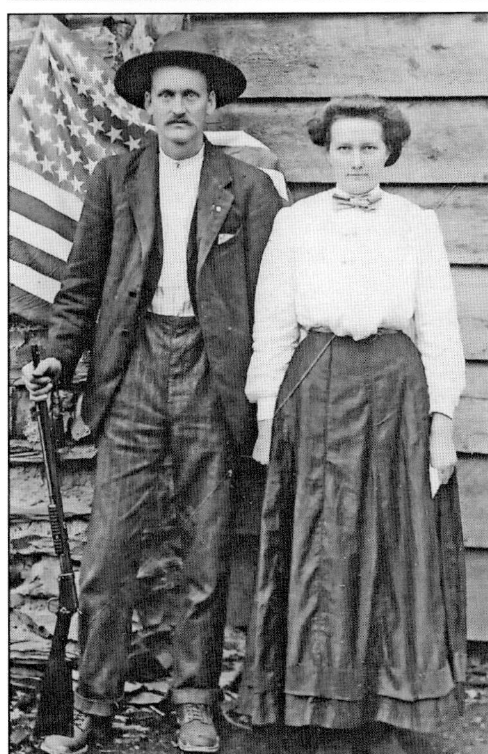

Leason Hearon and Barbara Elizabeth Gourley Hearon were married on February 26, 1912. Leason came from the Happy Valley area; he was the son of Jeremiah "Jerry" Hearon and Rachel Whitehead Hearon. Barbara was born on September 30, 1891, to Charles "Charlie" Gourley and Dolly Smith Gourley. (Courtesy of Hilda Gourley Long.)

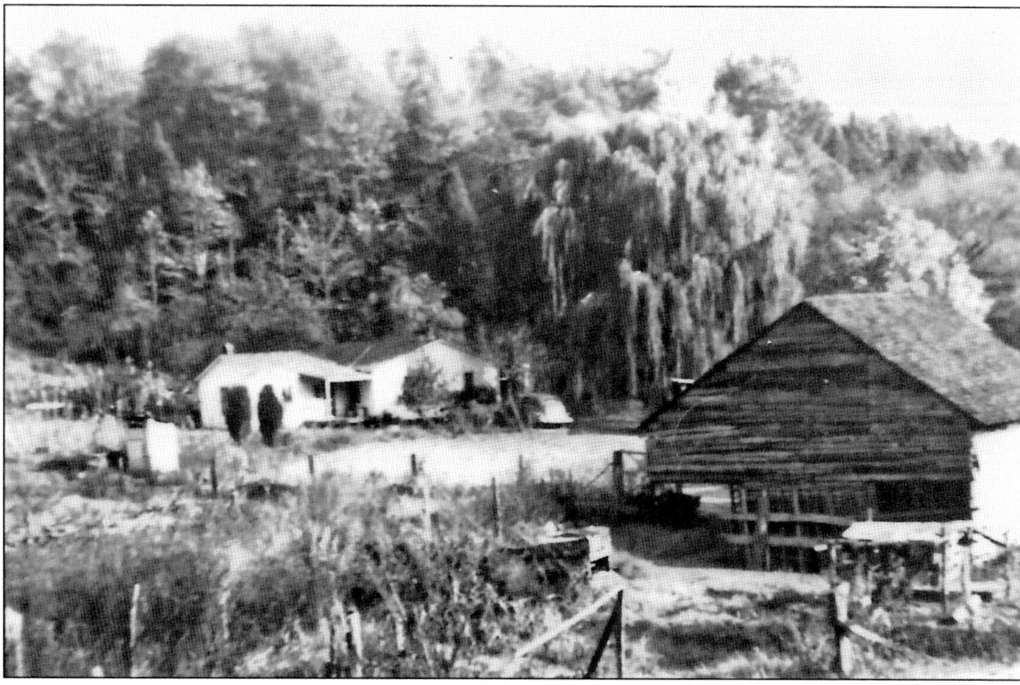

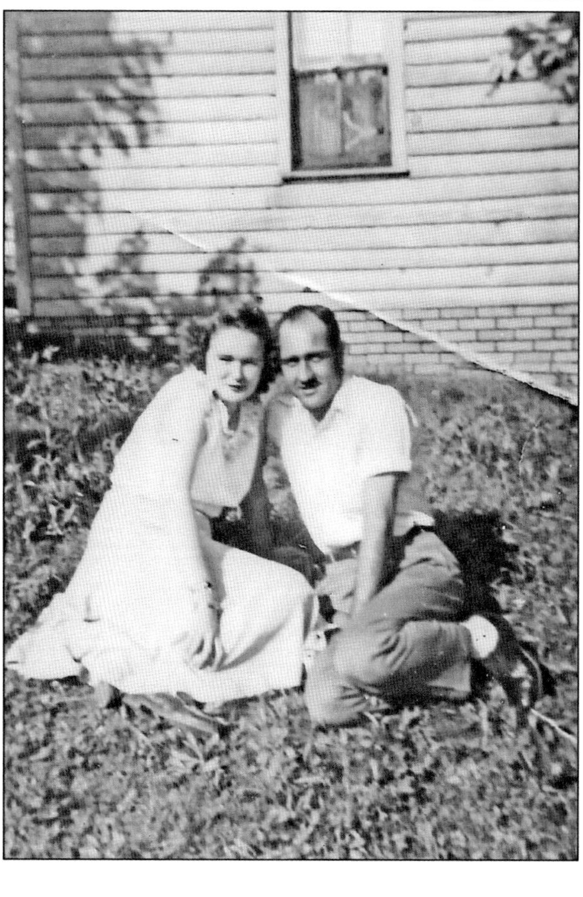

William Carson McCauley built this house and barn after moving from Cades Cove to West Miller's Cove about 1920. Notice that the cantilever barn has an overhang that protects the livestock from rain as well as protecting the structure. Leason Hearon and Barbara Gourley Hearon lived on this farm after the McCauley family. (Courtesy of Earl Adams Jr., Inez McCauley Adams Collection.)

William Raymond Myers and Princess Gourley lived in West Miller's Cove. William Raymond was born on June 3, 1920, to John Henry Myers and Mary Tina Flynn Myers. Princess was born on May 1, 1927, in Cades Cove to James Harrison Gourley and Lura Myrtle Gregory Gourley. (Courtesy of Rodney Myers.)

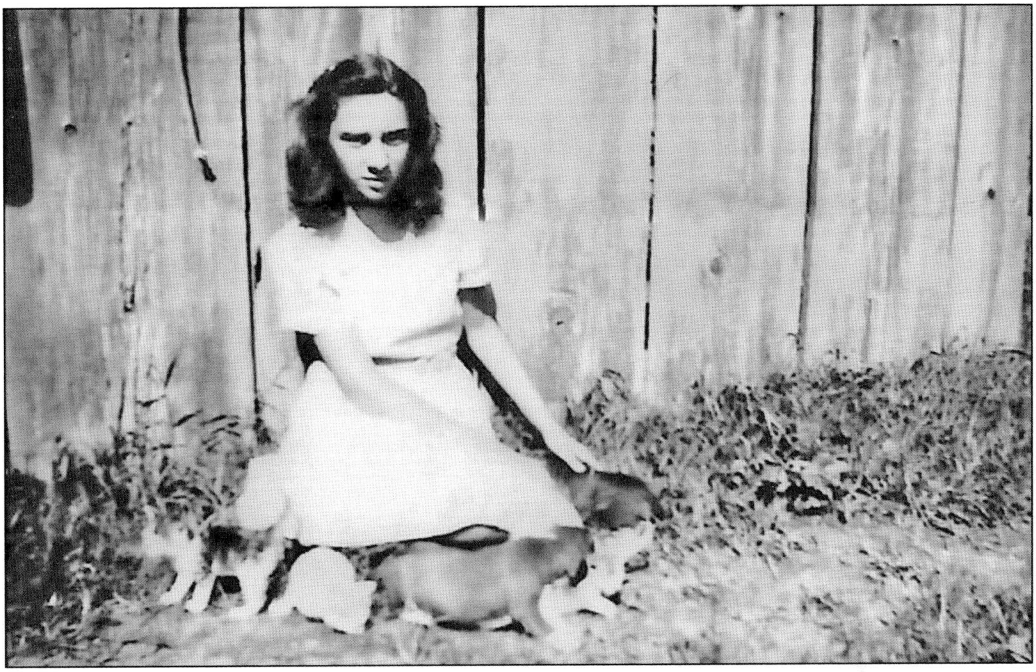

Aileene Myers enjoys time with her pets at her home in West Miller's Cove. Aileene was the daughter of John Henry Myers and Mary Tina Flynn Myers. (Courtesy of Kim Emert Leonard.)

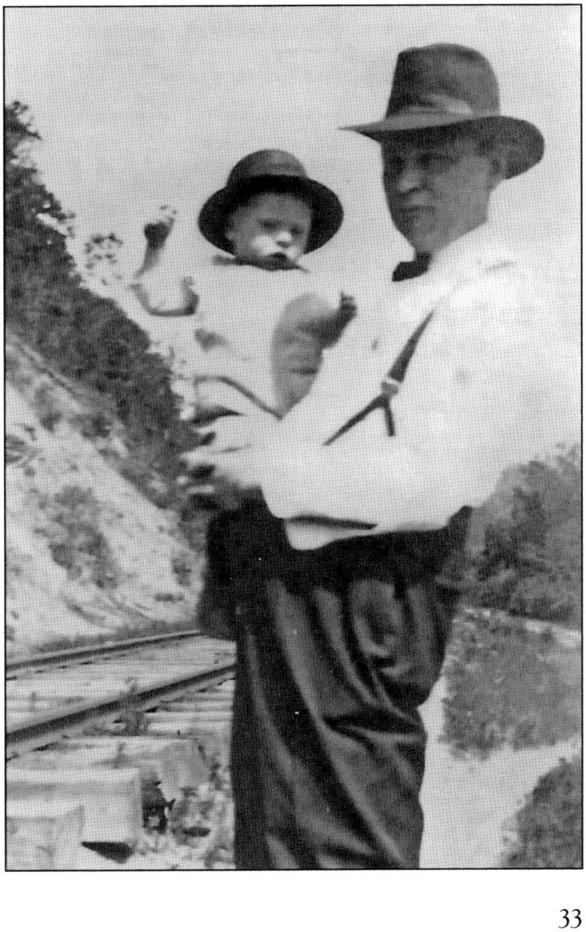

William Ira Emert and son Paul stand next to the railroad tracks in Walland. Ira, as he was known to everyone, was born on April 20, 1882, to Fredrick Emert and Martha Anne Perry Emert. On December 25, 1918, Ira married Belle Tipton from nearby Happy Valley. Belle was born on November 30, 1898, to John Tipton and Bettie L. Tipton. (Courtesy of Kim Emert Leonard.)

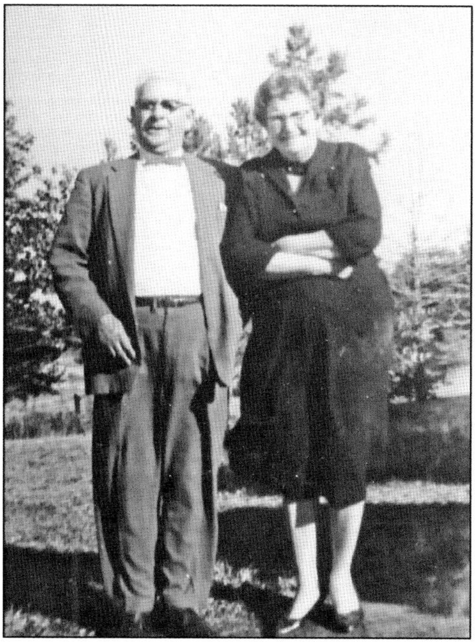

Sampson Flynn and his wife, Bonnie Cagle Flynn, lived in Miller's Cove. Sampson was born to Joseph Winfield Scott Flynn and Sarah Jane Settlemire Flynn on October 30, 1902, in Miller's Cove. While working at the tannery, Sampson met his wife, Bonnie Cagle, who had spent most of her childhood around the tannery, where her father was employed. Sampson and Bonnie were married on November 10, 1920. (Courtesy of Velda Flynn Powell.)

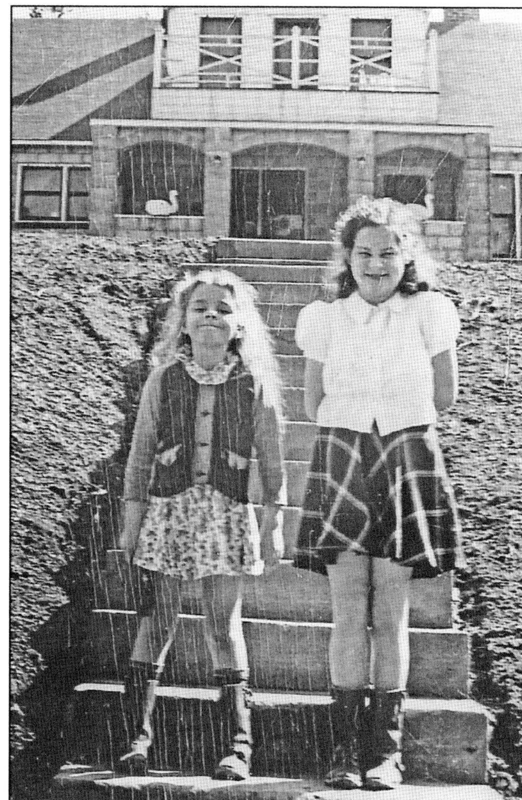

Vonnie (left) and Dee Flynn (right), daughters of Sampson and Bonnie Flynn, are pictured on the steps leading to the Flynn home in West Miller's Cove. The farm had a splendid view of the Chilhowee Mountains rising steeply to the north, with Hess Creek flowing through the rich valley between. (Courtesy of Vonnie Flynn Walker.)

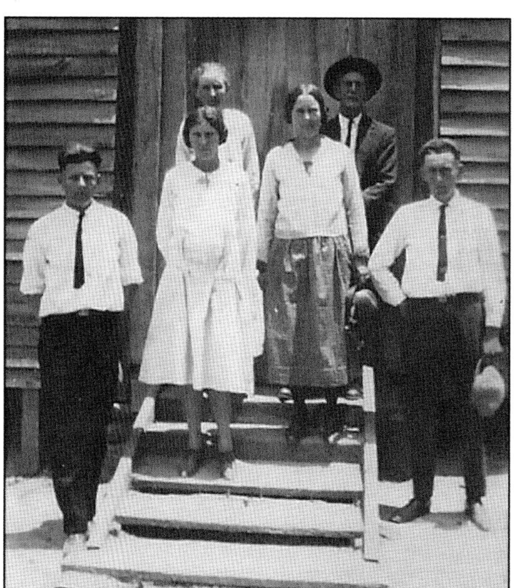

Pictured from left to right are (first row) Glenn and Clyde; (second row) Daisy and Pearl; (third row) their parents, Martha Caroline "Mattie" Caughron Lane and Alfred "Alf" Lane. "Mattie" was born in 1874 to Levi Patterson Caughron and Eliza Elliott Caughron of Miller's Cove Tennessee. (Courtesy of Carolyn Lane.)

Howard Lee Flynn and Susan "Susie" Ogle are pictured here. Howard was born to Joseph Winfield Scott Flynn and Sarah Jane Settlemire Flynn of West Miller's Cove on September 28, 1914. Susie was the daughter of James A. Ogle and Nancy E. Potter Ogle. (Courtesy of Earl Adams Jr., Inez McCauley Adams Collection.)

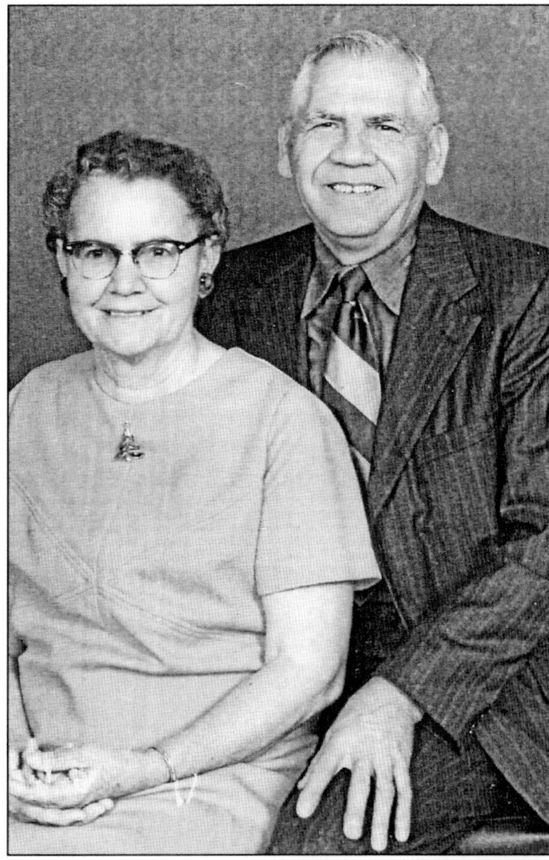

Theodore "Ted" Roosevelt Gourley is thought to have built this house in West Miller's Cove. Ted married Myrtle Bell Cooper Gourley, and they lived in this house for a time. In the early 1960s, Alice Braun and her family moved to Tennessee and bought this house. They lived in it for many years. (Courtesy of Jeanne Braun Whitehead.)

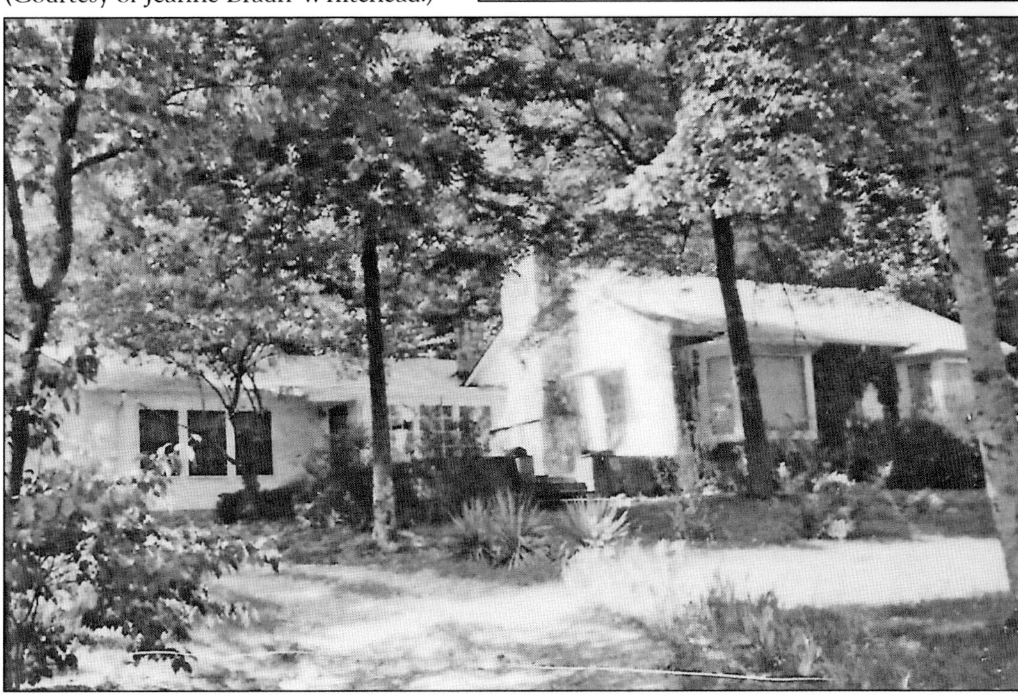

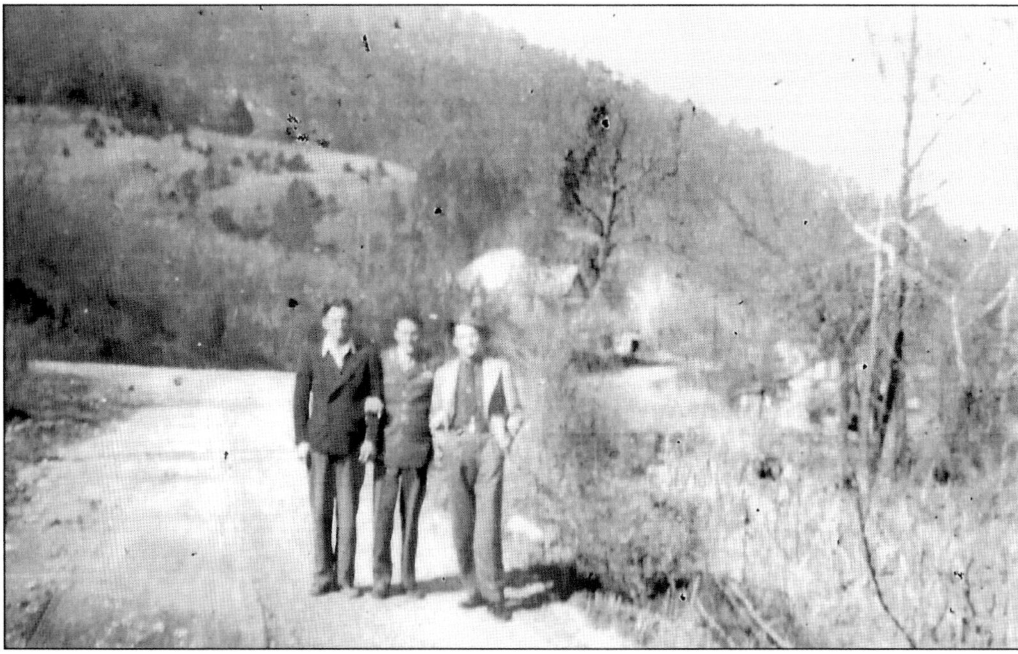

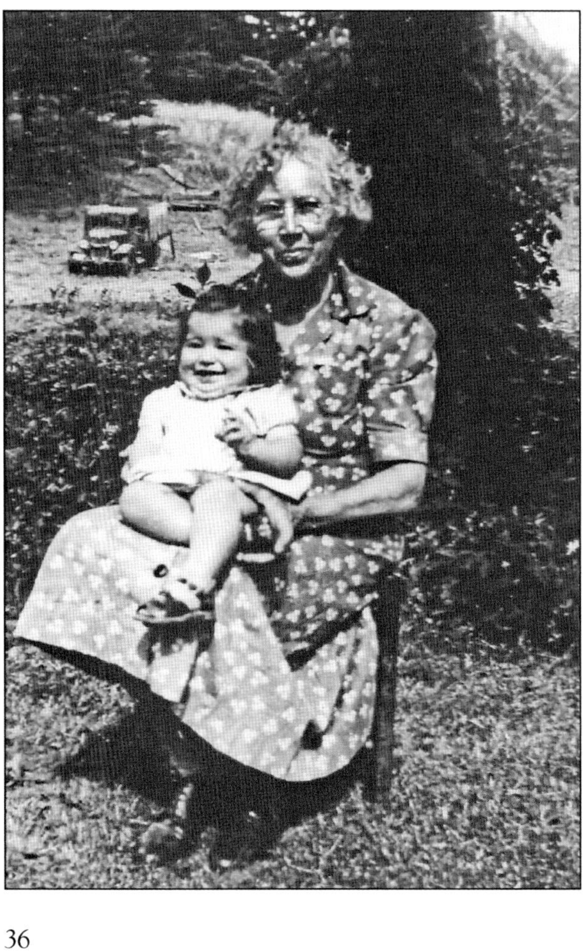

Pictured from left to right, brothers Walter, Charlie, and Lillard White walk down the road at Blue Springs on Little River after Walter returned from World War II. The Whites, Charlie, Hubert, Lillard, and Walter, came to the Walland area after working for the Civilian Conservation Corps in Tremont and Cades Cove. (Courtesy of Mike White.)

Winnie Tech Hannah is pictured with her great-granddaughter Billie Payton. Winnie was married to Doc Brewer; she once lived in a tent in the Miller's Cove Cemetery with snow on the ground with her son Harve and daughter Dockie Alice. Doc was killed while building the railroad that ran through the Blue Springs area; Winnie then married Levi Patty and had three sons, Perry, Shirley, and Mayford. Levi was killed, and Winnie raised all her children and her granddaughter Hazel Rathbone by herself. Winnie was thought of as an amazing person by her family and friends. (Courtesy of Mike White.)

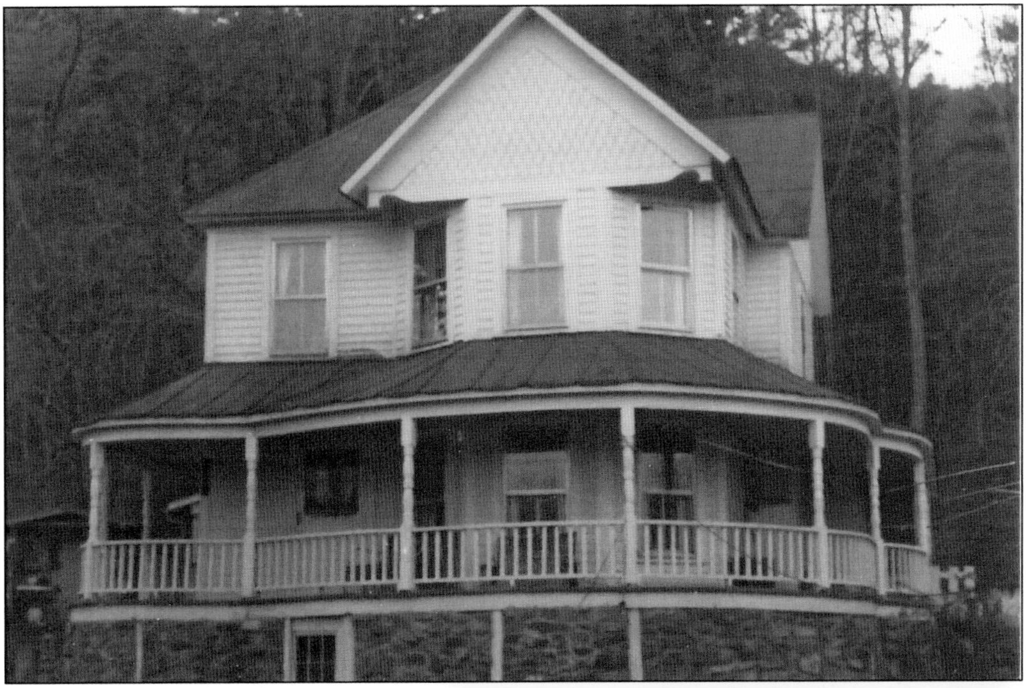

John Martin, "Snaky John" as he was known to most, built this house, and Hattie Hatcher Burns and John Luther Burns lived there. Hattie Leona Hatcher was born on January 24, 1890, to Joseph Walker "Joe" Hatcher and Rebecca Jane Walker Hatcher. John was the pastor at Miller's Cove Missionary Baptist Church from 1927 to 1930. (Courtesy of Earl Adams Jr., Inez McCauley Adams Collection.)

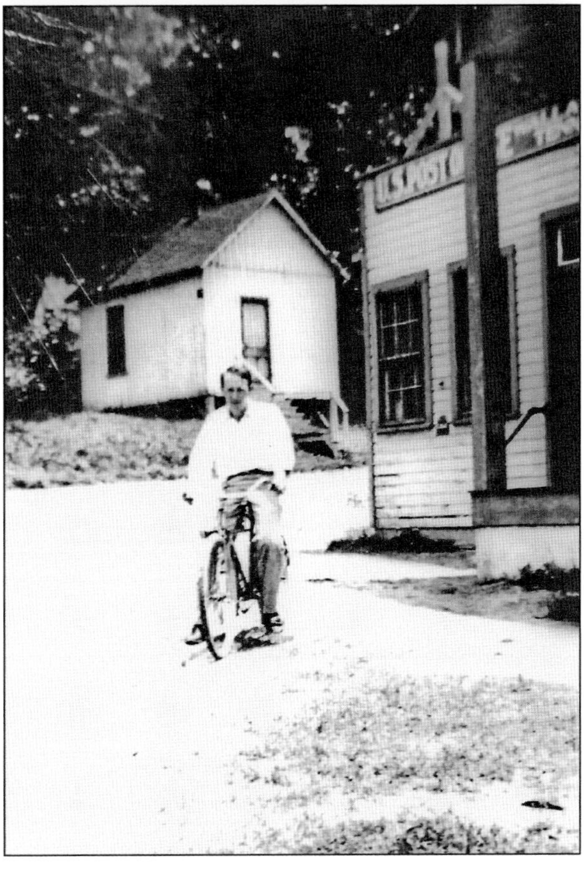

Earl Clayton Rudd rides his bicycle in front of Emert's Store and the Walland Post Office. Earl was born on June 30, 1908, to George Edgar Rudd and Nancy Adaline Fry Rudd. (Courtesy of Earl Adams Jr., Inez McCauley Adams Collection.)

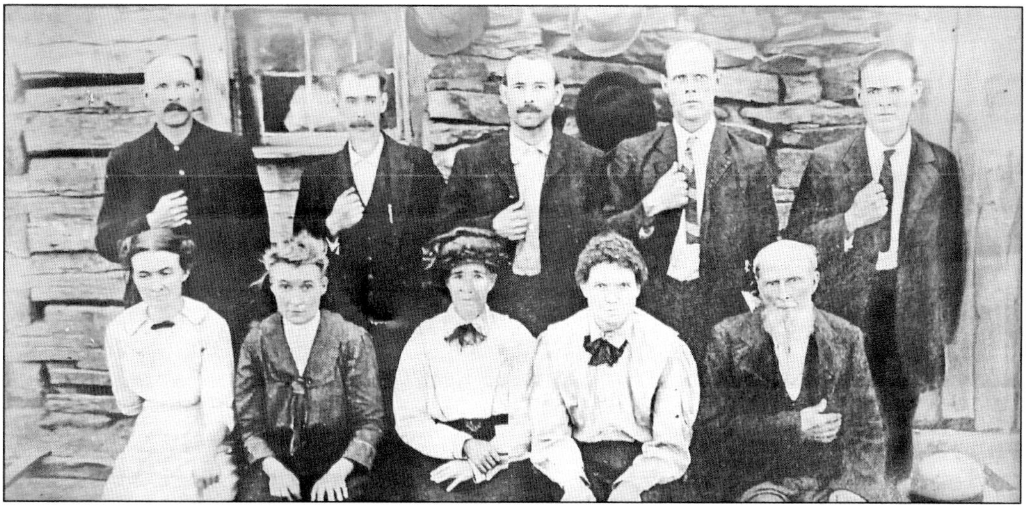

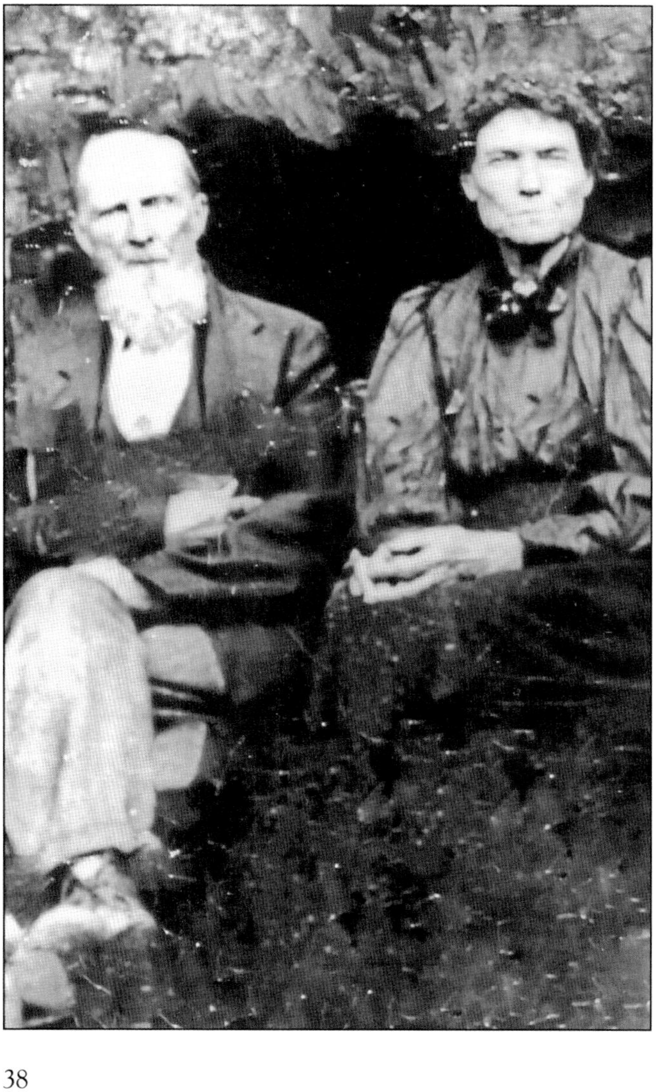

The family of Noah Hatcher and Rebecca Blair Hicks Hatcher is, from left to right, (first row) Noah, Rebecca, Elizabeth Jane, Mary, and Alice Florence Hatcher; (second row) James Houston, Robert Alexander, Joseph Bartley, William Richard, and Christopher Columbus. Noah Hatcher was born on January 12, 1845; he married Rebecca Blair Hicks in 1869. Noah's parents were William Elijah Hatcher and Rebecca Walker Hatcher. (Courtesy of the Ledbetter family.)

Noah Hatcher and his wife, Rebecca Blair Hicks, are pictured in front of the Hatcher cave in West Miller's Cove. Union sympathizers would hide their valuables and livestock from bushwhackers in limestone caves on the Hatcher property. Noah Hatcher's father, Elijah Hatcher, who was too old to serve in the war, was hiding in one the caves with other sympathizers when bushwhackers found them and shot and killed Elijah Hatcher. (Courtesy of Carol Hatcher Ellis.)

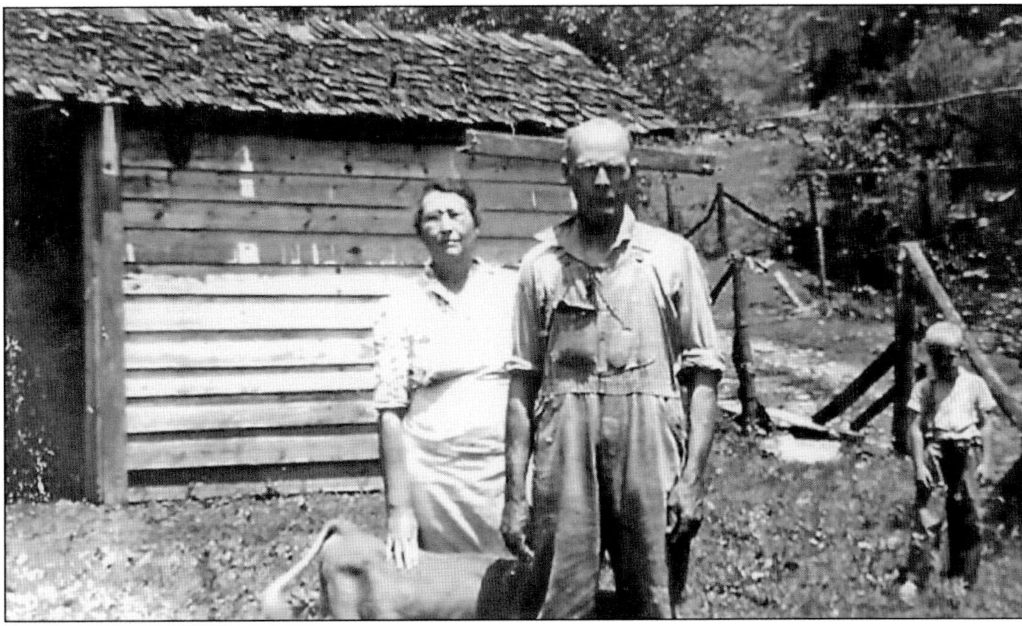

"Cordie" Murr Hatcher and Richard Hatcher pose in front of the spring house on their farm. (Courtesy of Allen Ledbetter.)

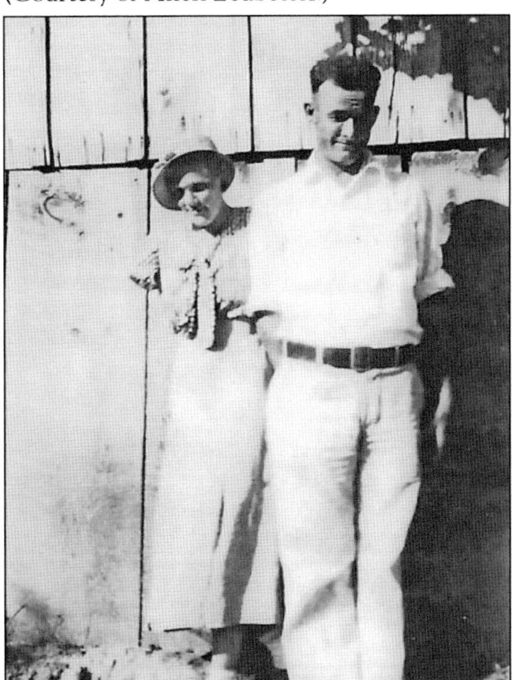

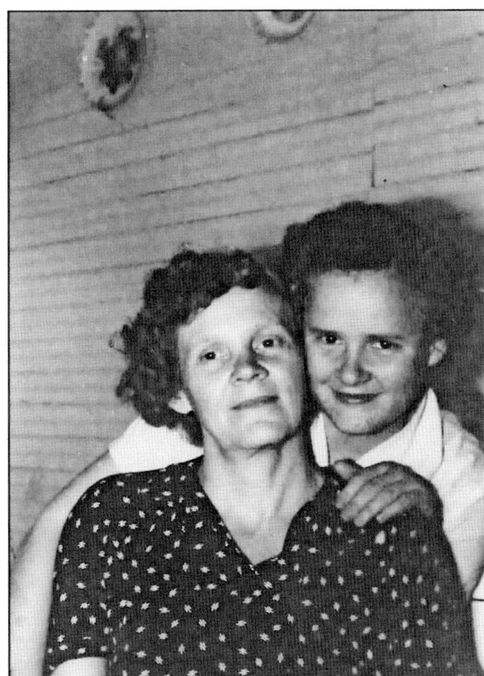

Noah Campbell "Cam" Hatcher (left) was born on April 13, 1909, to James Houston Hatcher and Alice Caldonia Blair of Miller's Cove in Walland. Cam married Ella Lawson, the daughter of Daniel Jasper Lawson and Martha Lawson. Ella was born on June 4, 1914, in Cades Cove. She is pictured at right with daughter Marie in their home in Miller's Cove. The 1930 census shows the family living in Miller's Cove. (Both, courtesy of Marie Hatcher McClanahan.)

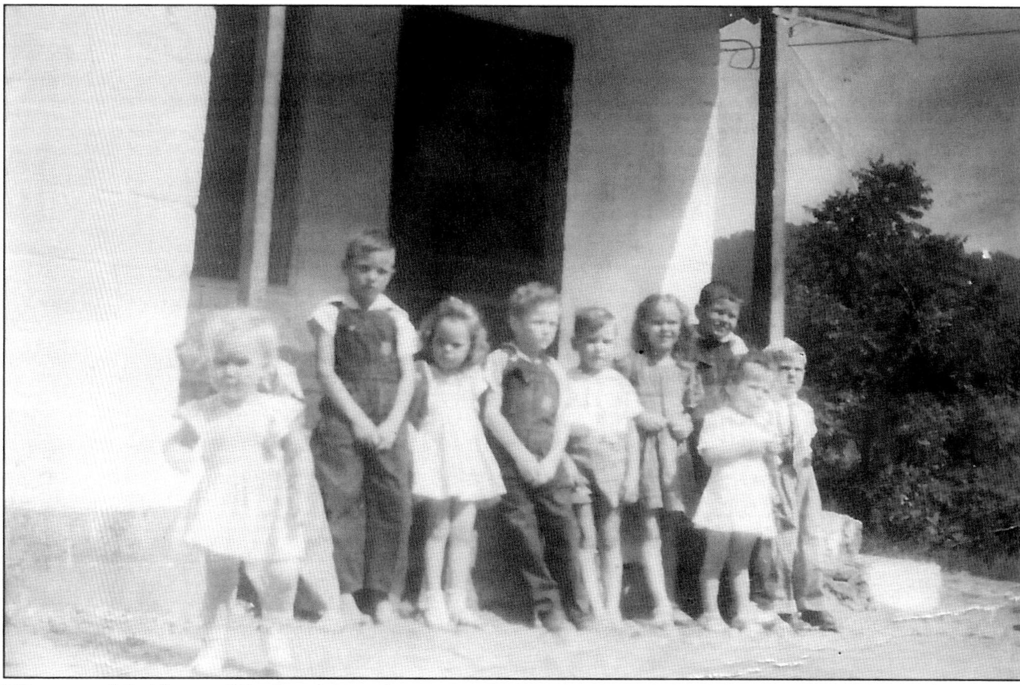

The grandchildren of Richard Hatcher and Cordie Murr Hatcher, pictured from left to right, are Irma Hatcher, Ray Headrick, Carol Hatcher, Max Headrick, Jackie Headrick, Geneva Headrick, Sammy Headrick, Janice Headrick, and Clay Ledbetter in 1946. (Courtesy of Carol Hatcher Ellis.)

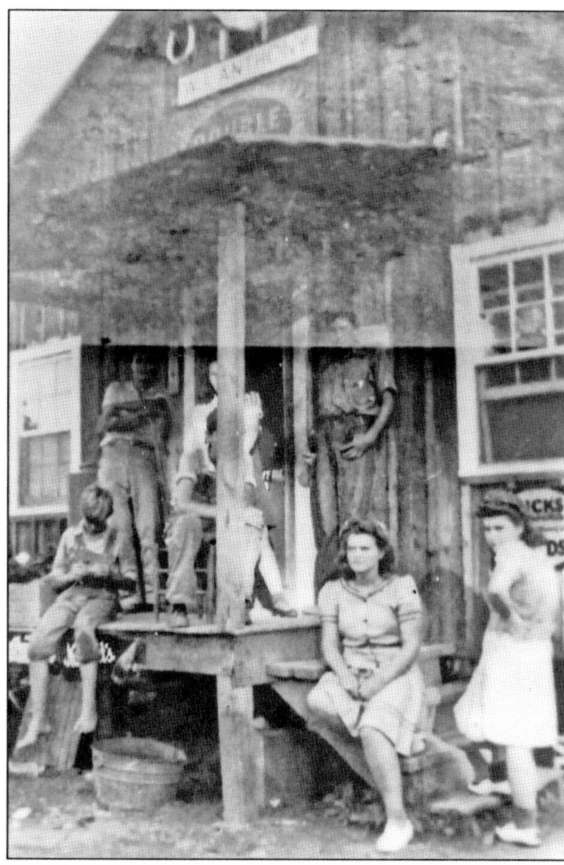

The W.I. Anthony Country Store is pictured in West Miller's Cove. Most stores had a front that was decorated with tin signs advertising tobacco, cigars, soft drinks, hardware, and more. The porch also served as the social center where residents gathered to talk weather, politics, the price of crops, and more. (Courtesy of Earl Adams Jr., Inez McCauley Adams Collection.)

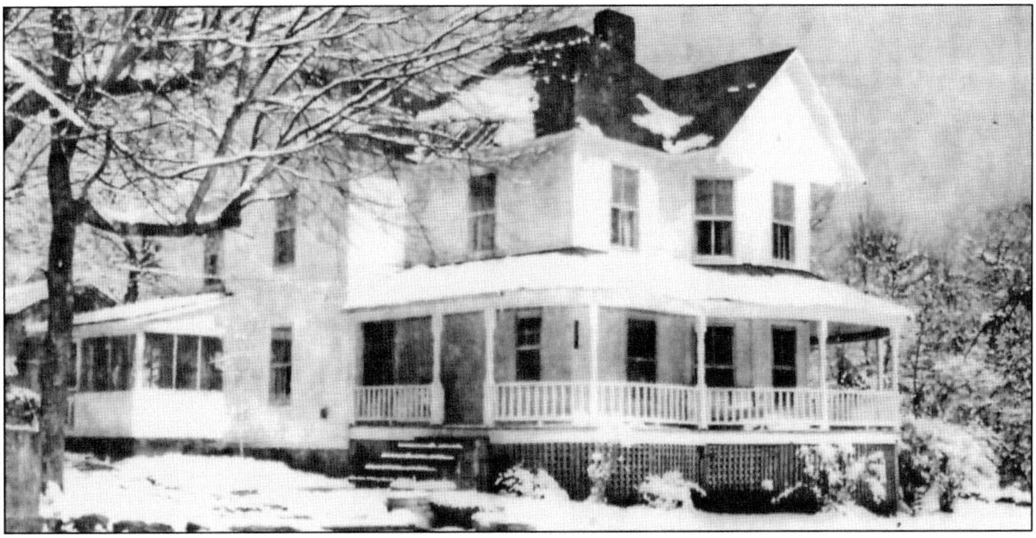

The David and Bertie West family lived in this West Miller's Cove home. David and Bertie moved from North Carolina to Tennessee for David to work for the Aluminum Company of America (ALCOA) about 1942–1943. The West family moved into this house in 1965. It was the former home of Ed and Hattie Hatcher Burns. (Courtesy of Bertie West.)

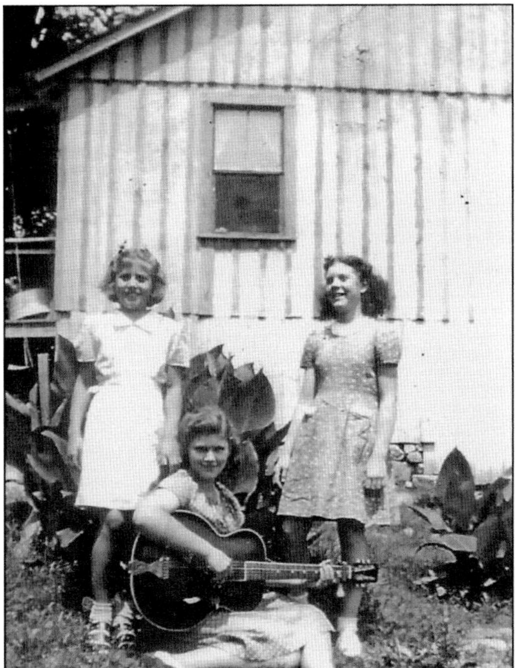

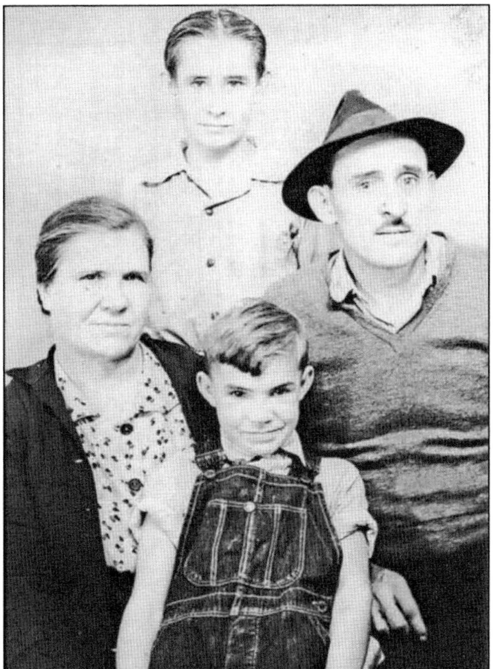

At left, pictured from left to right, Lura, Joyce, and Evelyn West, daughters of David and Bertie West, attended Walland schools and were involved in many activities. At right, Cora Everett and John Moses Everett are pictured with sons Raymond (back) and Max (front). John Moses was the son of Layfette "Fate" Everett and Della Lane Everett of the Rocky Branch area. Cora was the daughter of Rachel Ann Gamble Everett and Thomas James "Bish" Everett. (Left, courtesy of Bertie West; right, courtesy Sandy Everett Johnson.)

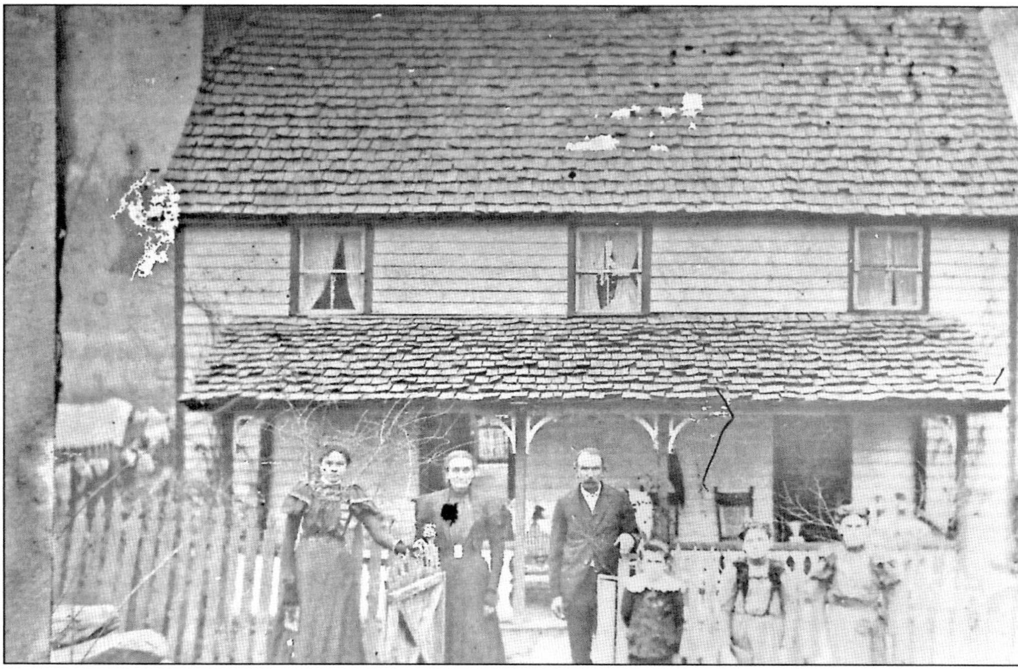

The Walker family is, from left to right, daughter Elizabeth "Lizzie," mother Isabella Amanda Burchfield Walker, father "Red" Vance Walker, son Oscar, and daughter Cora and Bertha. Red was the son of Spencer Walker and Orpha McDonnell Walker. Isabella Amanda Burchfield Walker was the daughter of Nathan Burchfield and Elizabeth Blair Burchfield of Cades Cove. (Courtesy of Earl Adams Jr., Inez McCauley Adams Collection.)

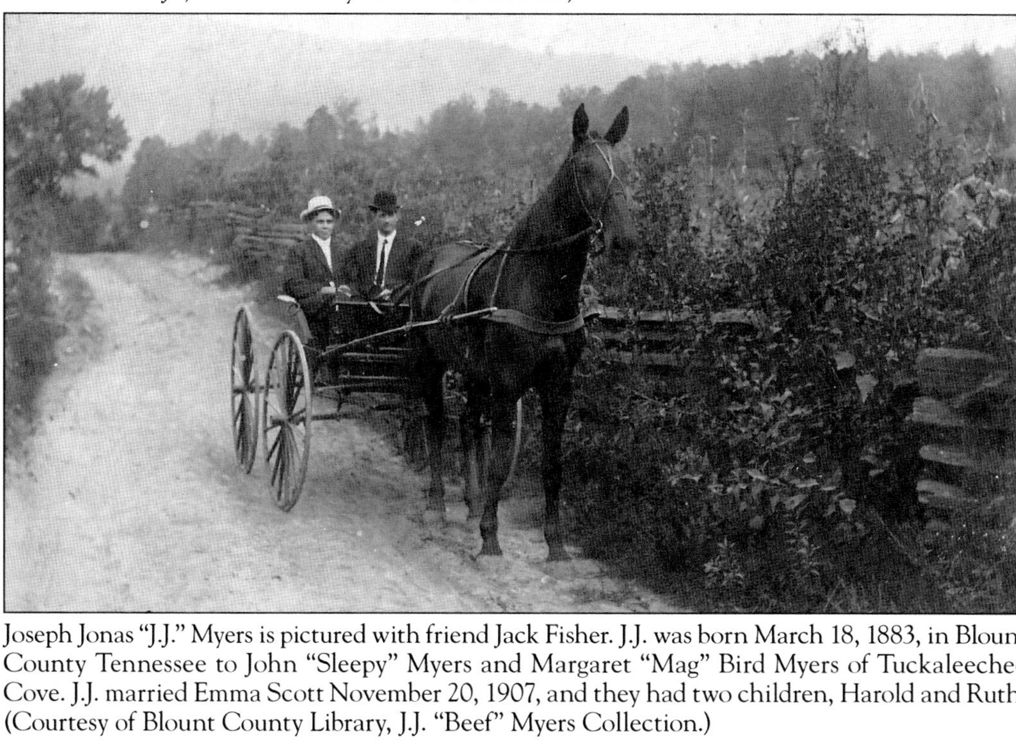

Joseph Jonas "J.J." Myers is pictured with friend Jack Fisher. J.J. was born March 18, 1883, in Blount County Tennessee to John "Sleepy" Myers and Margaret "Mag" Bird Myers of Tuckaleechee Cove. J.J. married Emma Scott November 20, 1907, and they had two children, Harold and Ruth. (Courtesy of Blount County Library, J.J. "Beef" Myers Collection.)

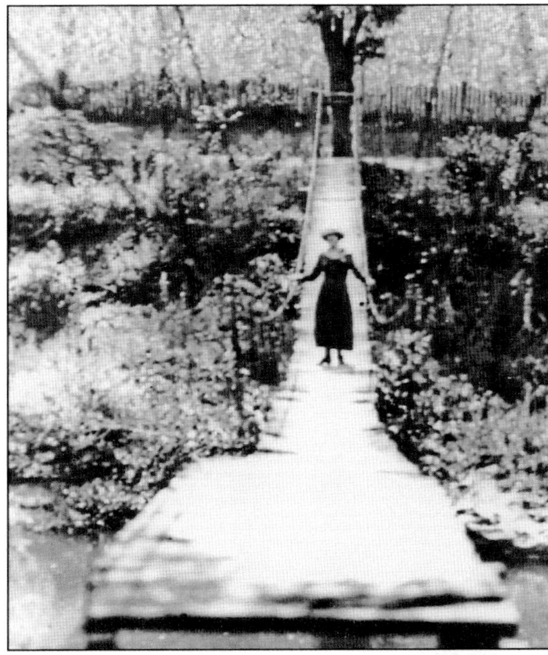

This swinging bridge from the Old Walland Highway to the New Walland Highway crossed Little River. The Walker children grew up on the banks of Little River. The Walker farm fronted about a mile along Little River Railroad. Walkers Station was the stop in the area for the train to bring incoming freight. (Courtesy of Jack and Vonnie Walker.)

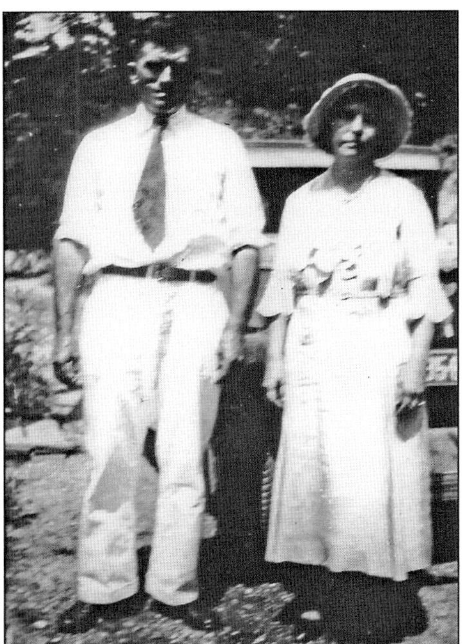

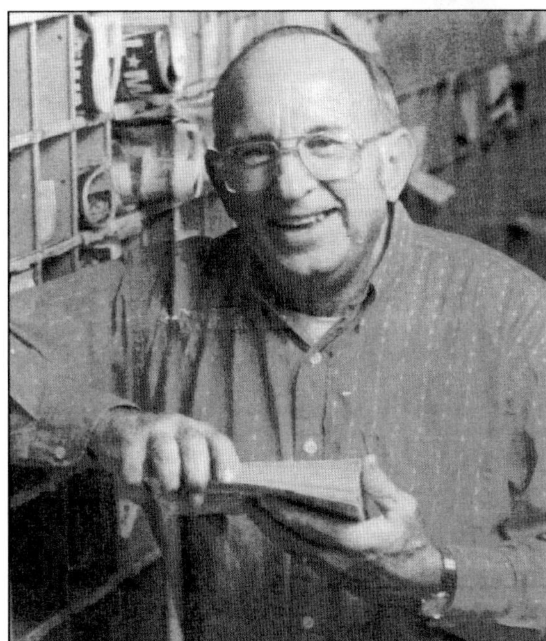

In 1918, Oscar Lafayette Walker Sr. (left photograph, wearing tie), a young farmer, married Nora Elizabeth McNeilly (left photograph, in hat), a teacher at Caughron School in Miller's Cove. Nora was the daughter of William Kelley McNeilly and Malinda Malvina "Mallie" Caughron. Oscar was born June 21, 1890, to Vance B. Walker and Isabella Amanda Burchfield. The Burchfield family was from the Cades Cove area. Jack Walker (right photograph), son of Oscar Walker and Nora McNeilly Walker, started working as the Walland postmaster in 1962; he retired 30 years later in 1992. Jack married Vonnie Flynn, daughter of Sampson Flynn and Bonnie Cagle Flynn. (Both, courtesy of Jack and Vonnie Walker.)

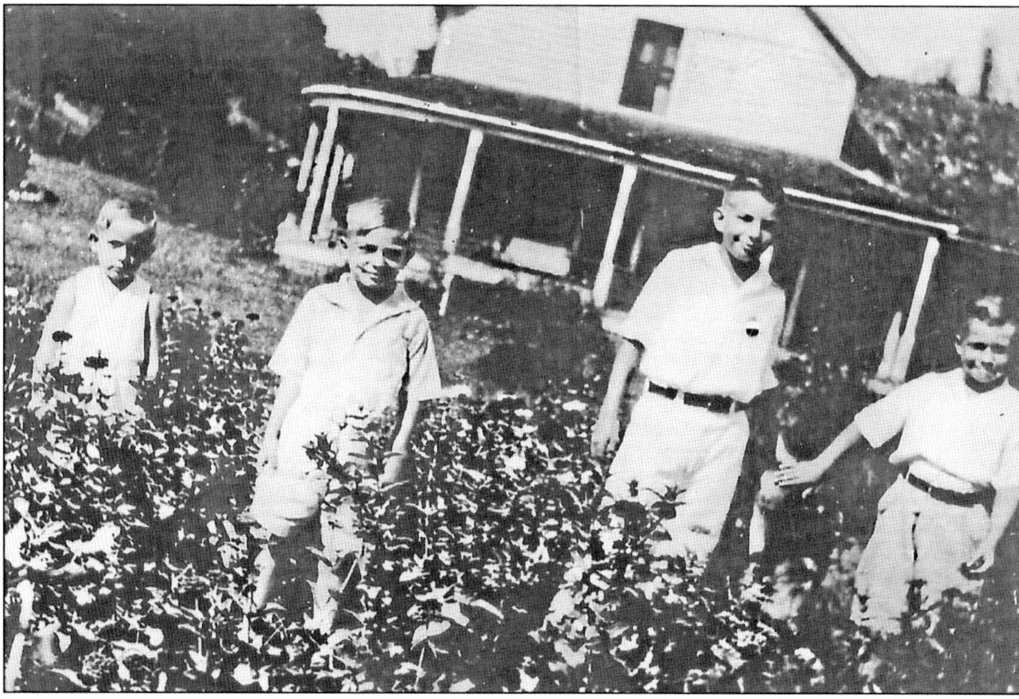

From left to right are Max, Harvey, Gene, Oscar Jr., and Vance Walker, five boys of Nora and Oscar Walker. All six of the Walker boys served their country in the military. (Courtesy of Jack and Vonnie Walker.)

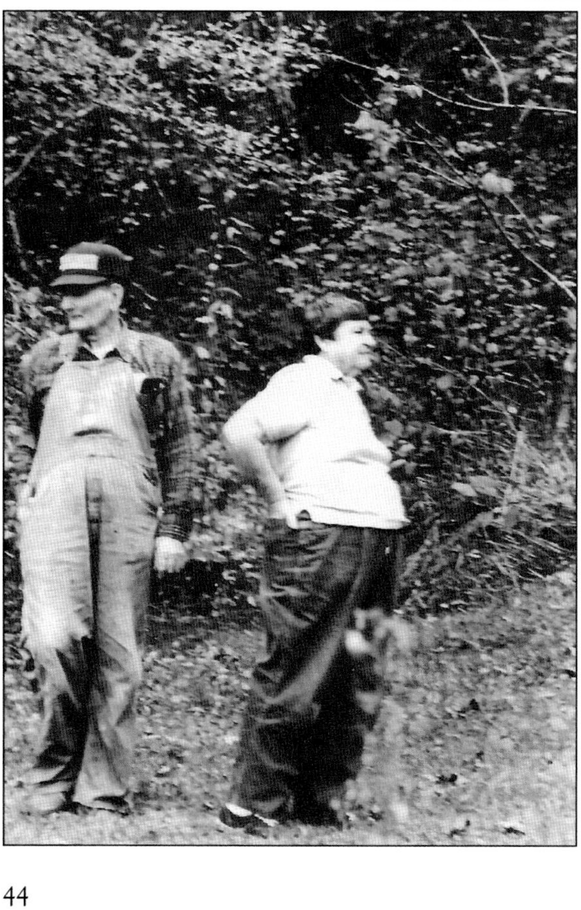

Pictured are Dewey Davis and Thelma Davis of Miller's Cove. Dewey worked for many years for Blount County as a road grader. (Courtesy of Sandy Davis Butler.)

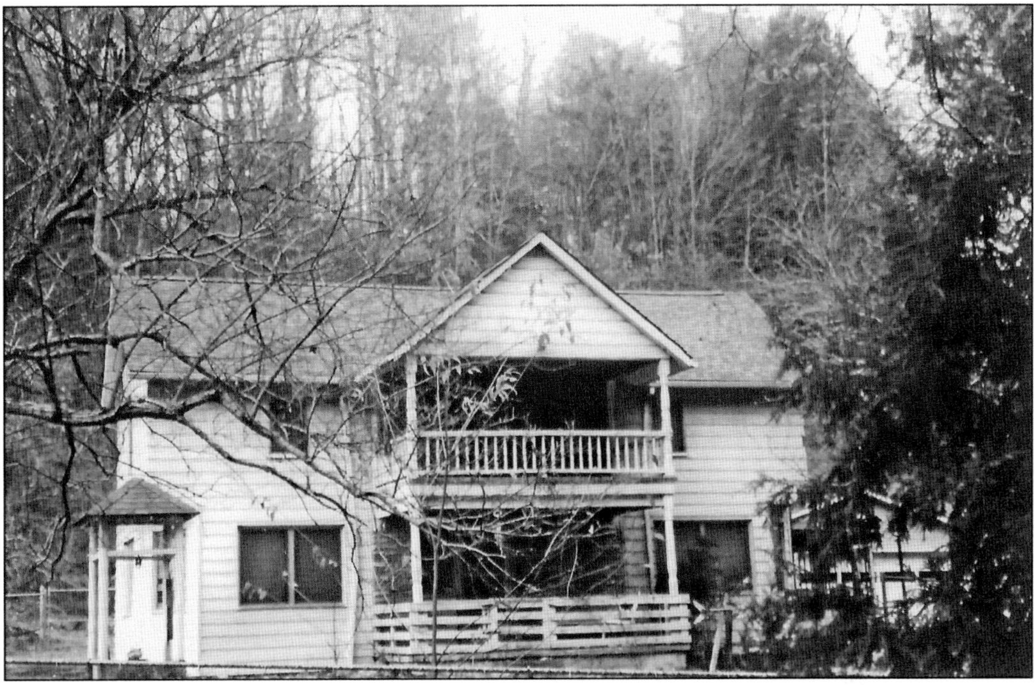

"Snaky John" Martin built this house that the miller resided in near Martin Mill, a gristmill that ground corn and wheat for the community. Martin Mill is on Hess Creek, and the waters of the creek are used to turn the millstone, which runs a corn sheller and an emery wheel. John Hess was issued permission in 1795 to build a mill on Murphy's Creek, now known as Hess Creek. In 1834, there was a mill listed as Hess' Mill. This could have been the predecessor of Martin Mill. (Courtesy of Earl Adams Jr., Inez McCauley Adams Collection.)

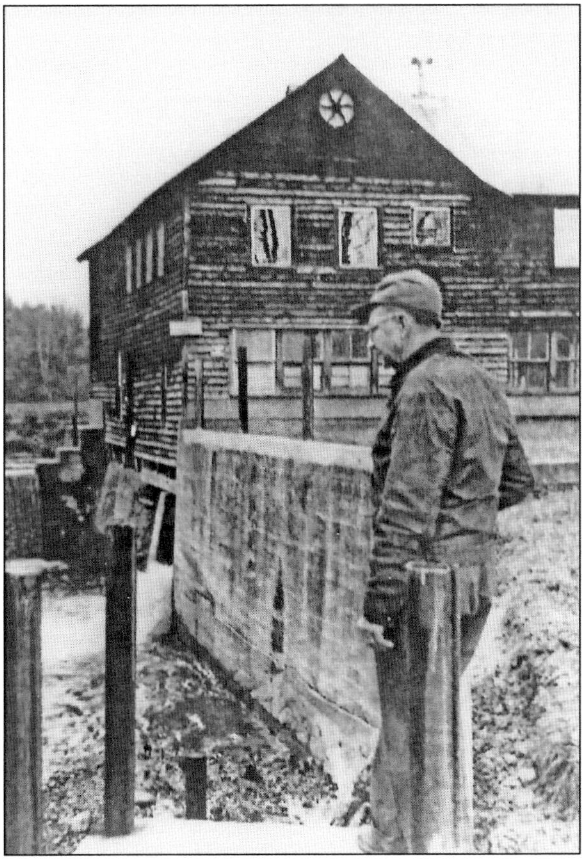

The Martin-Coada Mill is a turbine mill; the waterwheel is made to rotate by water falling across the blades and into buckets suspended from them. Charlie Coada, who took over ownership of the mill, had a toll board to measure the amount he would charge customers. (Courtesy of Earl Adams Jr., Inez McCauley Adams Collection.)

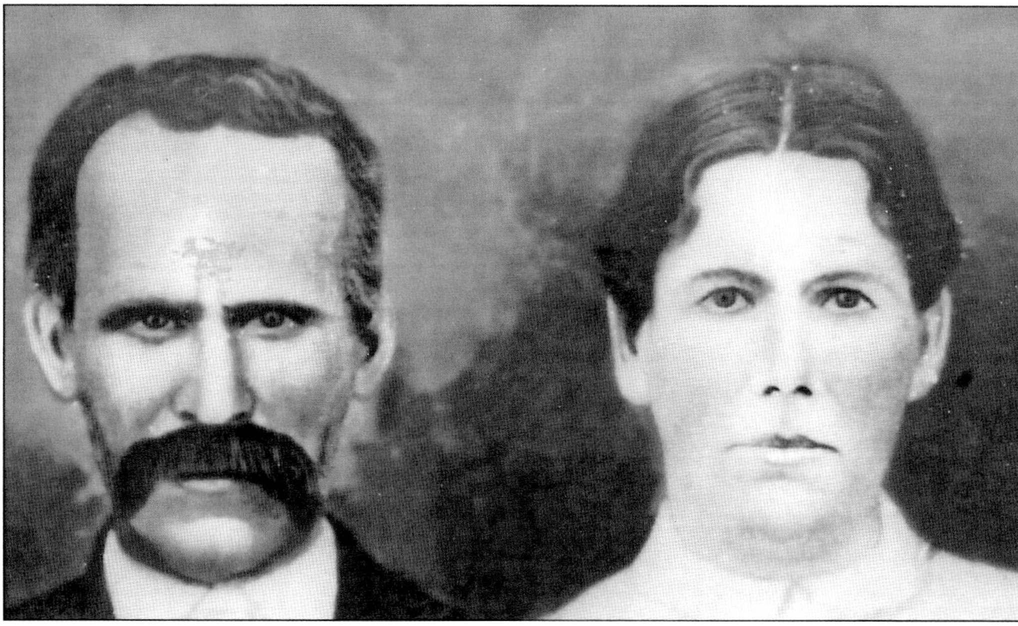

George Washington Everett was born on July 31, 1854, to Noah Everett and Rebecca Hatcher Everett. George's wife, Clementine McIntosh, was born on August 3, 1860. They were joined in marriage on September 26, 1878, by Spencer Walker, justice of the peace for Blount County. (Courtesy of Missy Tipton Green.)

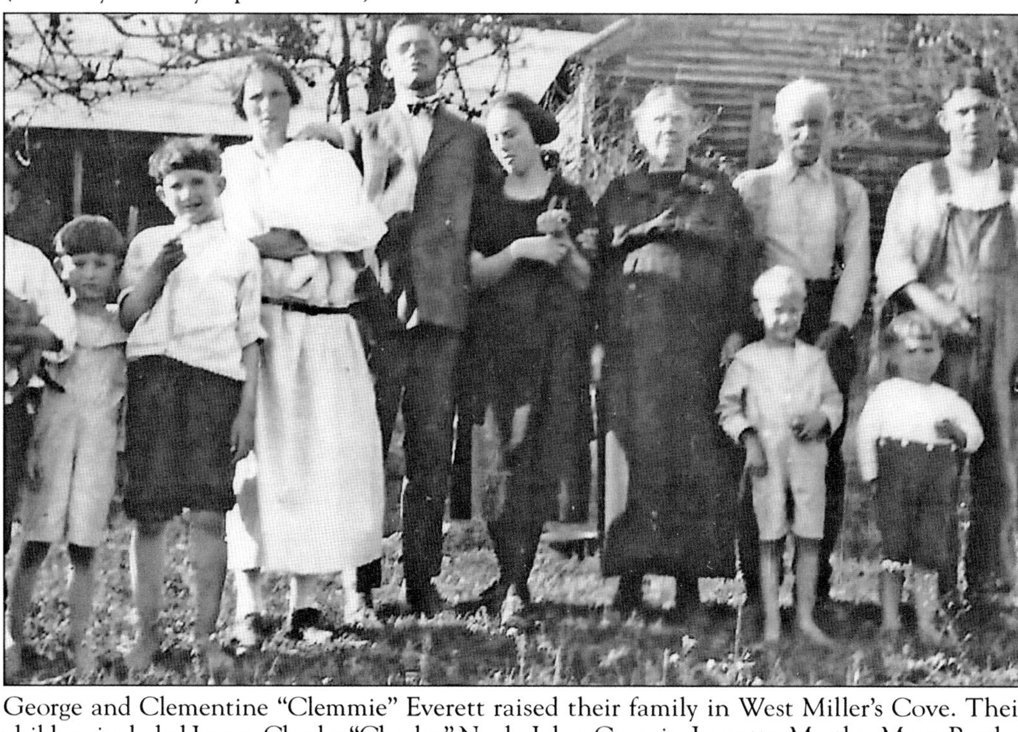

George and Clementine "Clemmie" Everett raised their family in West Miller's Cove. Their children included James, Charles "Charley" Noah, John, Georgia, Jeanette, Martha, Mary, Bertha, and Flora. Pictured in front of the Everett house are George and "Clemmie" and some of their children and grandchildren. (Courtesy of Missy Tipton Green.)

John Alexander Everett and Josephine "Joe" Catherine Henry were married on October 25, 1924. John was the son of George and Clemmie Everett, and Joe was the daughter of Susannah Everett Henry and Joe Henry. (Courtesy of Missy Tipton Green.)

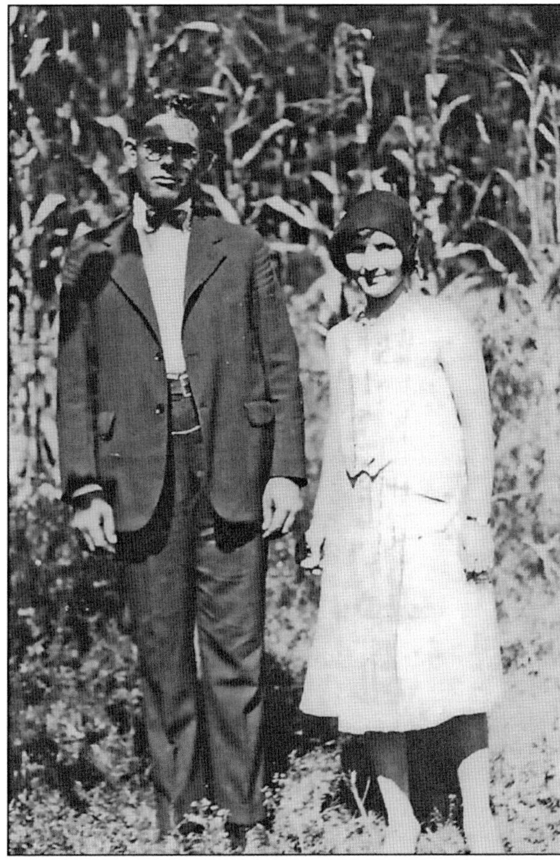

John Everett built his house on land he acquired from his father, George Washington Everett. John ran a pipe from his spring on the mountain, and he pumped running water from his spring house into his house. (Courtesy of Missy Tipton Green.)

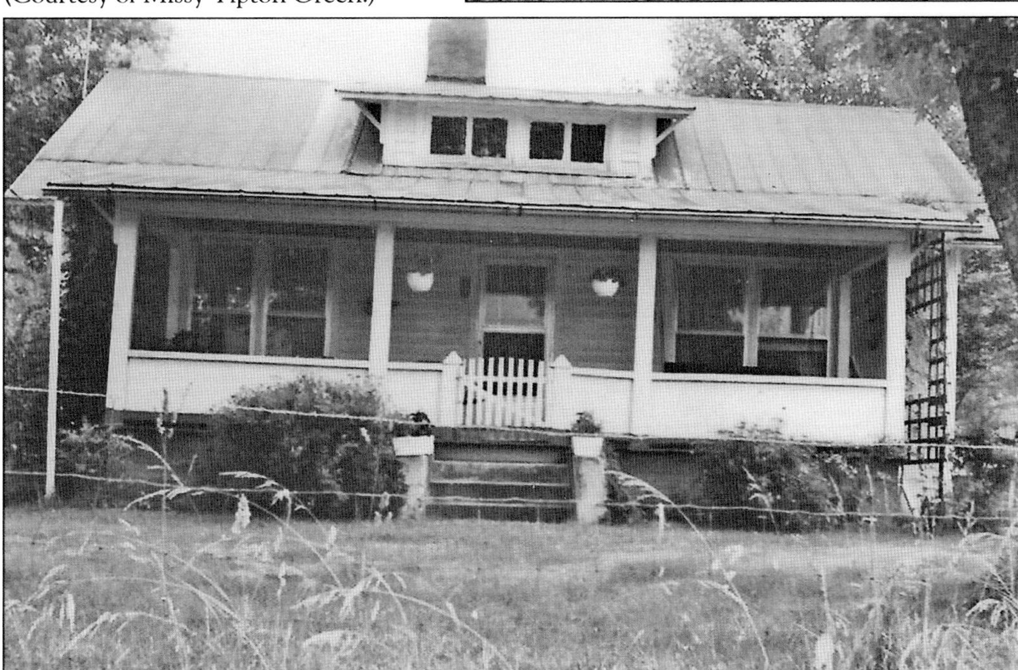

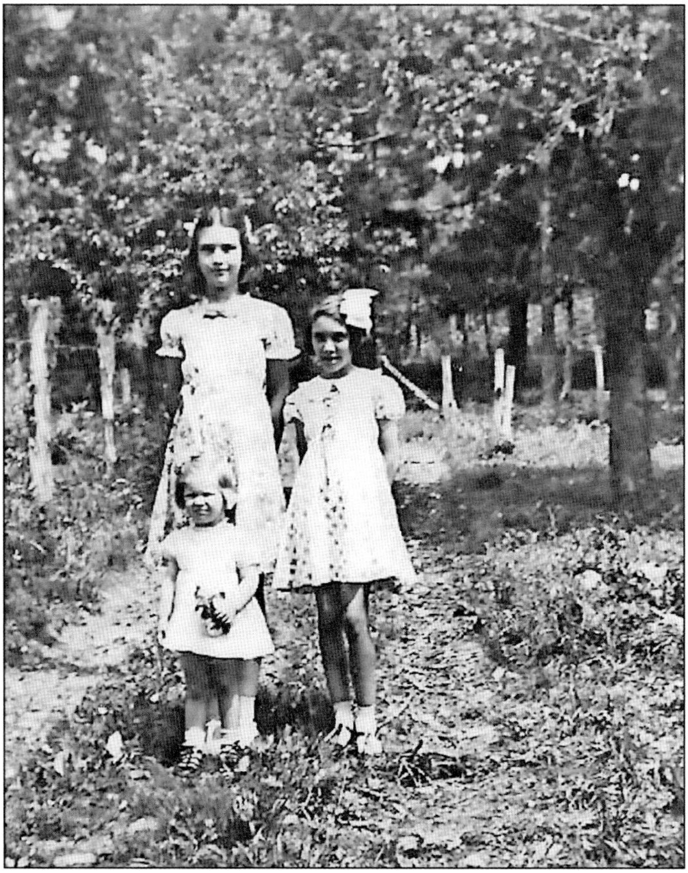

When John and Joe Everett started having children, the good Lord saw fit to give them all girls. Ruby Rowena (back, left) was born on January 1, 1927, Juanita (right) on July 1, 1930, Lois Faye (front) on February 25, 1938, and Martha Jo "Jody" on June 9, 1940. (Courtesy of Missy Tipton Green.)

Faye (left) and Jody Everett (right) are pictured as youngsters. All of the girls of John and Joe Everett attended Walland School from first grade to graduation. They enjoyed basketball and became very good players at Walland School. (Courtesy of Missy Tipton Green.)

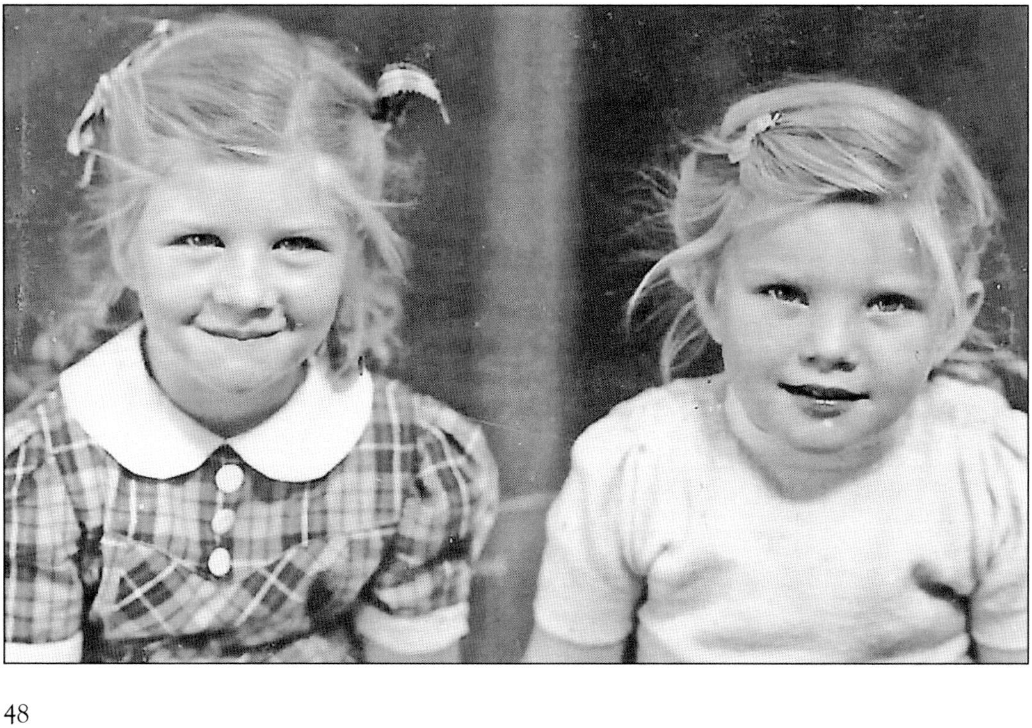

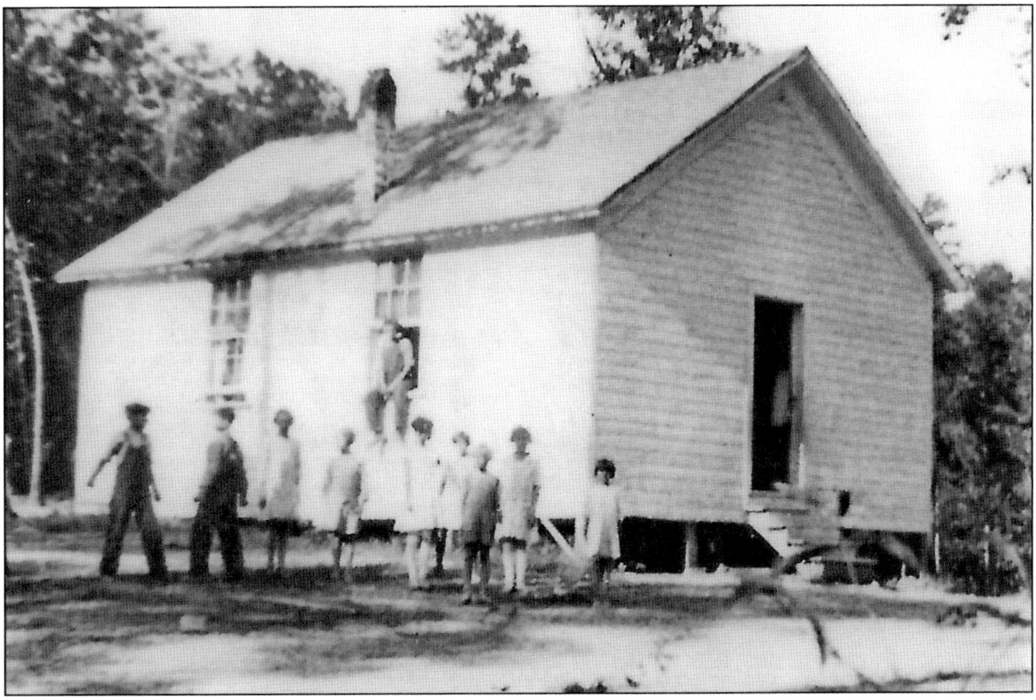

Webb School was on the Blackberry Farm property in West Miller's Cove. This was one of the earlier schools of the area and probably closed in the early 1920s. These students would have consolidated with students of nearby Caughron School. The school building became the guest house of Blackberry Farm. (Courtesy of Earl Adams Jr. Inez McCauley Adams Collection.)

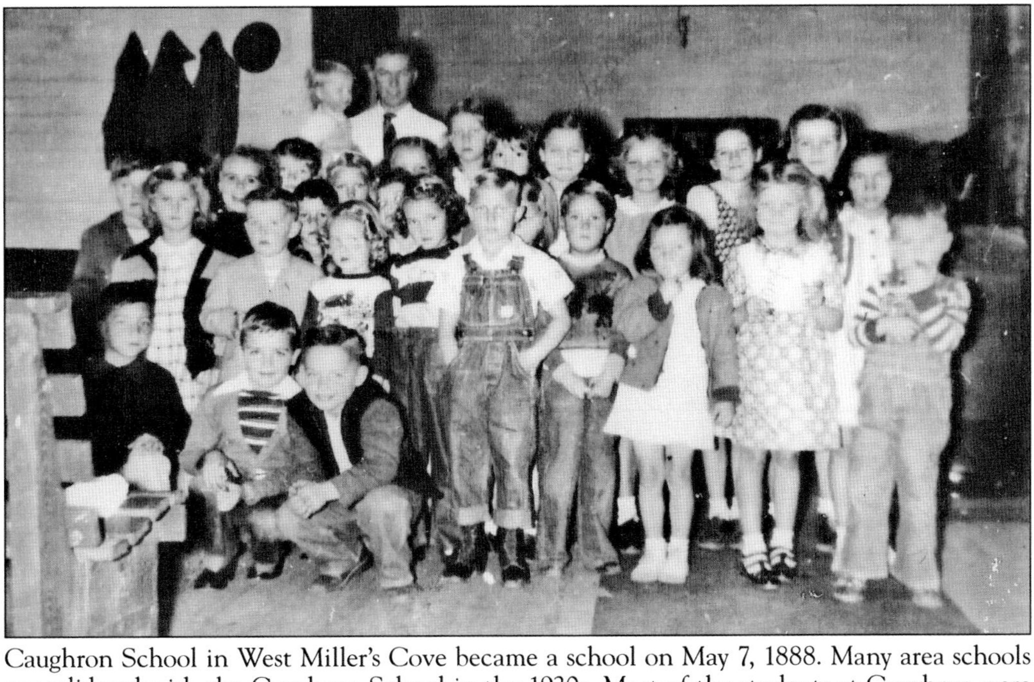

Caughron School in West Miller's Cove became a school on May 7, 1888. Many area schools consolidated with the Caughron School in the 1920s. Most of the students at Caughron were residents of West Miller's Cove. (Courtesy of Allen Ledbetter.)

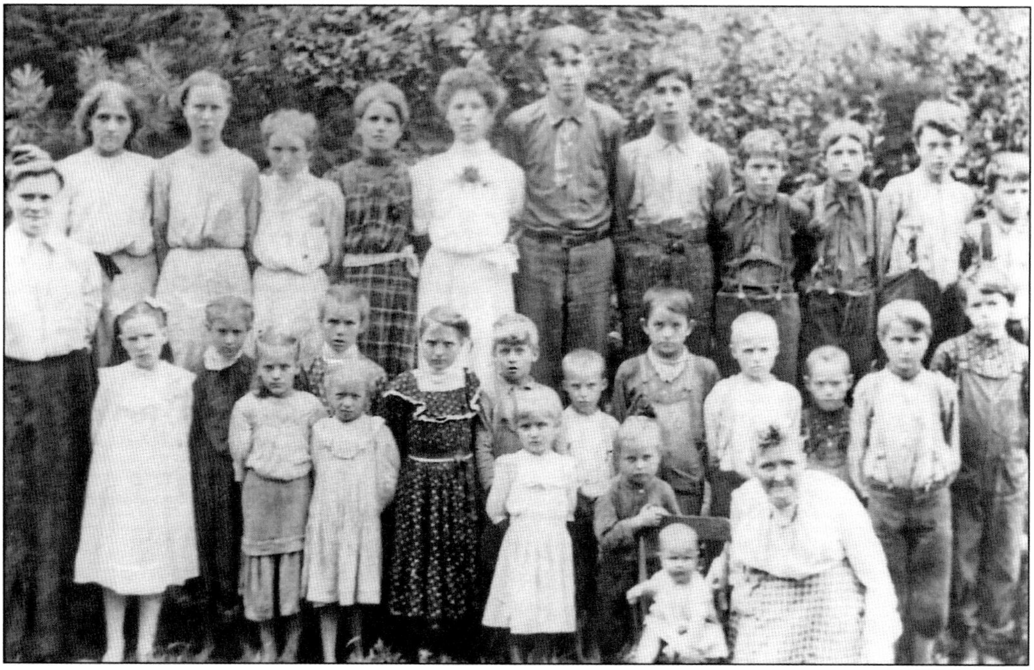

The Garland School, or Canes School, was in the Cane area. It was built to provide an education for the children of a large lumber and logging camp in 1903. Like most students of this era, the children attended school barefoot. This photograph was taken in 1908. The lady in foreground with her grandchild is Helen Harmon; they were visitors to the school. From left to right are (first row) teacher Ann Nuchols, Lydia Buchanan, Martha Garland, Ida Payne, Lillian Buchanan, Retta Harmon, Robert Buchanan, Braska Harmon, Melvin Harris, Austin Harmon, Frank Payne, Champlin Harris, Ed Garland, General Harmon, and Hamp Garland; (second row) Leonard Payne, Laura Harmon, Sally Garland, Lillie Garland, Pearly Woody, Jim Woody, Robert Garland, Manasseh Buchanan, Eugene Buchanan, Willie Harmon, and Cary Buchanan. (Courtesy of Earl Adams Jr., Inez McCauley Adams Collection.)

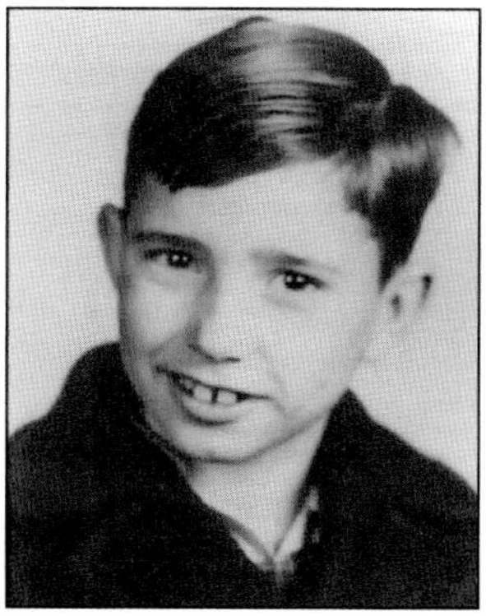

Johnny Headrick, son of James "Jim" Robert Headrick and Vedith Everett Headrick, was born on January 8, 1941. Johnny attended school at Walland. (Courtesy of Mary Headrick.)

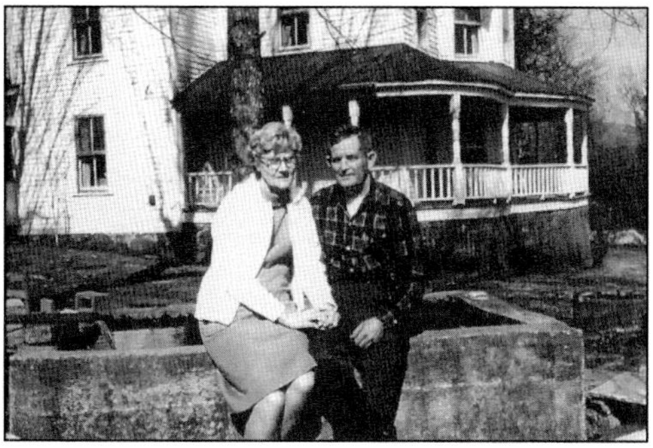

Bertie and David West are pictured in front of the house they bought from Hattie Burns in 1965. The West family moved to the Walland area from North Carolina about 1942–1943 for David to work at the Aluminum Company of America. (Courtesy of Bertie West.)

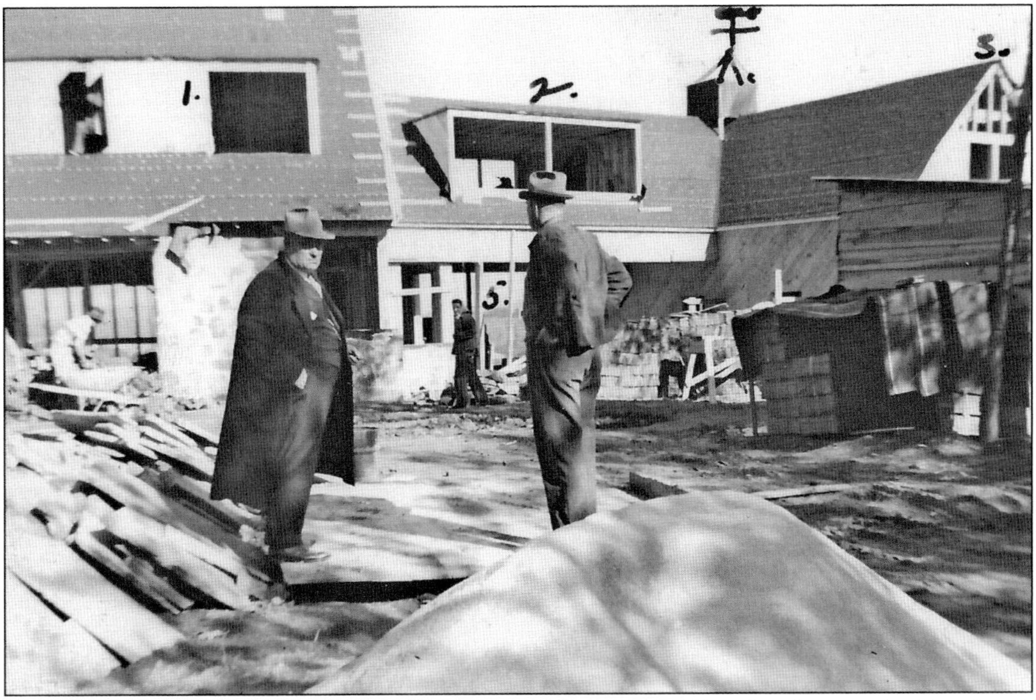

On March 21, 1940, David Lasier bought 158 acres of wooded land bordered in part by Hess Creek for $3,500. This photograph shows builder Jim Vineyard (left) with owner David Lasier (right) working on the construction of Lasier's inn. (Courtesy of *Blackberry Farm: The Beginning* by John Edmondson and the Harris-Edmondson family archives.)

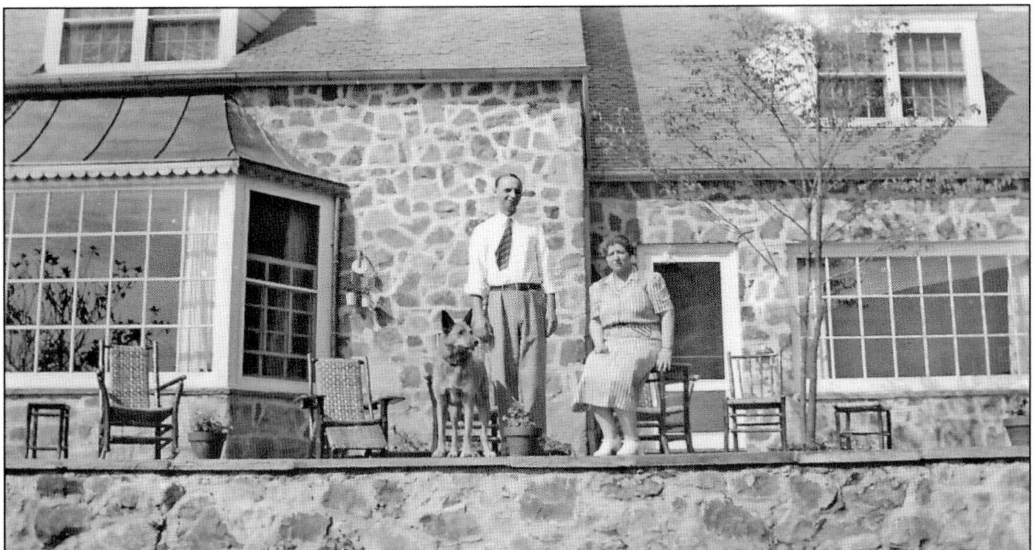

David Lasier and his wife, Florida, decided to call their new inn Blackberry Farm. They opened it in the spring of 1941, and Jim (called Jase by his family and friends) and Ruth Harris welcomed many guests. Jase and Ruth Harris are pictured on the porch of Blackberry Farm with their dog in 1941. (Courtesy of *Blackberry Farm: The Beginning* by John Edmondson and the Harris-Edmondson family archives.)

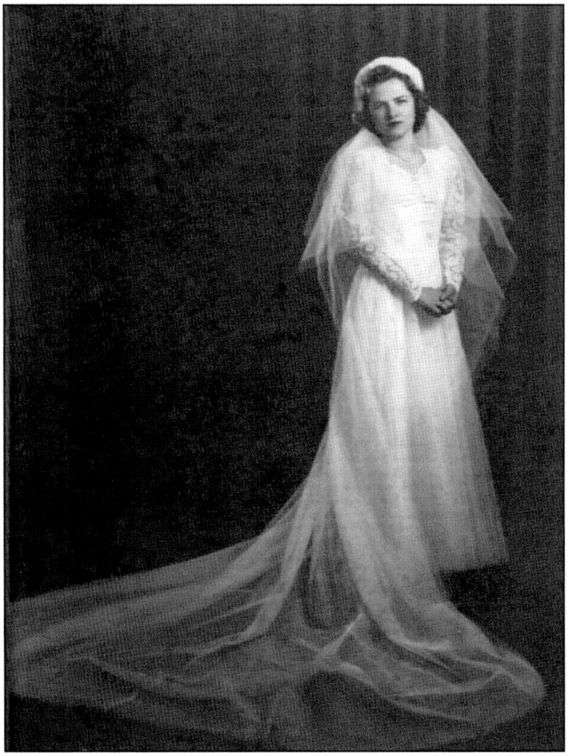

Ruthie Lorna Harris had the first wedding at Blackberry Farm on March 7, 1942, when she married John Henry Edmondson. She was the daughter of James and Ruth Harris, who managed Blackberry Farm at this time. (Courtesy of *Blackberry Farm: The Beginning*, John Edmondson, and the Harris-Edmondson family archives.)

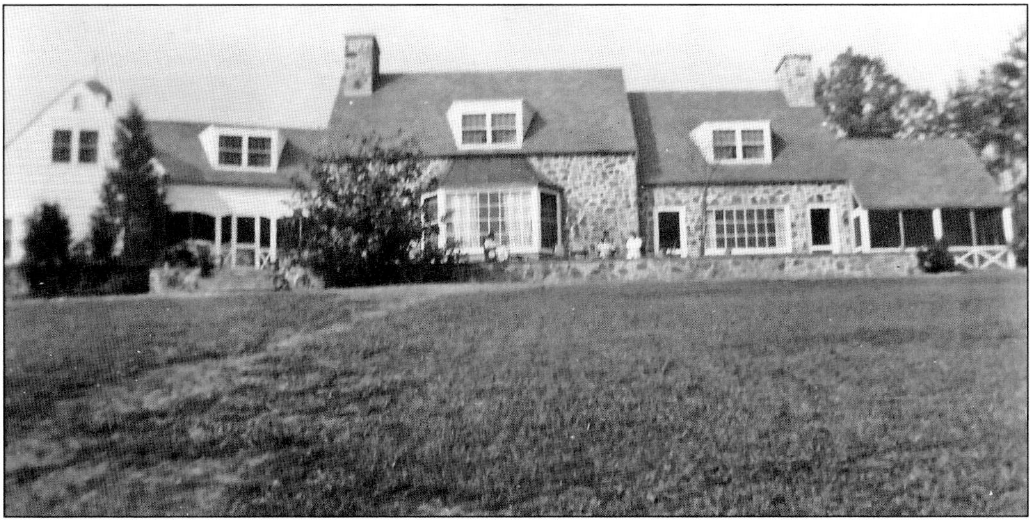

Pictured in 1941, the year it was built, the guest house at the Blackberry Farm Inn was constructed of stone, shingles, and slate, and was a retreat where guests could go to enjoy rest, fun, and contentment. There was always some sort of fun going on at the inn, such as hiking, outdoor games, and outside relaxation. Blackberry Farm was within walking distance to the Great Smoky Mountains National Park. Guests could enjoy the many hiking trails of the Smokies or just take in the natural wonders. Blackberry was located in the southeastern portion of Blount County, known as Miller's Cove. Blackberry Farm Inn is surrounded by the beautiful Chilhowee Mountains. (Courtesy of *Blackberry Farm: The Beginning* by John Edmondson and the Harris-Edmondson family archives.)

Blackberry Farm raised its own chickens and pigs and had a large variety of row crops as well as blackberries. Vern Elseth shows the first crop of blackberries grown at Blackberry Farm. (Courtesy of *Blackberry Farm: The Beginning* by John Edmondson and the Harris-Edmondson family archives.)

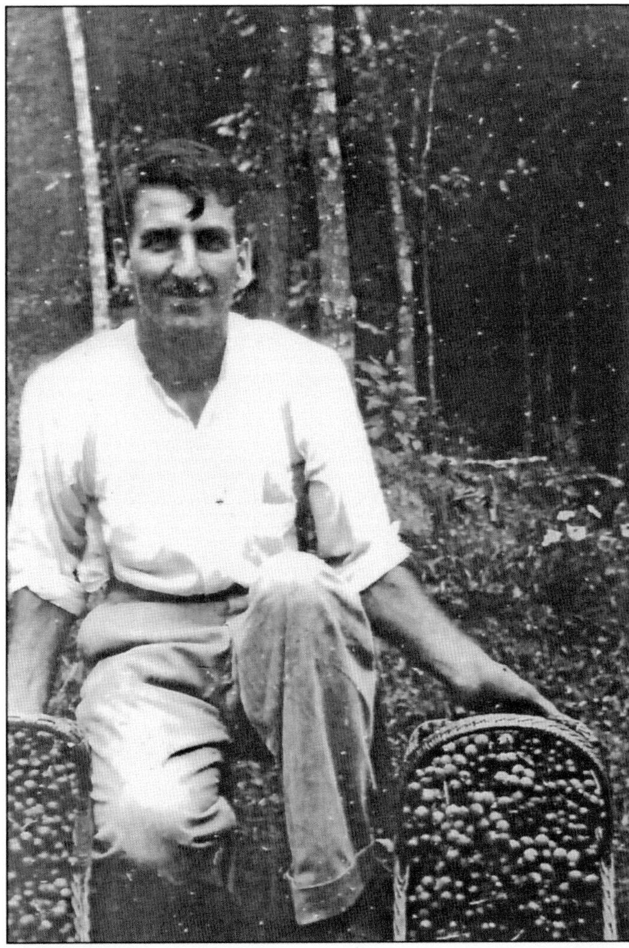

Gladys and Hugh Howard were among the key workers at Blackberry Farm. (Courtesy of *Blackberry Farm: The Beginning* by John Edmondson and the Harris-Edmondson family archives.)

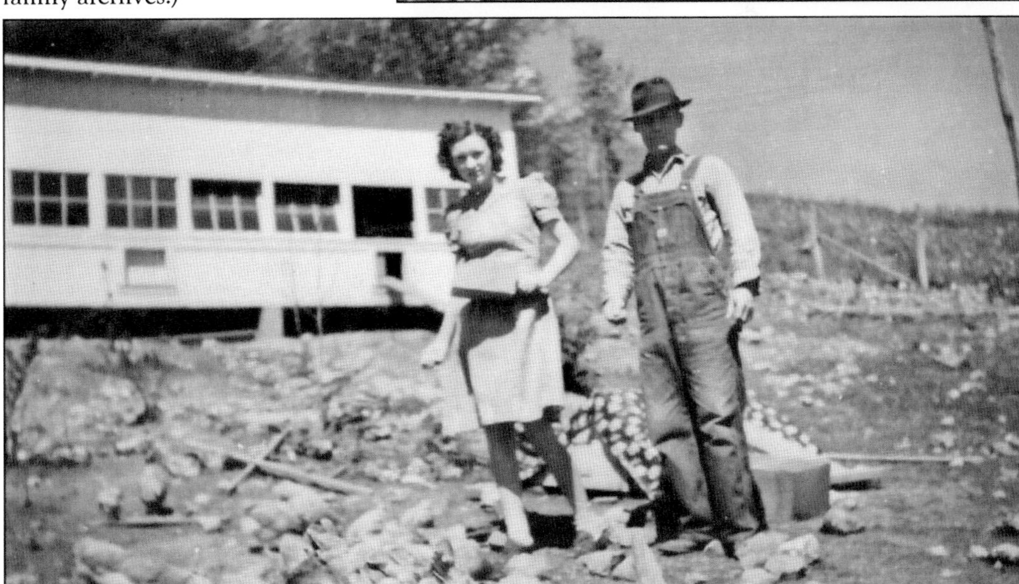

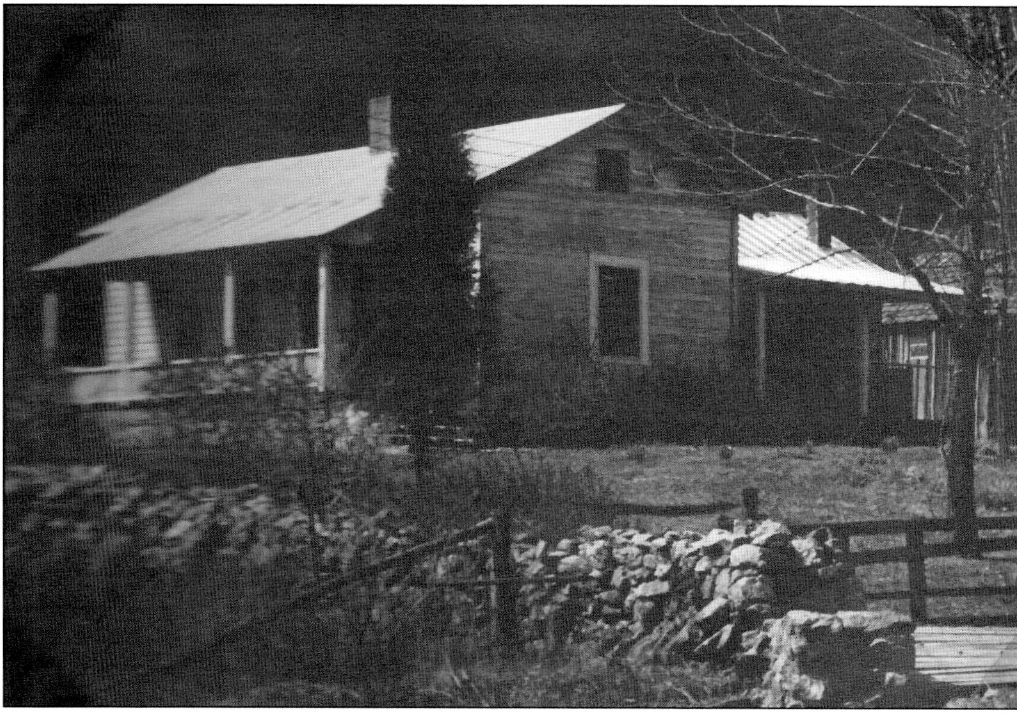

When David Lasier met J.W.F. "Chief" Davies, Davies soon realized that Lasier had a wonderful plan and decided to purchase land just down the road from Blackberry Farm in 1945. Chief and his wife, Cora, coined the name of their recent purchase "Singing Brook Farm." (Courtesy of *Blackberry Farm: The Beginning,* John Edmondson, and the Harris-Edmondson family archives.)

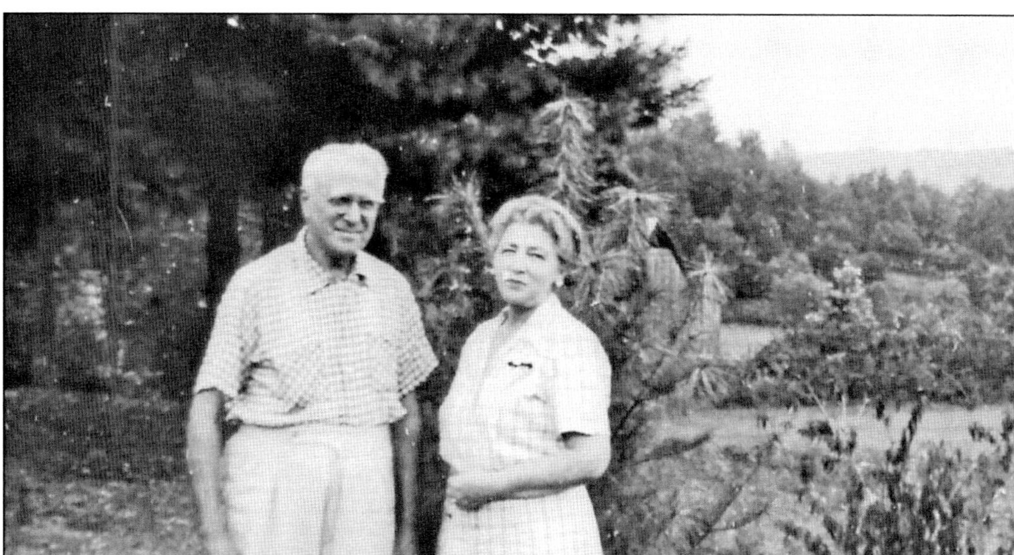

"Chief" and Cora Davies were enjoying retirement when Cora suddenly passed away. Chief was reunited with a longtime friend, Ruth Lasier. Chief and Ruth started their life together, becoming husband and wife on Valentine's Day, 1949. (Courtesy of *Blackberry Farm: The Beginning* by John Edmondson and the Harris-Edmondson family archives.)

Two

East Miller's Cove

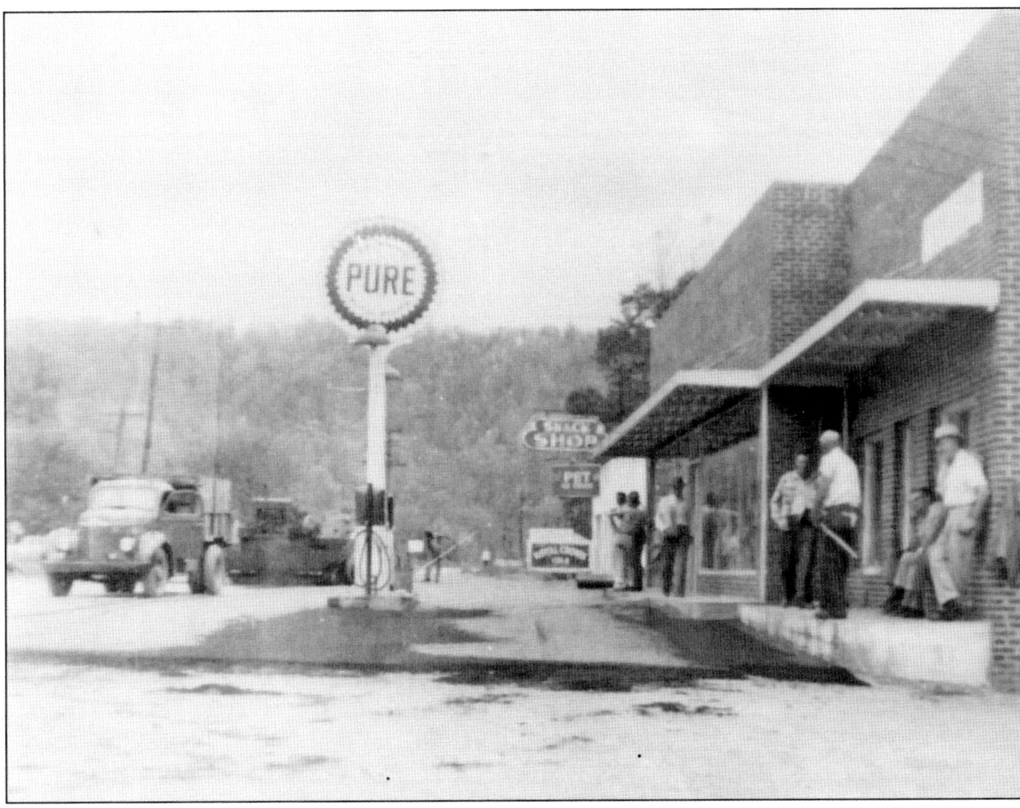

Rock King's Store was located close to the site of Schlosser Leather Company. Rock bought the store in 1941 from Raymond Moles. Rock sold PURE brand gasoline to his customers. There was a snack shop, Barton's Barber Shop, and the US Post Office beside King's Store. Belle Tipton Emert was the postmistress at this post office. The post office was located in the general store, and many of the operators of the store also served at postmaster. (Courtesy of Jeremy Stephens, King Family Collection.)

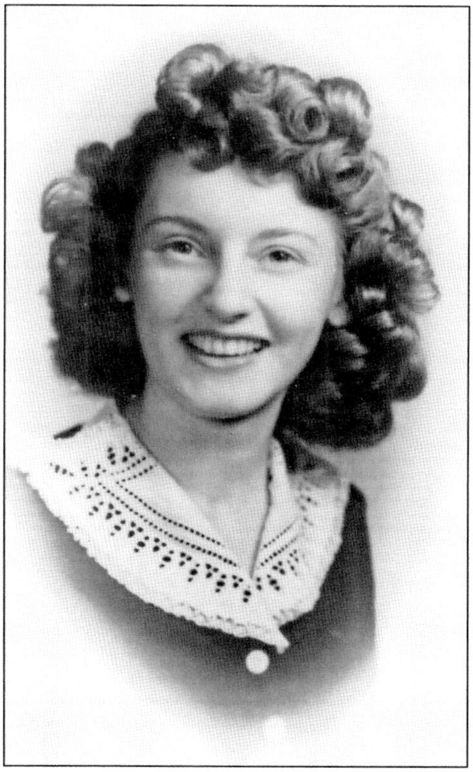

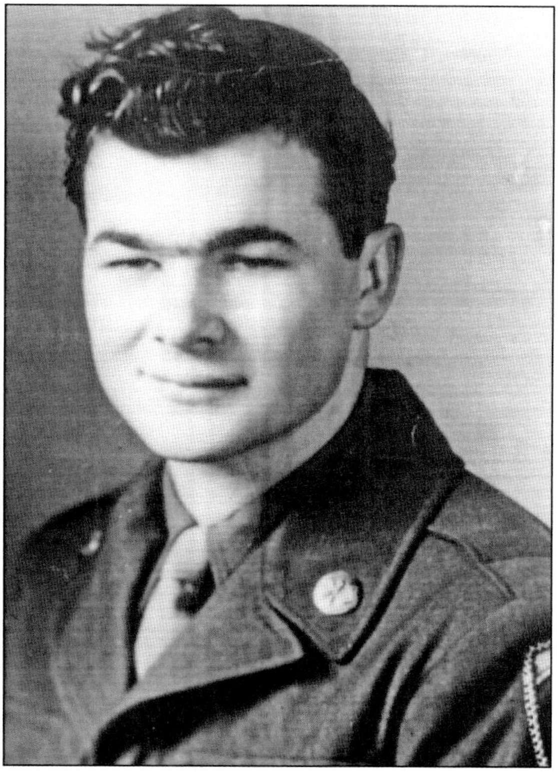

Della Inez McCauley Adams (left) was born October 11, 1926, in Cades Cove, Tennessee, to Dulcie Abbott McCauley and Millard McCauley. The McCauley family left Cades Cove about 1934 when Cades Cove was made into a national park. Inez was known to many who loved her as "Granny." She was a historian and genealogist who loved to dig into the history of the local region. Pfc. Earl Adams McKinley Jr. (pictured at right in 1946) joined the US Army in 1945. He was the son of Earl McKinley Adams Sr. and Cora Adams. Earl and Inez married September 1947 and were married 68 years before the passing of Inez. (Courtesy of Earl Adams Jr., Inez McCauley Adams Collection.)

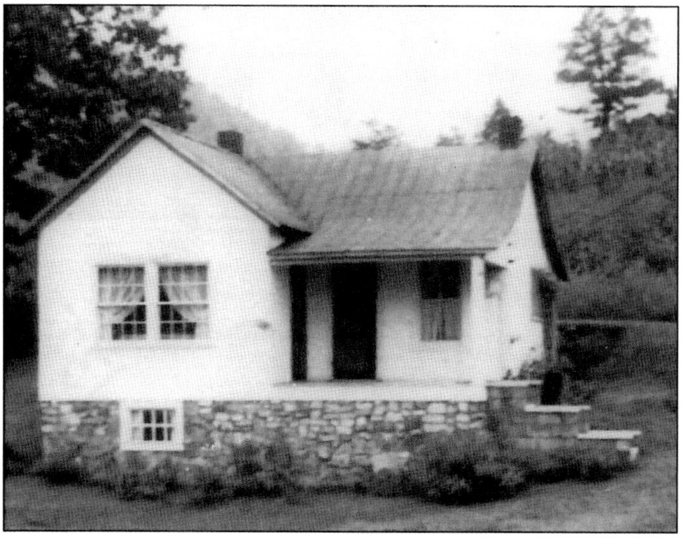

Earl McKinley Adams was discharged from the US Army in 1947 and soon purchased this house on East Miller's Cove Road. In September of the same year, Earl married the love of his life, Inez McCauley. They were married in Maryville and moved into this house and lived their 58 years before moving to nearby Maryville. (Courtesy of Earl Adams Jr., Inez McCauley Collection.)

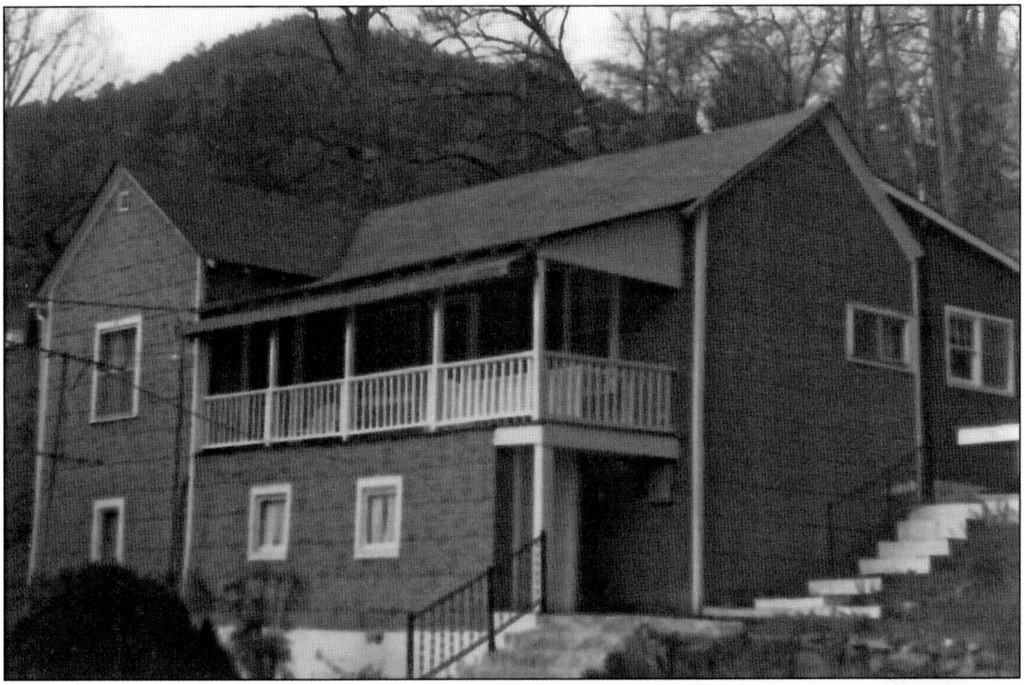

This was the residence of Earl Adams Sr. and Cora Adams from 1940 to 1984. Originally the home of Jim Shields, it also served as a tannery house. (Courtesy of Earl Adams Jr, Inez Adams McCauley collection.)

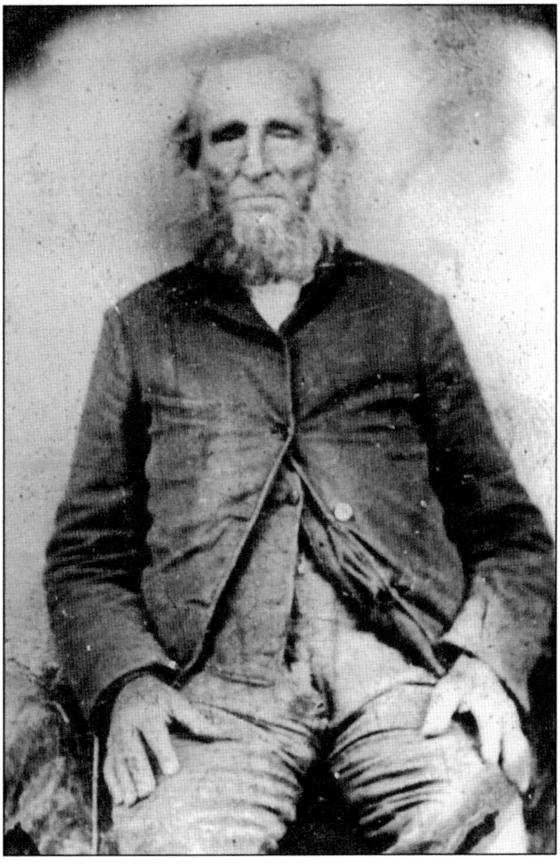

Adam Fagala Waters was born on February 22, 1819, in Miller's Cove, Tennessee, to John Gabriel Waters and Mary Catherine Fagala Waters. Adam was a Union Civil War veteran serving in Company B, 6th Regiment. On January 10, 1866, he married Temperance "Tempe" Lowe. (Courtesy of Gladys Oliver Burns.)

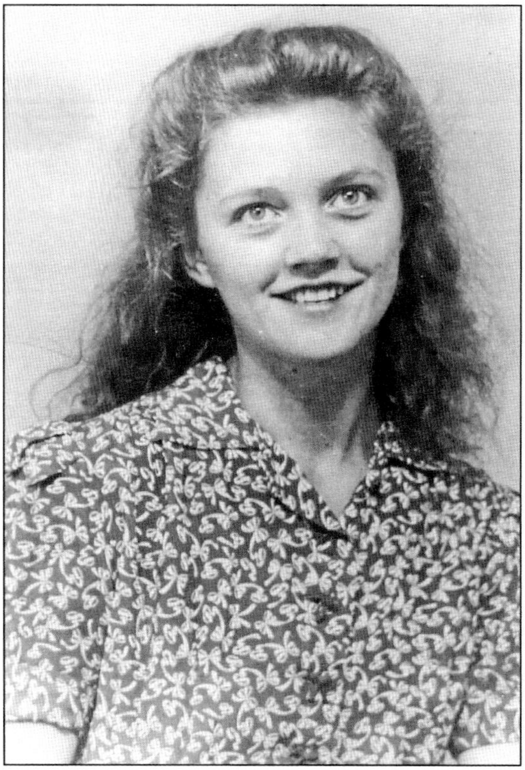

Maggie Mae Gredig Huskey was born on October 27, 1923, to Abraham Frank Gredig and Anna Belle Gredig. She married Samuel "Sam" Lawson Huskey, and they raised their family in East Miller's Cove. (Courtesy of Bill Huskey.)

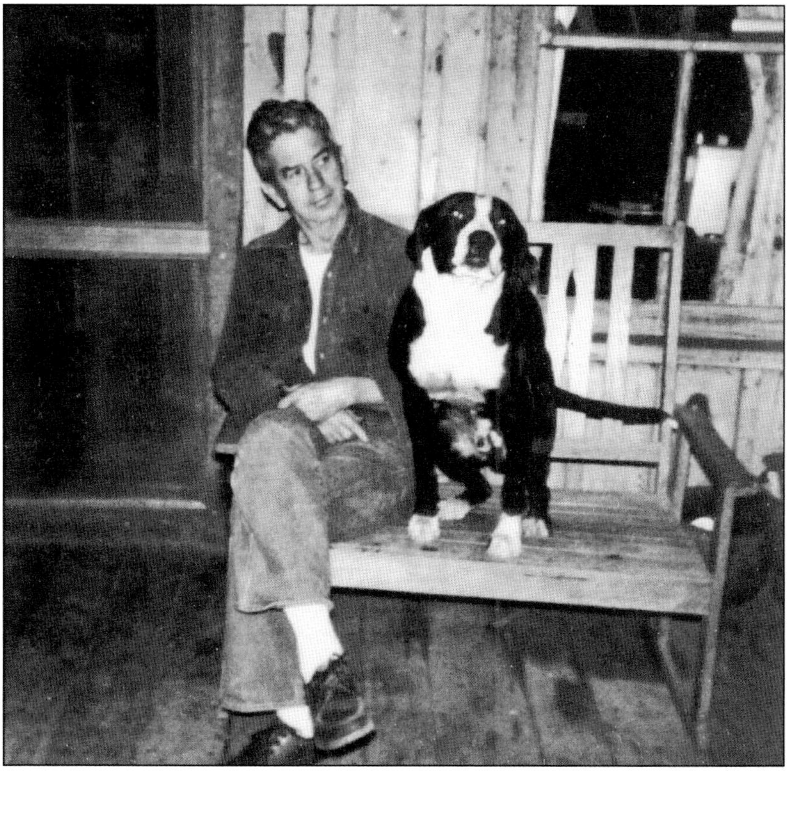

Samuel Lawson Huskey was born to Alexander Isaac "Alex" Huskey (1887–1952) and Alice Whitehead Huskey (1893–1923) on February 28, 1918. Sam and his wife, Maggie Mae Gredig Huskey, lived on East Miller's Cove Road. (Courtesy of Bill Huskey.)

Roy Lee Dalton and Eleanor Tate Dalton moved to the Walland area in the early 1940s. They made their home in East Miller's Cove. Pictured are Eleanor holding Doug, Roy holding Mike, Delores (center), and Evelyn and Bob in front. (Courtesy of Benny and Beverly Dalton.)

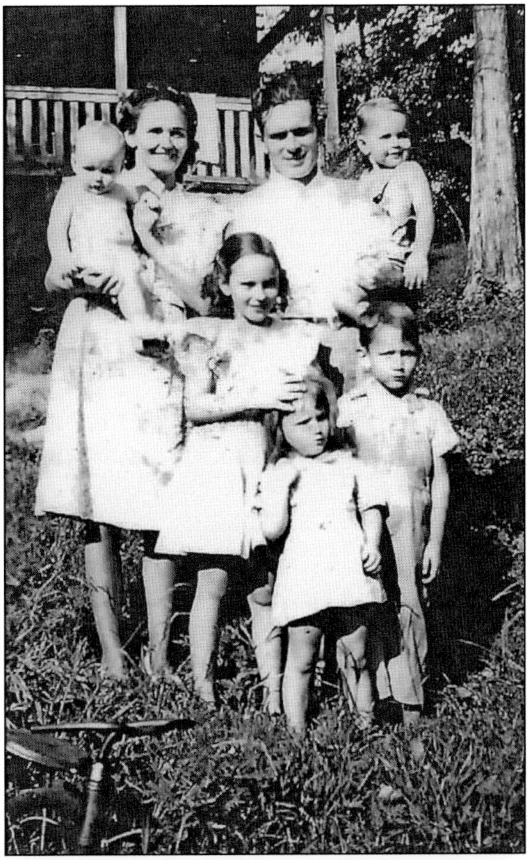

The Dalton gang of Walland is, from left to right, (first row) Becky, Evelyn, Delores, Eleanor, and Roy; (second row) Benny, Doug, Mike, and Bob. Delores, the first child of Roy and Eleanor, graduated from Walland High School in 1956. Robert "Bob" played football and graduated as valedictorian in 1959. Evelyn Dalton played basketball at Walland High School and graduated in 1960. Michael "Mike" played football and basketball at Walland and graduated as valedictorian in 1962. Douglas "Doug" played football and graduated from Walland in 1964. Benjamin "Benny" played football and basketball at Walland and graduated in 1965 as valedictorian. The youngest of the gang, Rebecca "Becky," played basketball at Walland High School and graduated in 1969. (Courtesy of Benny and Beverly Dalton.)

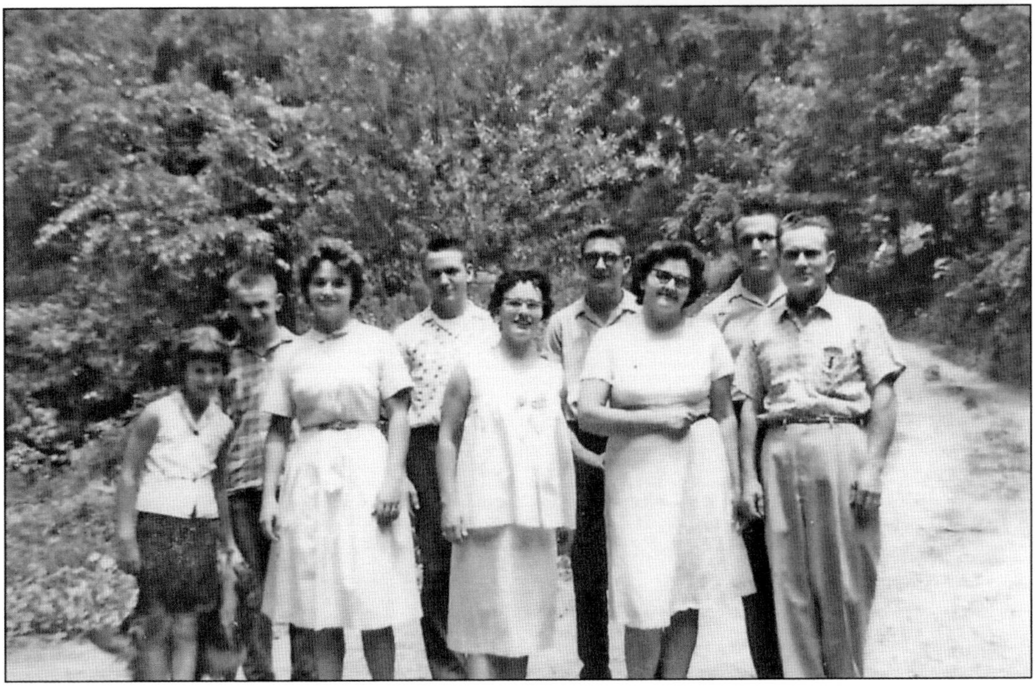

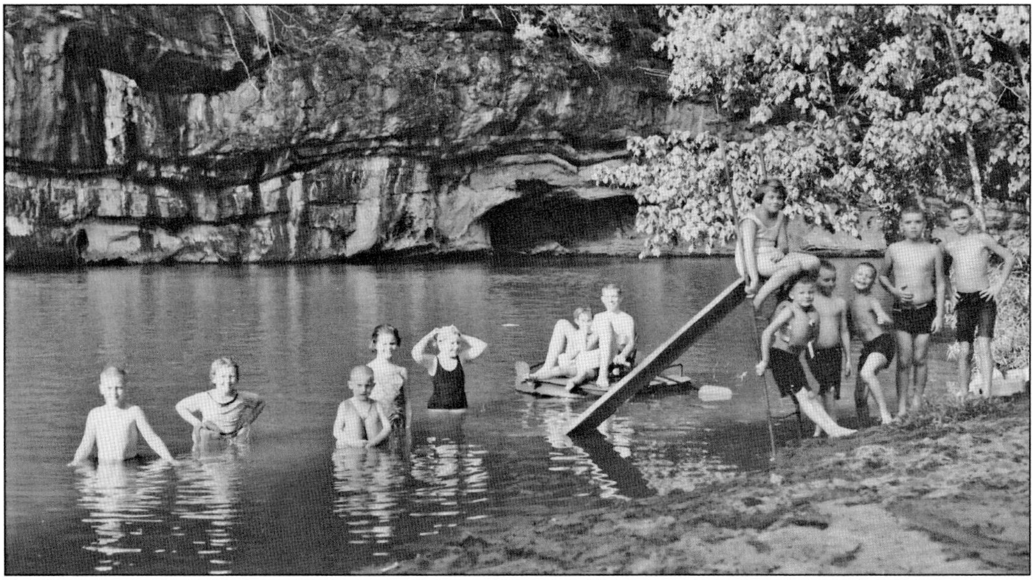

This swimming hole is on Little River near the home of J. Frank "Doc" Manning and Polly Walker Manning. Walker cousins enjoying their swimming time are, from left to right, David Love, Robby Love, Bob Teffeteller, Tina Schuch, Susie Osborne, Tommy Wilson, Nancy Schuch, Billy Love, Mike Osborne, Danny Schuch, Joe Wilson, and Tom Osborne. (Courtesy of Bobbie Walker King.)

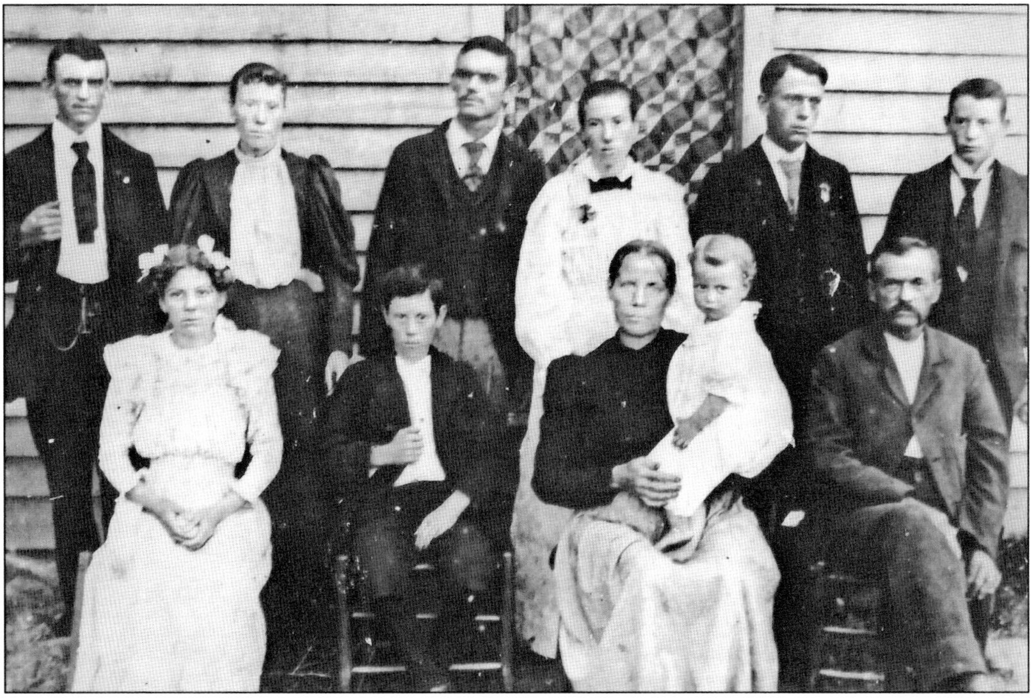

The family of Alexander Houston Walker and Mary Malinda Walker is, from left to right, (first row) Kate Walker Long, Robert Franklin Walker, Mary Malinda Walker holding Luke, and Alexander Houston Walker; (second row) Jim Martin, Maggie Walker Martin, John Martin, Susie Walker Martin, John Walker, and George Walker. (Courtesy of Bobbie Walker King.)

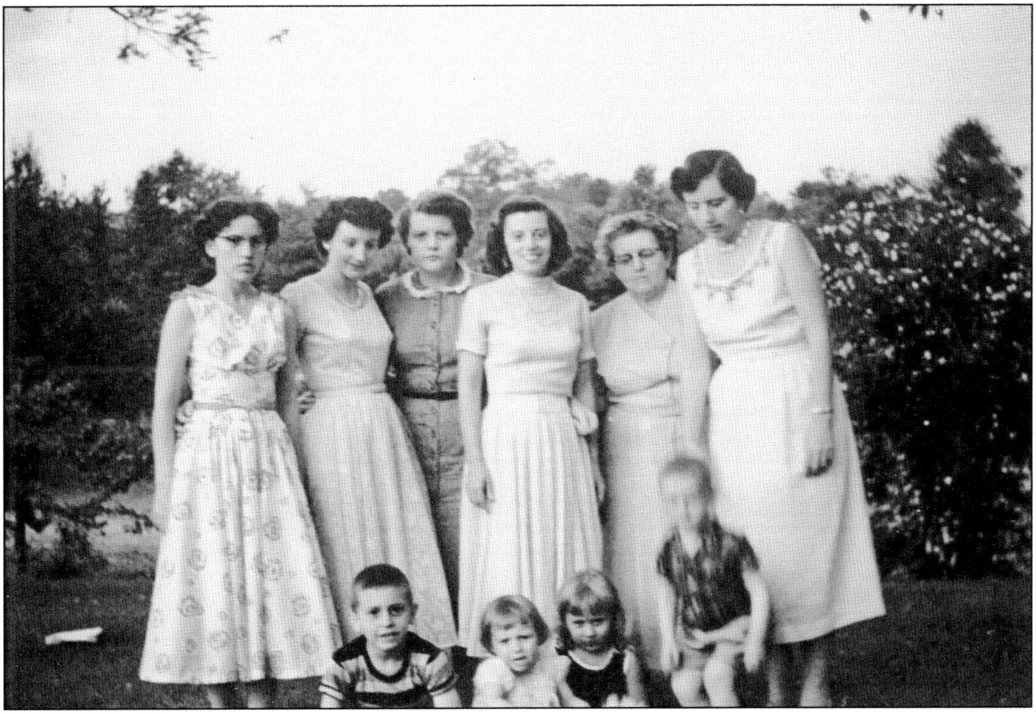

Children and grandchildren of Robert Franklin Walker and Minnie Belle Clendenen are, from left to right, (first row) Bill Joe Cameron III, Robbie Love, Teresa Thomas, and David Love; (second row) Jewell, Georgia, Sue, Kathy, Minnie, and Bobbie Walker. (Courtesy of Bobbie Walker King.)

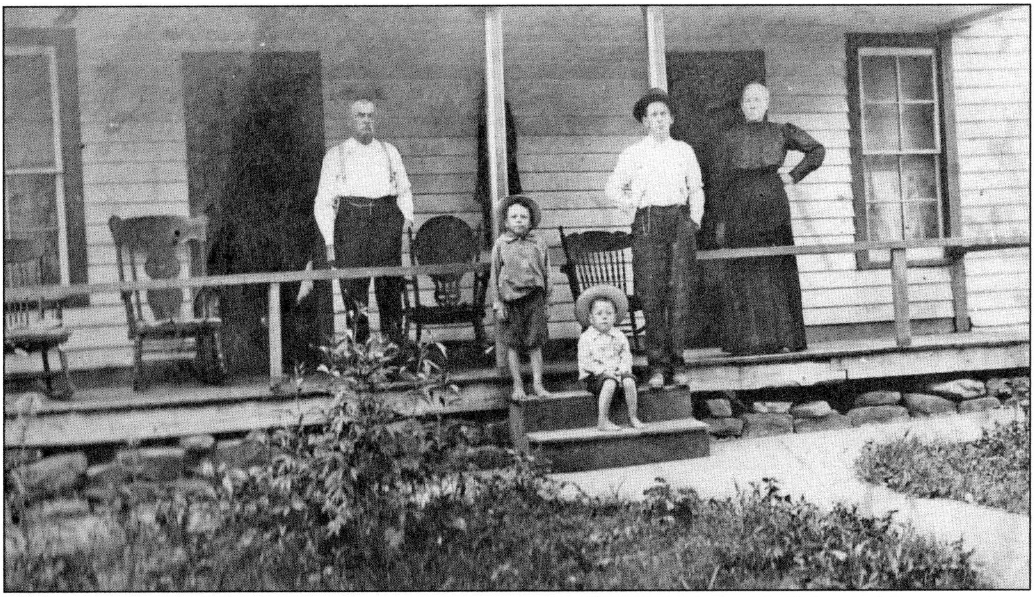

From left to right are Alexander Houston "A.H." Walker, sons John, Ralph, and Raymond on the steps, and mother Mary Malinda Walker. In 1870, the family lived in Civil District 15, which was Tuckaleechee and Miller's Cove, then the district changed to 18, which was Miller's Cove. (Courtesy of Bobbie Walker King.)

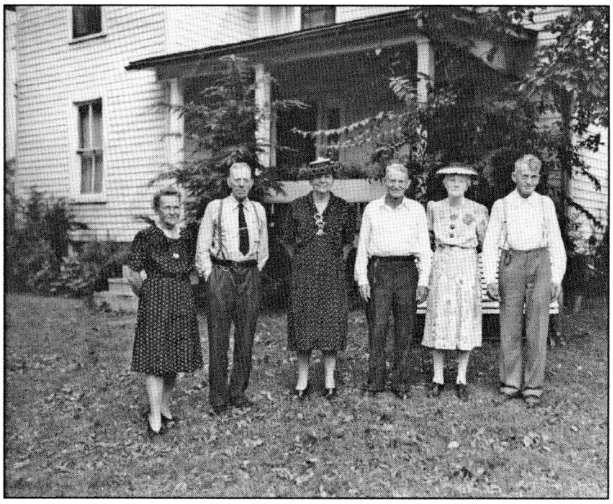

From left to right are Annie Tallent, Robert F. Walker, Kate Long Walker, George Walker, Maggie Martin Walker, and John Walker on Sunday, June 16, 1946. The reunion was held at the J. Frank "Doc" Manning and Polly Walker Manning house on Manning Lane at a place on Little River known as Blue Springs. The Manning house was built by Snaky John Martin in 1910. He operated a lumber mill and built many houses in the area. This house was known as the "two-by-four. The walls were built of two-by-four timbers stacked one on top of the other. (Courtesy of Bobbie Walker King.)

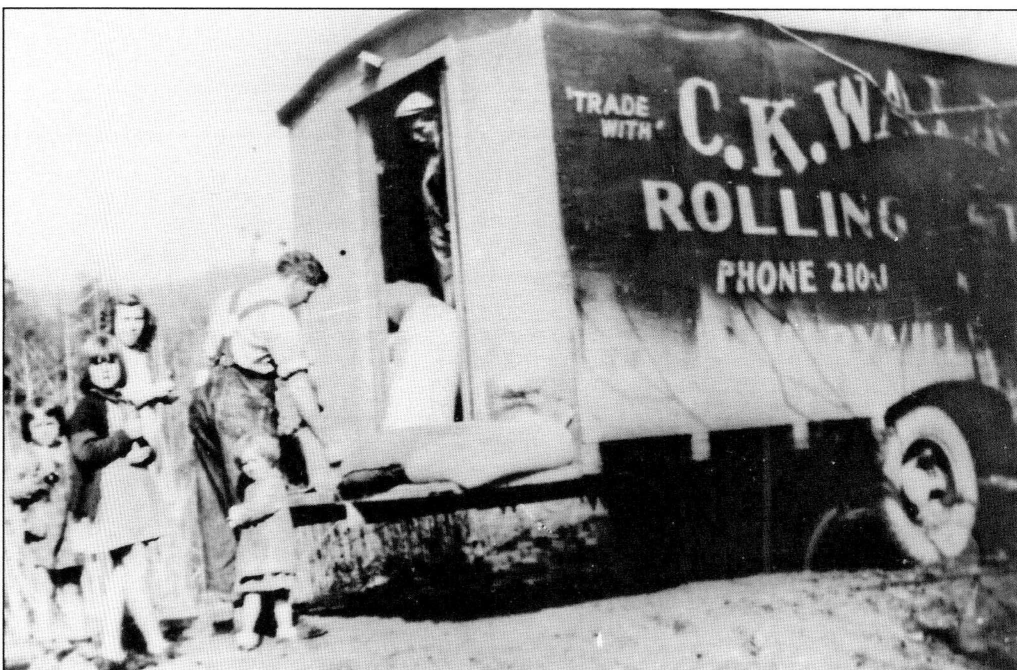

C.K. Walker was the owner of the "rolling store" and traveled through rural areas. Walker had his main store on Montvale Road in Maryville. Fred Houston Waters is pictured here purchasing items from the "rolling store" with his children (from left to right) Rena, Betty, Anna Mae, and Mildred. Fred Waters was the son of Jefferson Poland "Jeff" Waters and Susan J. "Susie" Headrick Waters of East Miller's Cove. The "rolling store" only traveled in rural areas where housewives could not and did not go into town much. Many items were purchased from the "rolling store," such as flour, meal, sugar, salt and pepper, and household items such as needles and thread. Some stores offered sacks of laying pellets and feed for baby chickens and bartered fresh eggs with the storekeeper. Some trucks were equipped with fenced-in boxes in case customers wanted to barter chicken. (Courtesy of Earl Adams Jr., Inez McCauley Adams Collection.)

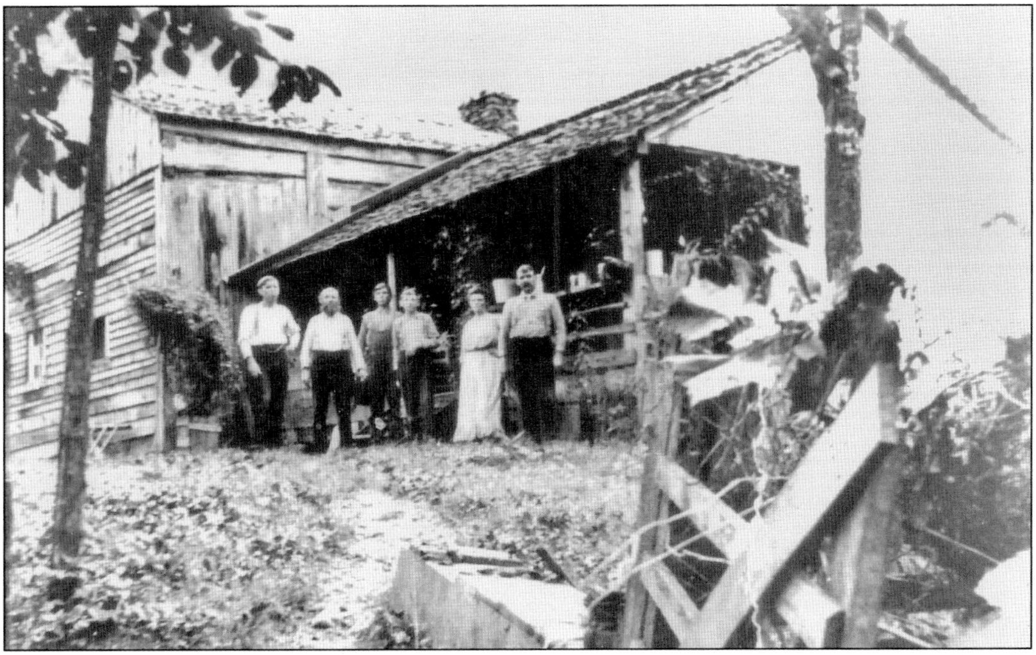

The home of Richard "Dick" Waters and Elizabeth Jane Burns Waters was in East Miller's Cove. From left to right are Jim, Richard, Sam, Jake, and Lara Waters. Dick was born on August 28, 1849, to Adam Fagala Waters and Temperance "Tempe" Elizabeth Lowe Waters. (Courtesy of Jeremy Stephens, King Family Collection.)

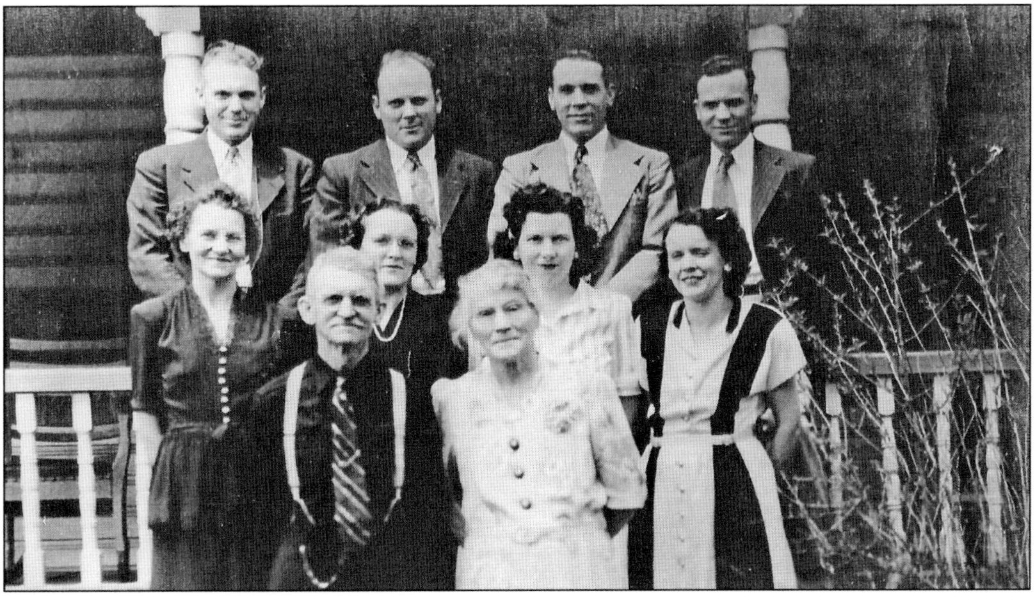

J.V. Martin (front, left) and Margaret "Maggie" Walker Martin (front, right) of East Miller's Cove are pictured with, from left to right, (second row) Grace, Ruth, Gladys, and Irma; (third row) Huse, Doyle, Bob, and Art. Two more sons, Clyde and Wade Martin, are not pictured. J.V. was the son of John Leander Martin and Amanda Marshall Martin. "Maggie" Walker Martin was the daughter of A.H. Walker and Mary Malinda Waters Walker. (Courtesy of Earl Adams Jr., Inez McCauley Adams Collection.)

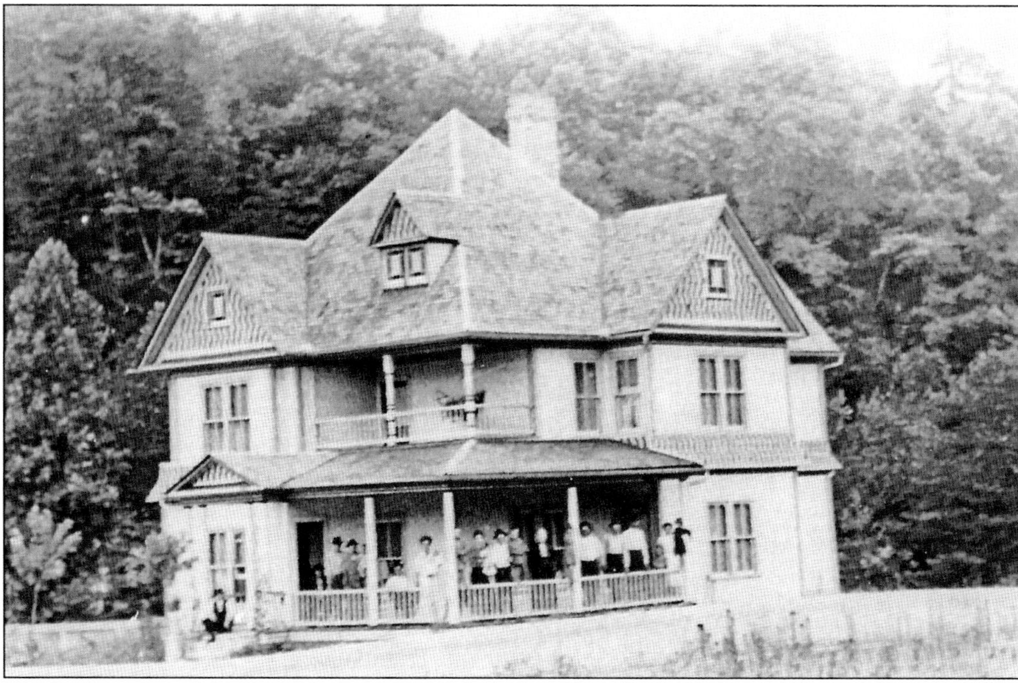

The home of James Vance "J.V." Martin and Margaret Ann "Maggie" Walker Martin was in East Miller's Cove. It was built by J.V.'s father on land acquired from Maggie's parents, A.H. Walker and Mary Malinda Walker. (Courtesy of Earl Adams Jr., Inez McCauley Adams Collection.)

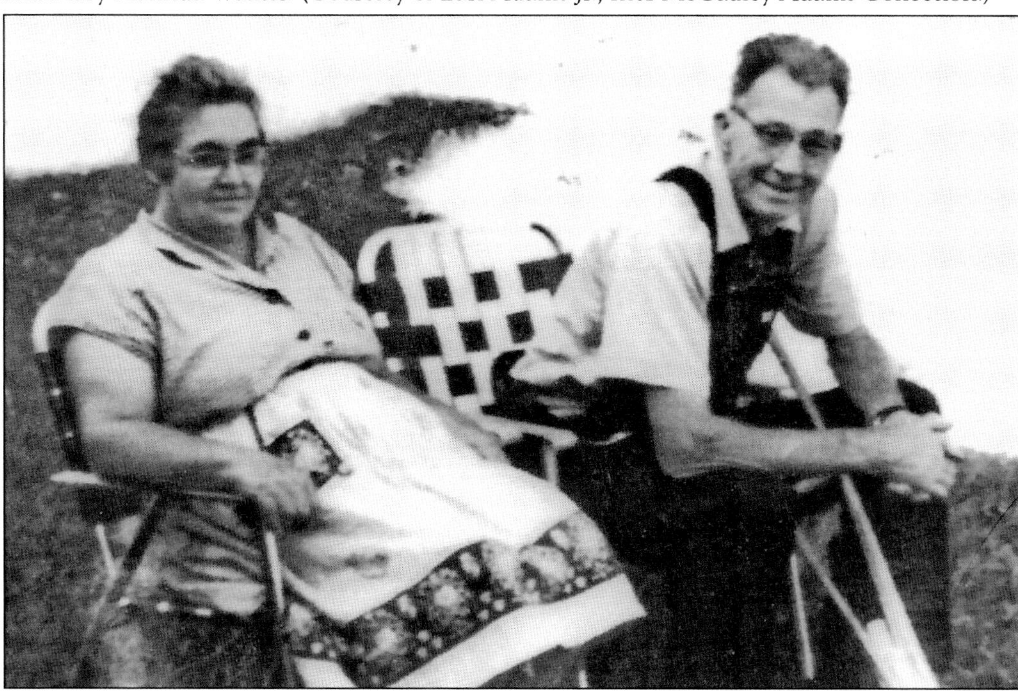

Aileene Waters Myers and George Myers lived in East Miller's Cove. Aileene was born on September 16, 1914, to Jefferson Poland Waters and Susan J. Headrick Waters. (Courtesy of Earl Adams Jr., Inez McCauley Adams Collection.)

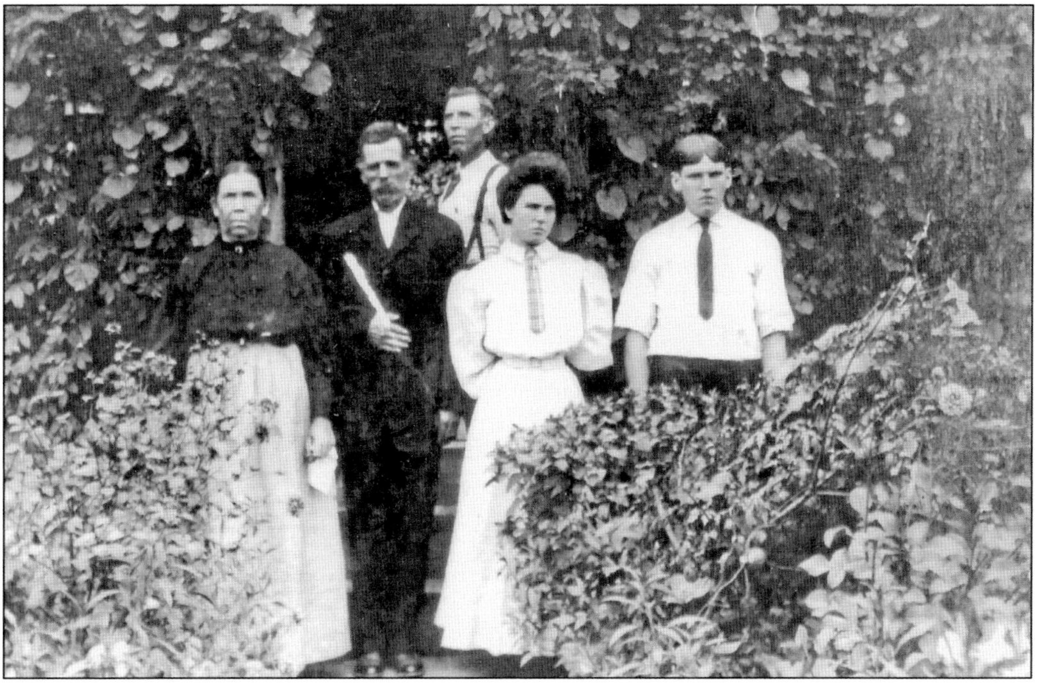

Pictured from left to right are Nancy P. Waters Burns, James Walker Burns, Jim Waters, Eliza Burns Helton, and Edward Burns of East Miller's Cove. Nancy Pauline Waters was born on June 7, 1846, to Adam Fagala Waters and Temperance Elizabeth Low Waters. (Courtesy of Jeremy Stephens, King Family Collection.)

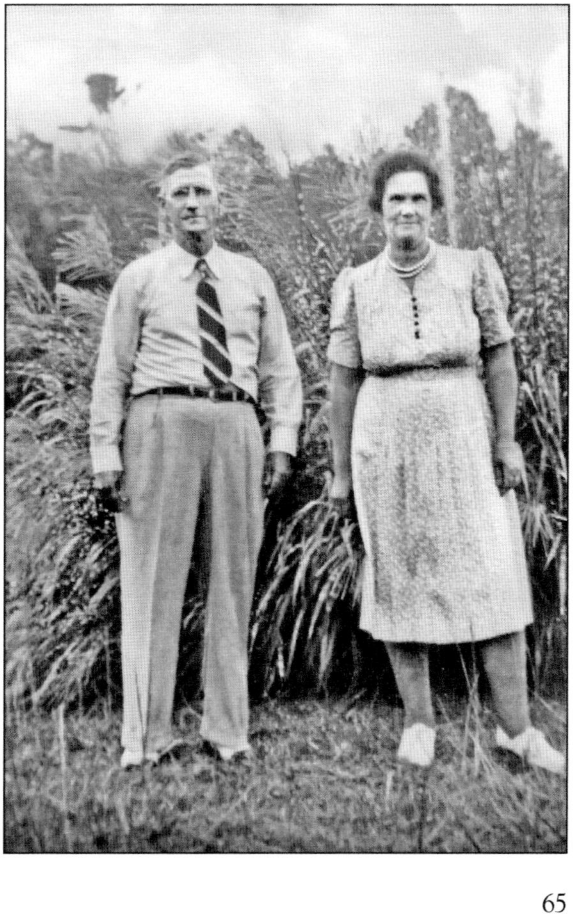

Charles Melvin "Mel" Helton and wife Eliza Jane Burns Helton lived in East Miller's Cove. Eliza Jane was born on May 27, 1891, to James Walker Burns and Nancy Pauline Waters Burns. Charles Melvin and Eliza Jane were married on October 3, 1915. (Courtesy of Jeremy Stephens, King Family Collection.)

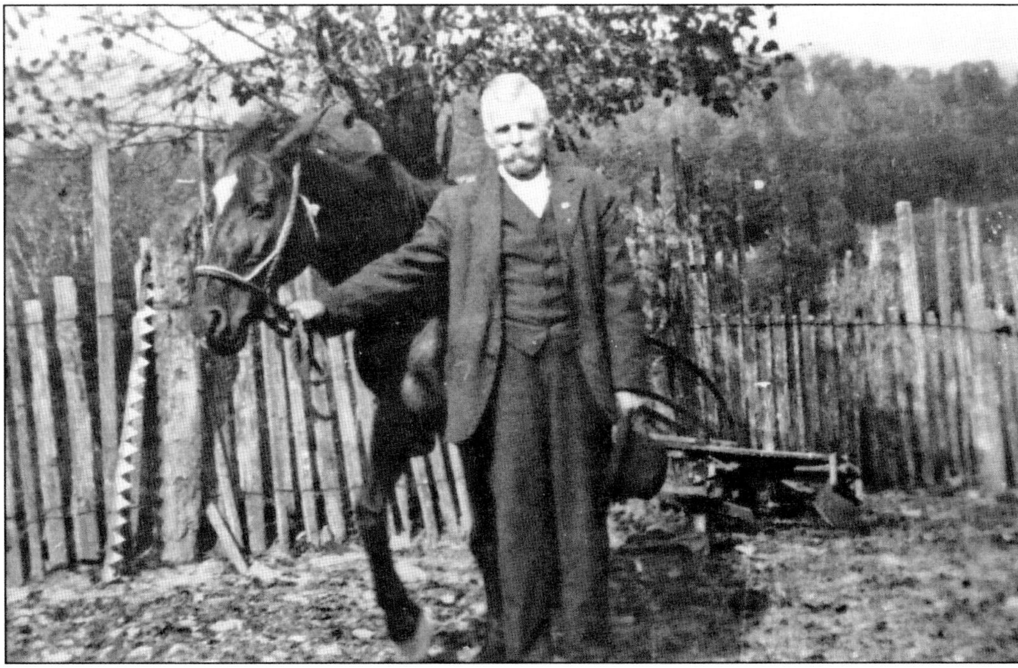

James Walker Burns poses in front of his workshop. He was born on October 10, 1849, in Miller's Cove to Aaron Tilgham Burns and Susannah Walker Burns of East Miller's Cove. (Courtesy of Jeremy Stephens, King Family Collection.)

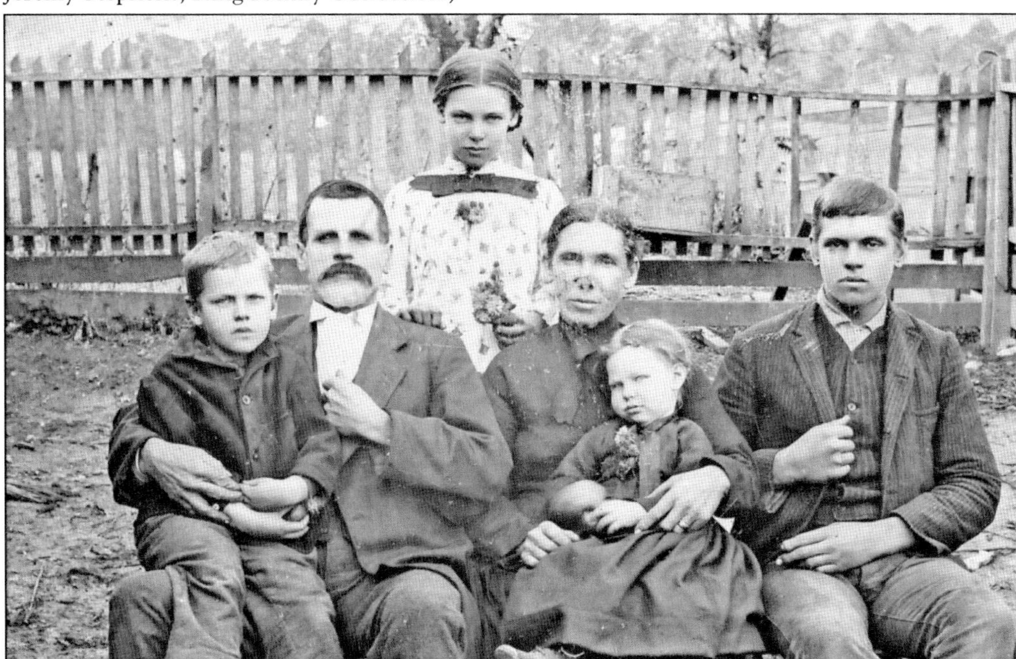

From left to right are James Walker "Jim" Burns holding Ed, Nancy Waters Burns holding Eliza Jane, and Rick Burns; in back is Elizabeth Susan Burns. James married Nancy Pauline Waters on February 4, 1869. (Courtesy of Jeremy Stephens, King Family Collection.)

Eliza Jane Burns (left) was born on May 27, 1891, to James Walker Burns and Nancy Pauline Waters of East Miller's Cove. Flora Ann Burns (right), a niece of Eliza Jane, was born on October 29, 1893, to John Gamble Burns and Sarah Texana Myers Burns. (Courtesy of Jeremy Stephens, King Family Collection.)

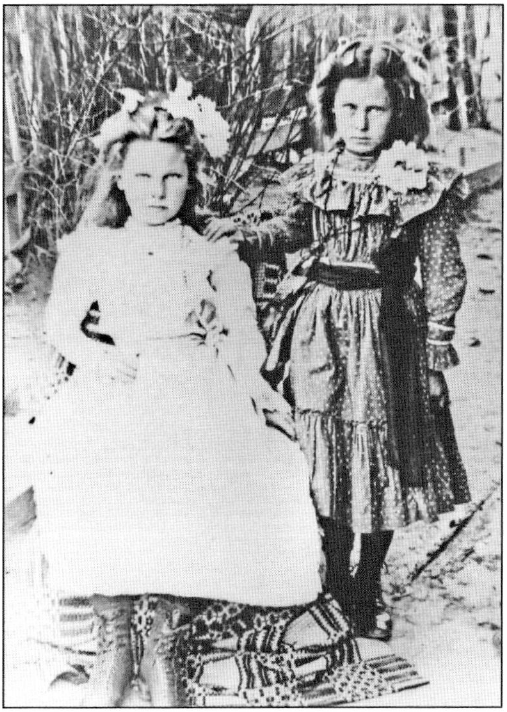

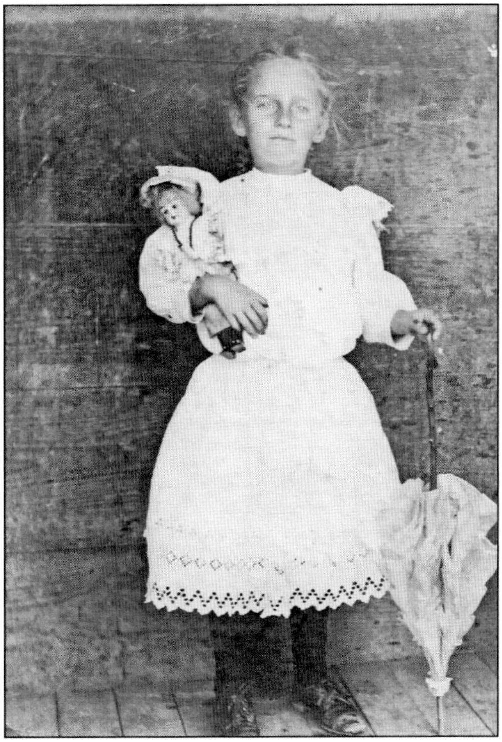

Sarah Frankie Burns was born on August 5, 1900, to Adam Fagala Burns and Hannah Keller Burns. In the 1920 and 1930 censuses, Frankie is listed as a public schoolteacher in Civil District 18. (Courtesy of Jeremy Stephens, King Family Collection.)

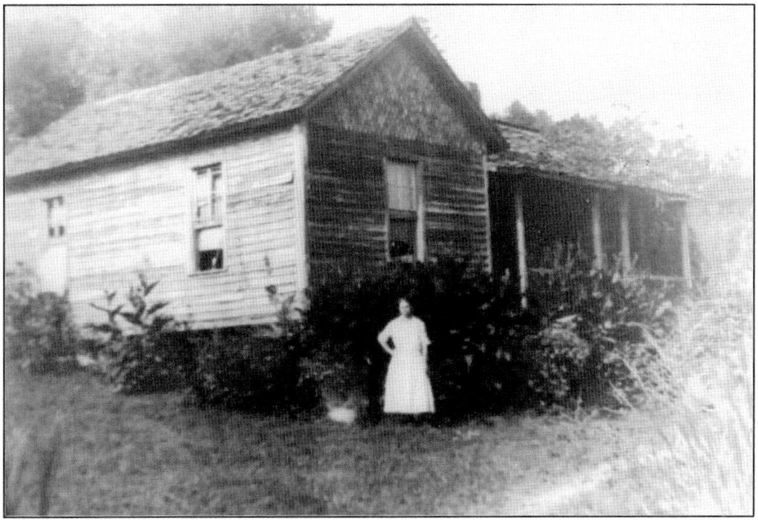

This house belonged to Aaron Tilghman Burns and Susannah A. Walker Burns in East Miller's Cove. Aaron was born on December 18, 1820, in Wears Valley Tennessee. Susannah A. Walker Burns was the daughter of James Magill Walker and Phoebe Taylor Walker. (Courtesy of Jeremy Stephens, King Family Collection.)

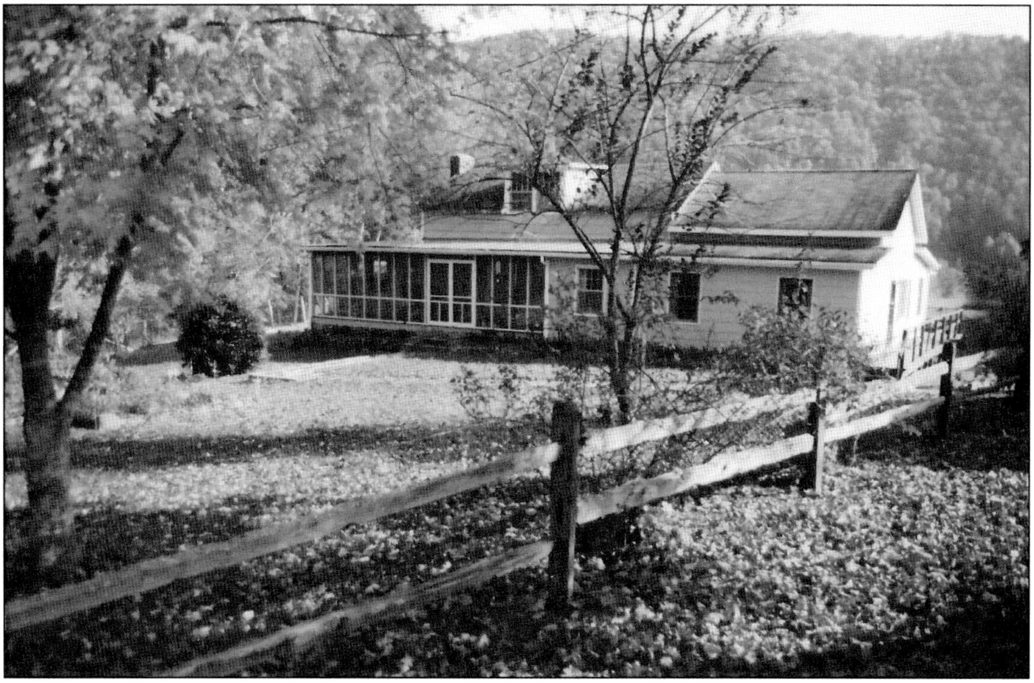

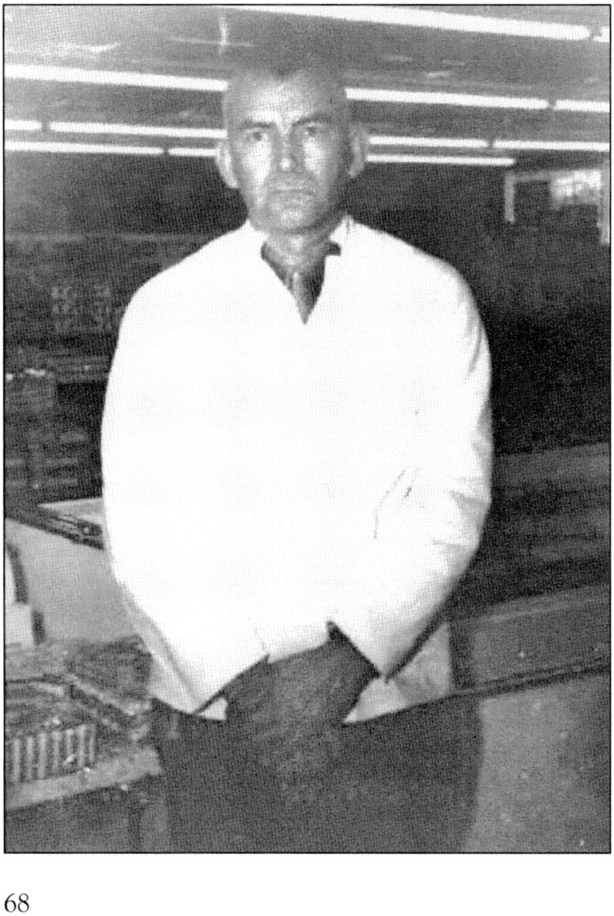

Gladys Helton King and Rocklan King lived in a house in East Miller's Cove that contained the log home of her grandparents, James and Nancy Burns. Gladys is the daughter of Charles Melvin Helton and Eliza Burns Helton. (Courtesy of Jeremy Stephens, King Family Collection.)

William Rocklan "Rock" King owned and ran King's Grocery in Walland. He first ran a store near Chilhowee Inn that he purchased from Russell Moles. In 1961, John Everett sold King a building across the river from King's current store. Rock was the butcher in the meat department of this store. Everyone loved to go to Rock King's store for fresh sandwiches. (Courtesy of Jeremy Stephens, King Family Collection.)

From left to right, the children of Rock and Gladys Helton King, Rolena, Linda, and Rocky, are pictured in 1956. Children spent most of their time outdoors playing with their pets or making up games of their own. (Courtesy of Jeremy Stephens, King Family Collection.)

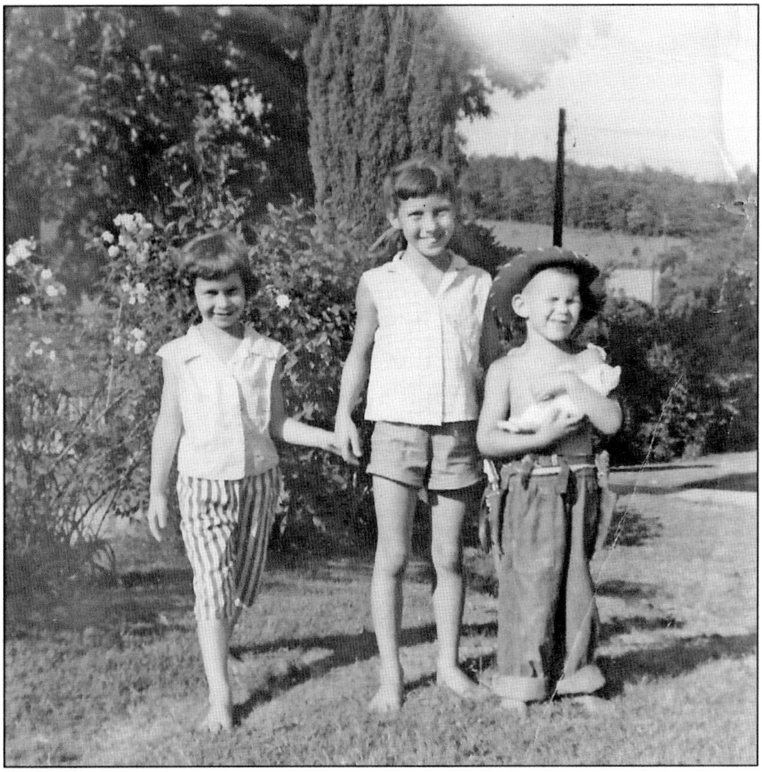

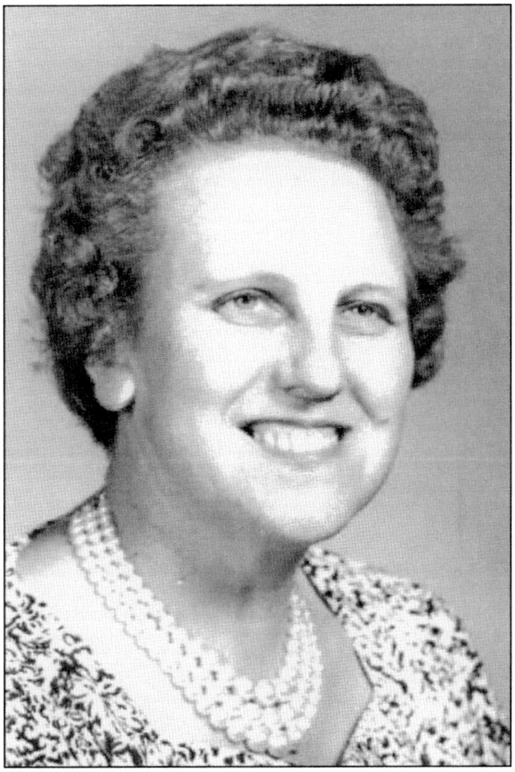

Gladys Helton King married Rocklan King and taught school for many years at Walland High School and Elementary School. (Courtesy of Jeremy Stephens King Family Collection.)

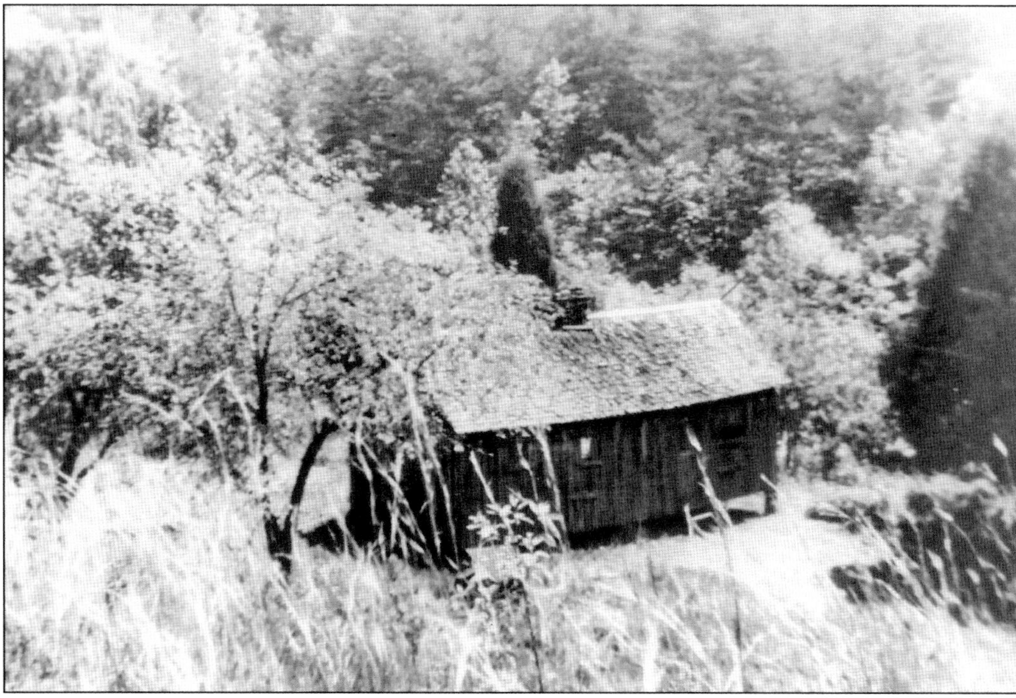

Ida Murphy Burns and Aaron Columbus Burns lived in this home on the Loop Road in East Miller's Cove. Ida was born to Rebecca Jane Hatcher Murphy and Micajah Rogers Murphy. Aaron was the son of William Thomas Burns and Mary Stillwell Burns; he was born on September 17, 1888. (Courtesy of Gladys Oliver Burns.)

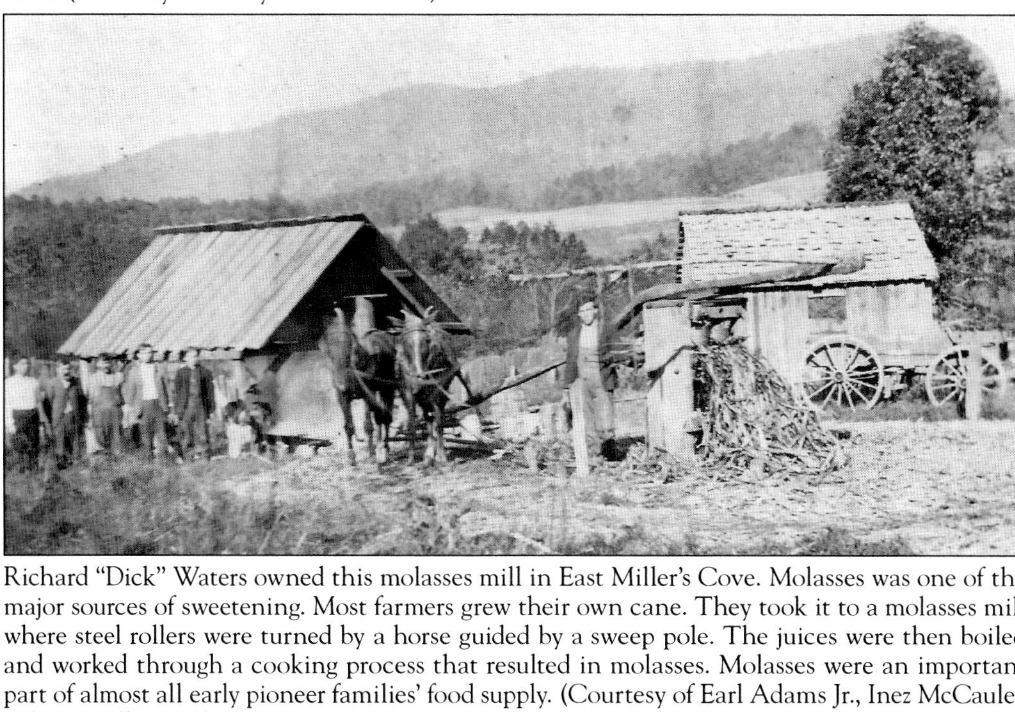

Richard "Dick" Waters owned this molasses mill in East Miller's Cove. Molasses was one of the major sources of sweetening. Most farmers grew their own cane. They took it to a molasses mill where steel rollers were turned by a horse guided by a sweep pole. The juices were then boiled and worked through a cooking process that resulted in molasses. Molasses were an important part of almost all early pioneer families' food supply. (Courtesy of Earl Adams Jr., Inez McCauley Adams Collection.)

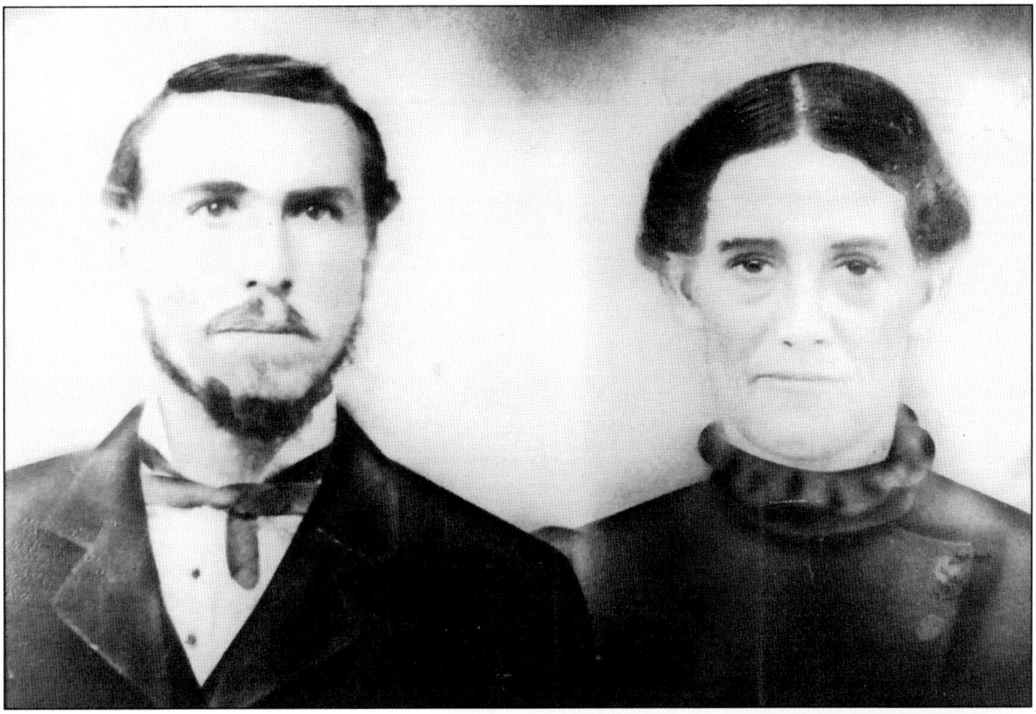

Thomas Jefferson Waters married Margaret Perkins on November 11, 1883, and they lived in the East Miller's Cove area. Thomas was the son of Adam Fagala Waters and Temperance Elizabeth Lowe. (Courtesy of Gladys Oliver Burns.)

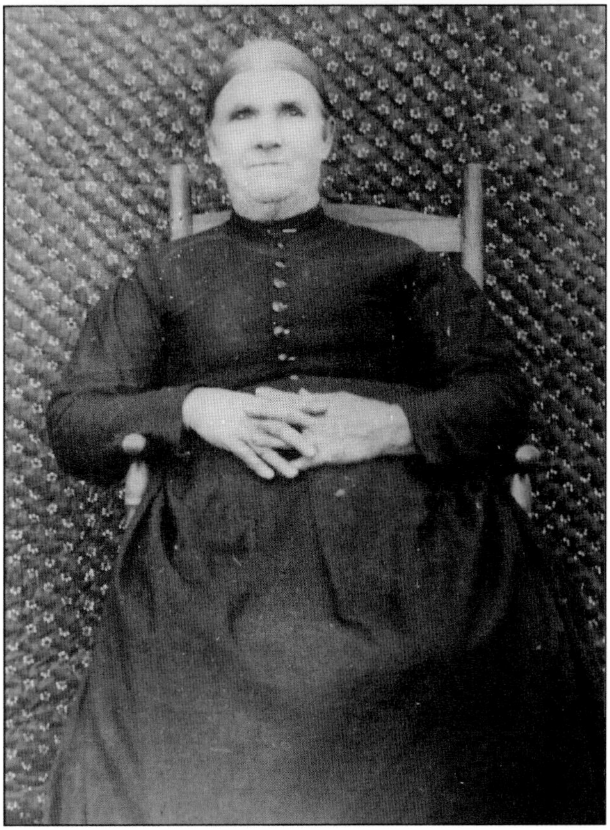

Temperance "Tempe" Lowe Waters of Millers Cove is pictured here. Born on June 16, 1821, in Blount County, Tennessee, Tempe married Adam Fagala Waters on January 10, 1866. (Courtesy of Gladys Oliver Burns.)

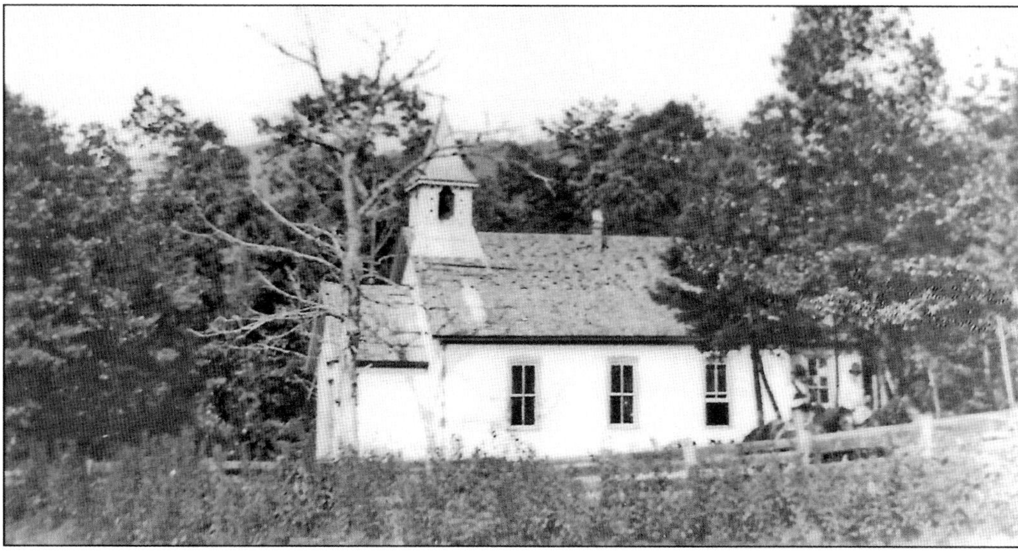

In 1867, Methodist minister J.B. Seaton and Baptist minister James Coulter held a revival in an old log school building in East Miller's Cove that led to a spiritual building of the community. James Walker donated some land, and a log house was built in the east end of Miller's Cove. A.H. Walker and his wife, Malinda Walker, donated the site for the current church. Aaron Burns, a notable carpenter of the day, worked faithfully on the construction of the church building along with his sons. When the church was dedicated on April 8, 1894, it was named Burns Chapel after the man who had so unselfishly given of his time and talent to construct this building for his community. (Courtesy of Earl Adams Jr., Inez McCauley Adams Collection.)

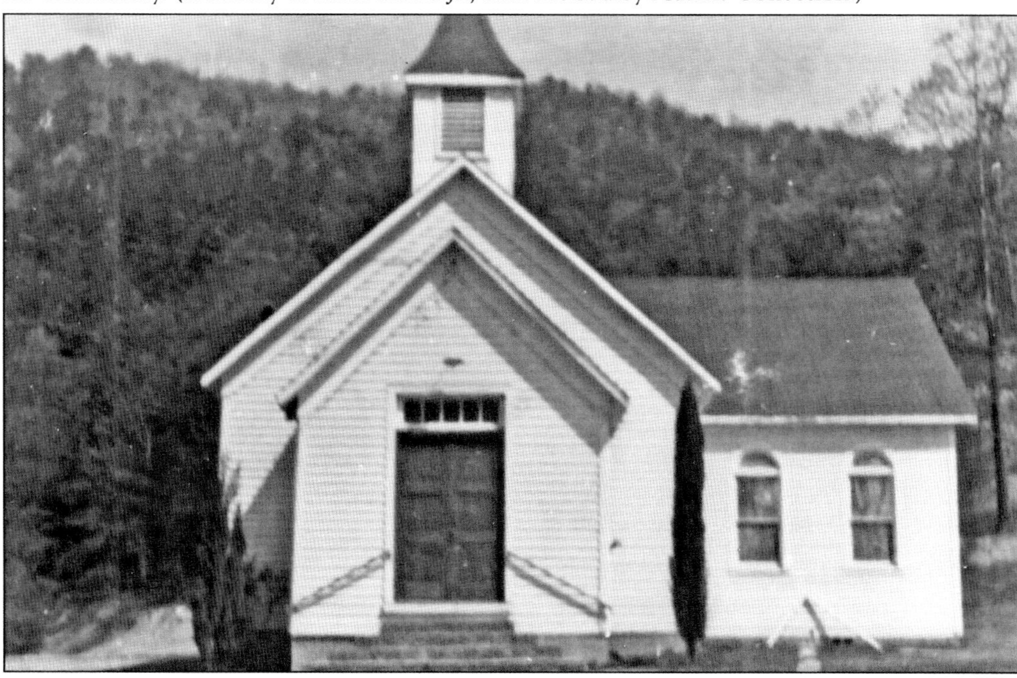

Walker's Chapel and Burns Chapel merged to form the Walland Methodist Church, which still stands today with many descendants of the early families attending. (Courtesy of Earl Adams Jr., Inez McCauley Adams Collection.)

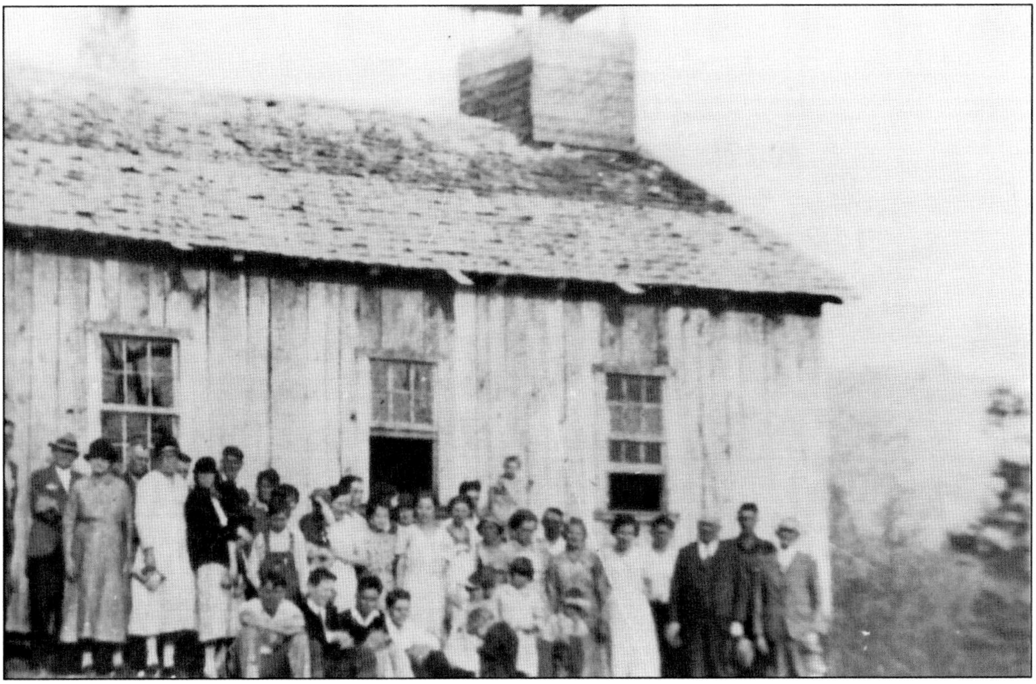

East Walland Baptist Church was in East Miller's Cove. Some of the children went to a school at East Mountain View Presbyterian Church after the closure of the nearby Waters School. The pews would be pushed back so students' desks could be moved to the middle of the room. (Courtesy of Earl Adams Jr., Inez McCauley Adams Collection.)

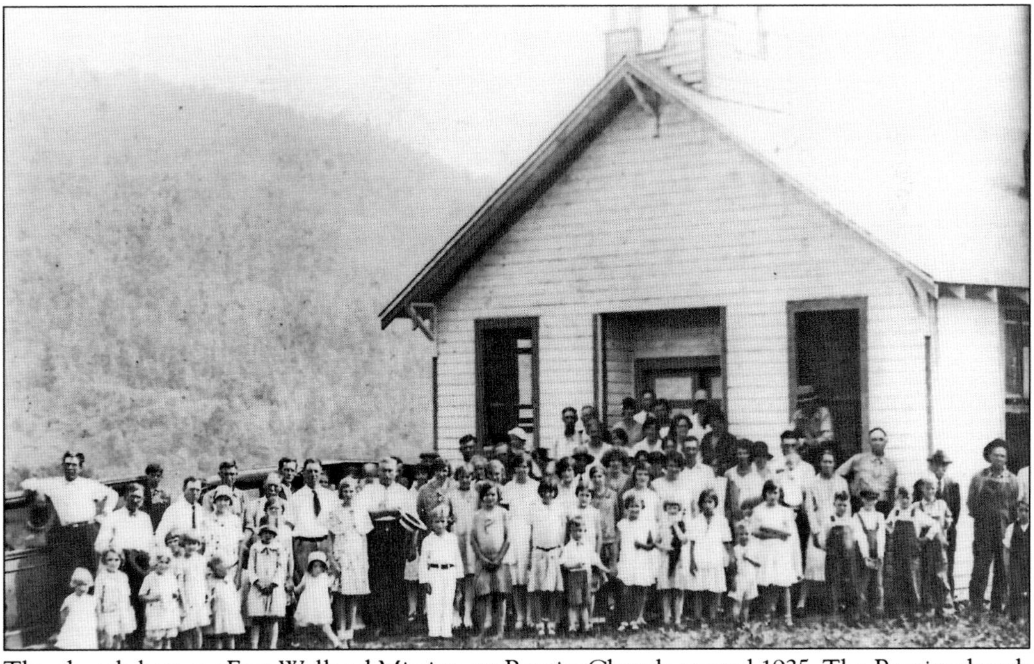

The church became East Walland Missionary Baptist Church around 1935. The Baptist church school was closed, and the students rode the bus to Walland School. (Courtesy of Earl Adams Jr., Inez McCauley Adams Collection.)

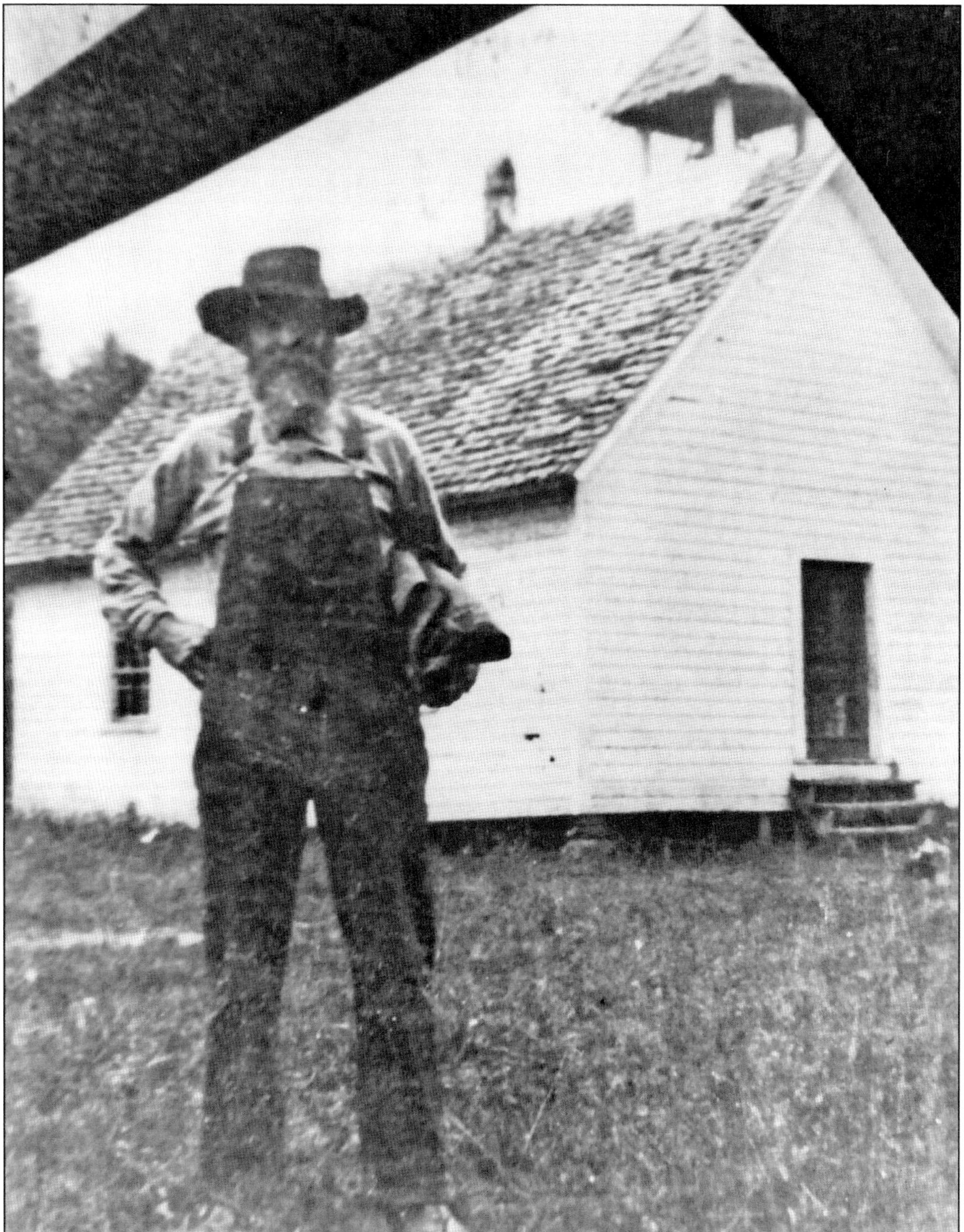

Waters School was on East Miller's Cove Road on Adam Waters's land. The schoolhouse was built by John Waters on his original land grant and passed on to Adam Waters after the death of John and Catherine Waters. The original land grant was split, and the portion containing the school was given to Adam's son, Lavator "Vate" Waters. Vate Waters attended this school in 1868 as well as many of the area children. It is thought that the original building was made of logs with split siding put on later. Around 1923, not many students attended Waters School, so it was closed and destroyed. (Courtesy of Gladys Oliver Burns.)

Three

Walland School

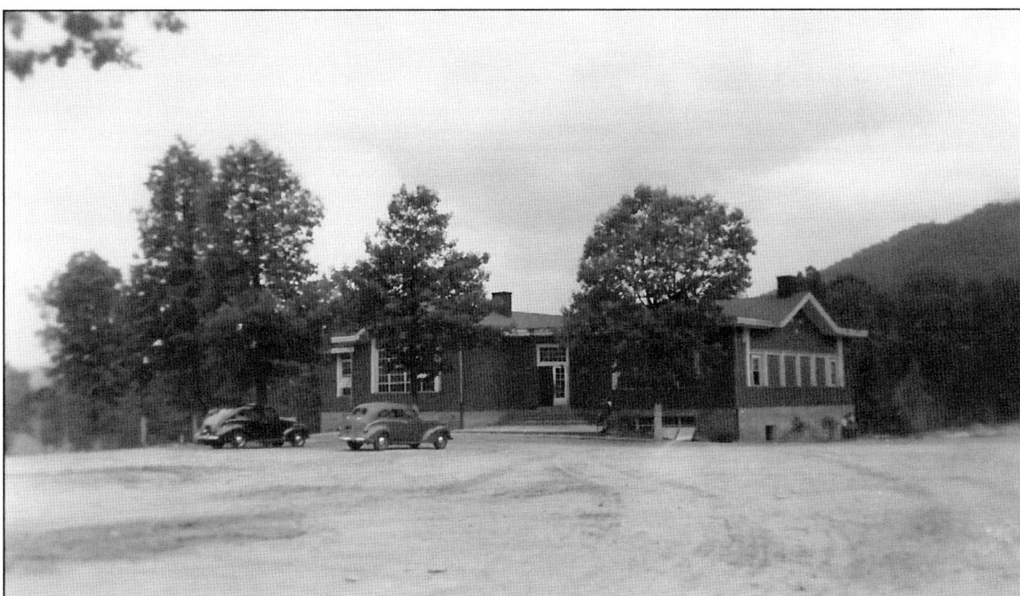

Walland High School was established in 1922, and the high school building was built in 1925 on East Miller's Cove Road. The school opened on September 28, 1925, with an enrollment of 50 students. A new building was built in 1963–1964 and occupied in the spring of 1964. In 1973, a new gymnasium was built to replace a wooden structure that had once been part of the Schlosser Leather Company. This high school building had replaced an earlier school built by the Walland High School in 1941. Many schools fed into the Walland High School, including Walland Elementary, Rocky Branch, Chilhowee View, Forest Hill, Union, and Hubbard. Some of the principals included Paul G. Houts (1926, with the first graduating class), O.M. Drinnen, George Dillingham, D.K. Whitehead, J.H. Davis, Loren Snelson, Charles Lemons, Ben A. Cunningham, P.G. Rice, and W.B. Rich. Clyde McMahan served as principal at Walland for 23 years. Walland graduate James "Jimmy" Carroll became principal and was there for three years before the Walland High School consolidated with other county schools to form the Heritage High School in 1977. (Courtesy of Paul Roberts.)

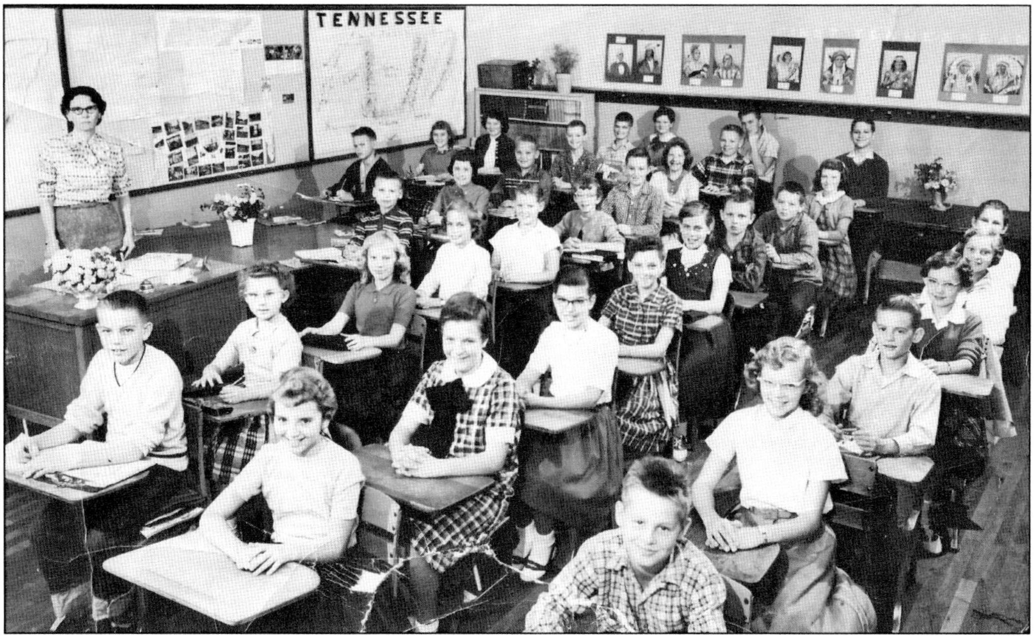

Nita Keeble Martin is shown with students, probably in fourth grade, at Walland Elementary School. This photograph is thought to be from the 1950s, by which time students were attending individual classes for each grade instead of multiple grades sharing a classroom. Reading, writing, and arithmetic were not the only classes taught; history and science were added in the 1950s. (Courtesy of Gladys Oliver Burns.)

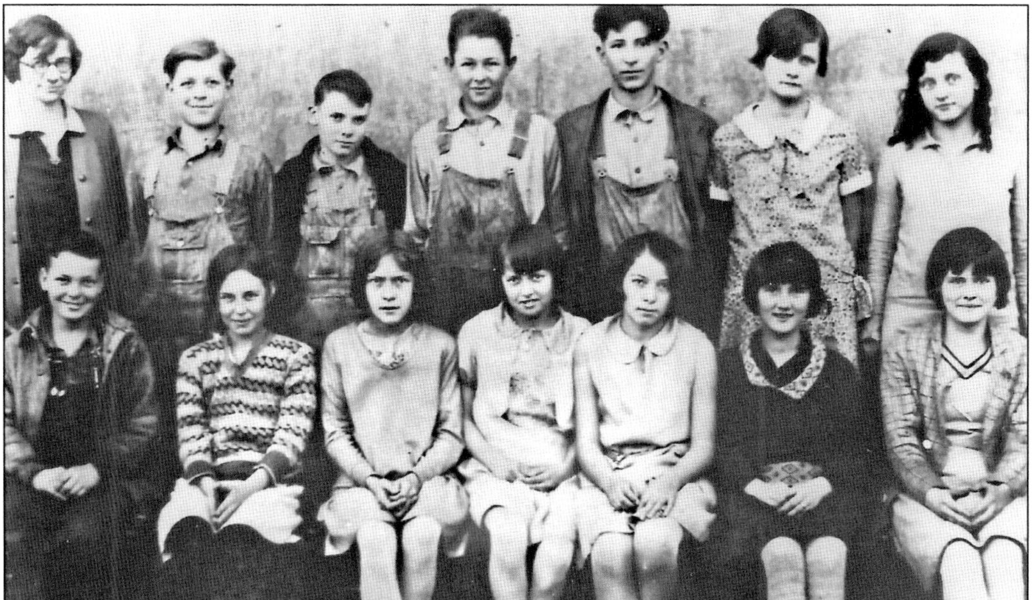

Walland School students are, from left to right, (first row) Houston Walker, Cora Bell Hatcher, Ruth Adams, Mildred Sams, Lucille Gillespie, Mattie Law, and Ailene Law; (second row) Carra Helton, John Wilson, Art Martin, Howard Pace, Raymond Chaney, Zelma Chaney, and Arlene Gamble. (Courtesy of Earl Adams Jr., Inez McCauley Adams Collection.)

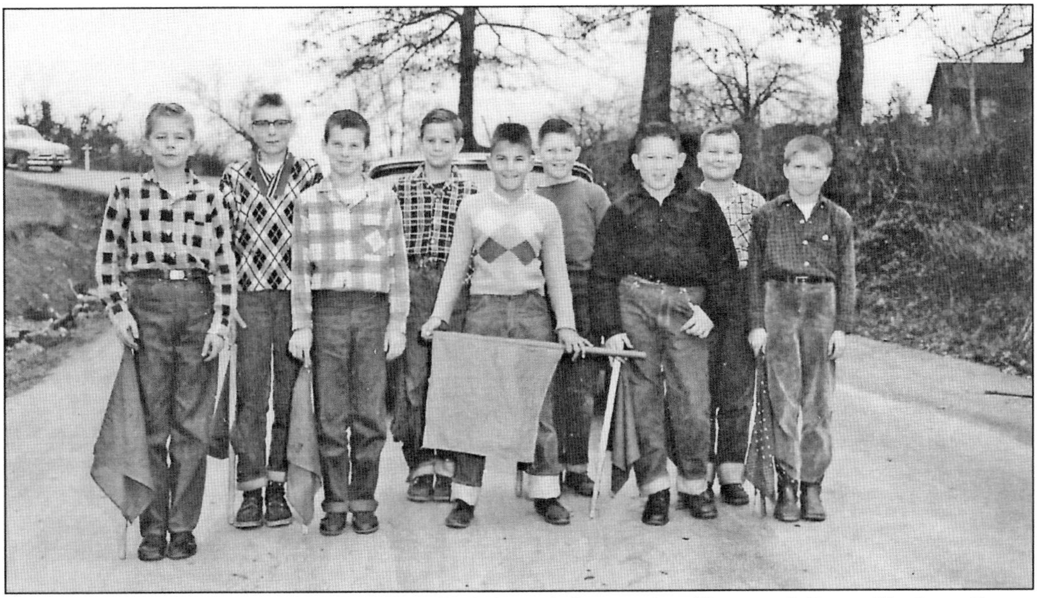

Walland School's safety patrol consisted of, from left to right, (first row) Steve Huskey, Curtis Wade, C.R. Dalton, Mike Hinchman, and Eddie Williams; (second row) Ronald Rollins, unidentified, Clarence White, and Terry Adams. (Courtesy of Earl Adams Jr., Inez McCauley Adams Collection.)

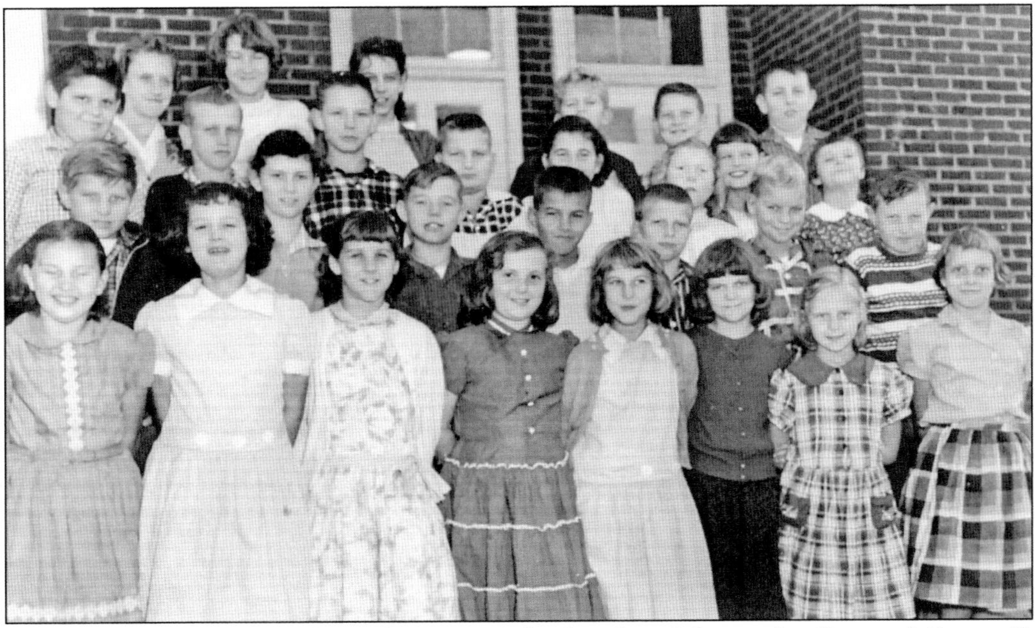

The fifth-grade class at Walland Elementary School is, from left to right, (first row) Donna K. Myers, Geraldine Effler, Kathy Watson, Charlotte Brewer, Mary Ann Murphy, Daisy Buchanan, May Price, and Ida Sue Hatcher; (second row) George Lowe, Linda Woodruff, David Ledbetter, C.R. Dalton, Eddie Williamson, Roy Lee Watkins, and Eugene Murphy; (third row) Joe Thomas, George Lowe, Jimmy Rollins, Terry Adams, Martha Patty, Margaret Stinnett, Phyllis Effler, and Charlotte McMahan; (fourth row) Millie Hutsell, Shirley Monday, Steve Huskey, unidentified, Clarence White, and Gary Suttles. (Courtesy of Earl Adams Jr., Inez McCauley Adams Collection.)

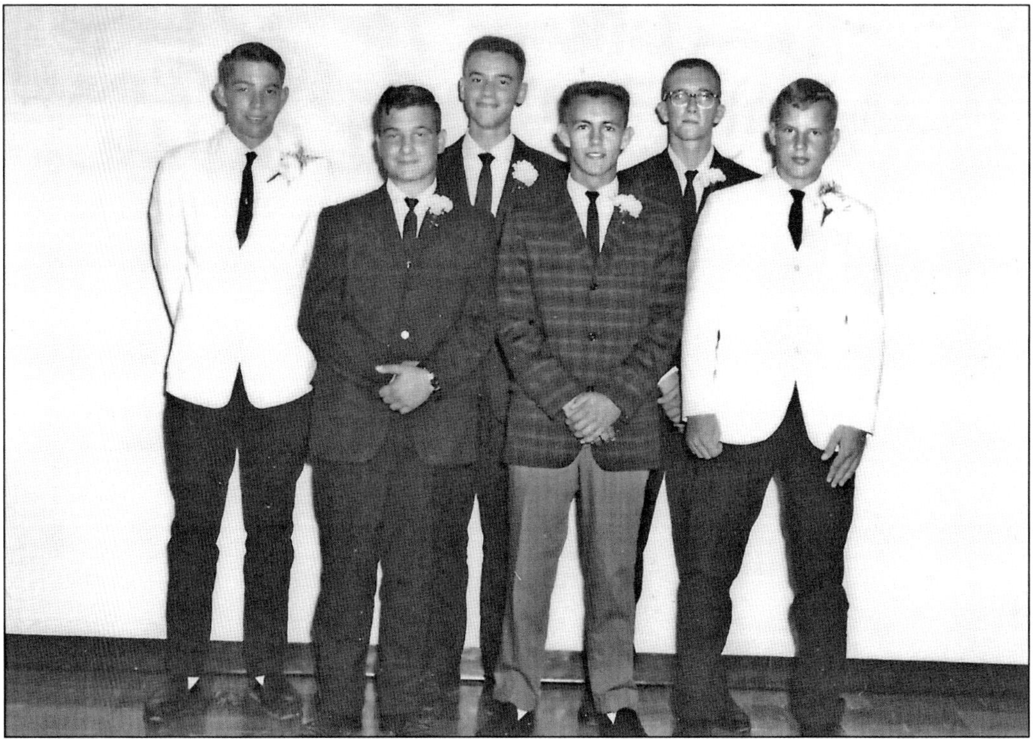

From left to right in 1967 are (first row) Terry Adams, Don Turbyfill, and Eddie Riddle; (second row) Tommy Wilson, Buddy Hill, and Ronald Patty. (Courtesy of Earl Adams Jr., Inez McCauley Adams Collection.)

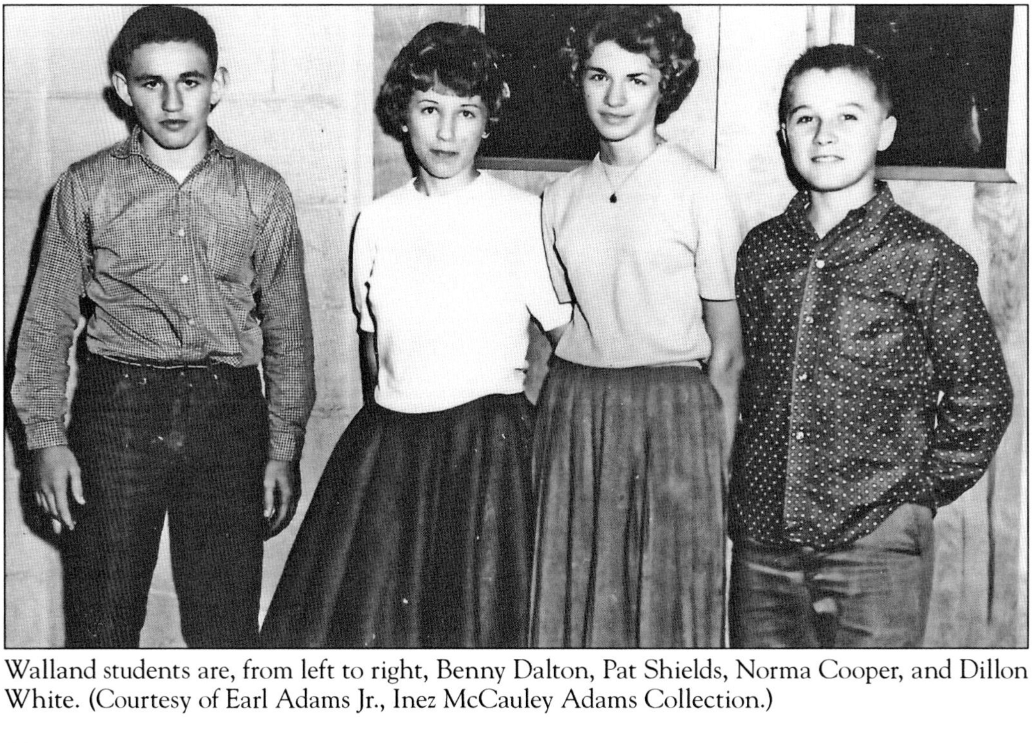

Walland students are, from left to right, Benny Dalton, Pat Shields, Norma Cooper, and Dillon White. (Courtesy of Earl Adams Jr., Inez McCauley Adams Collection.)

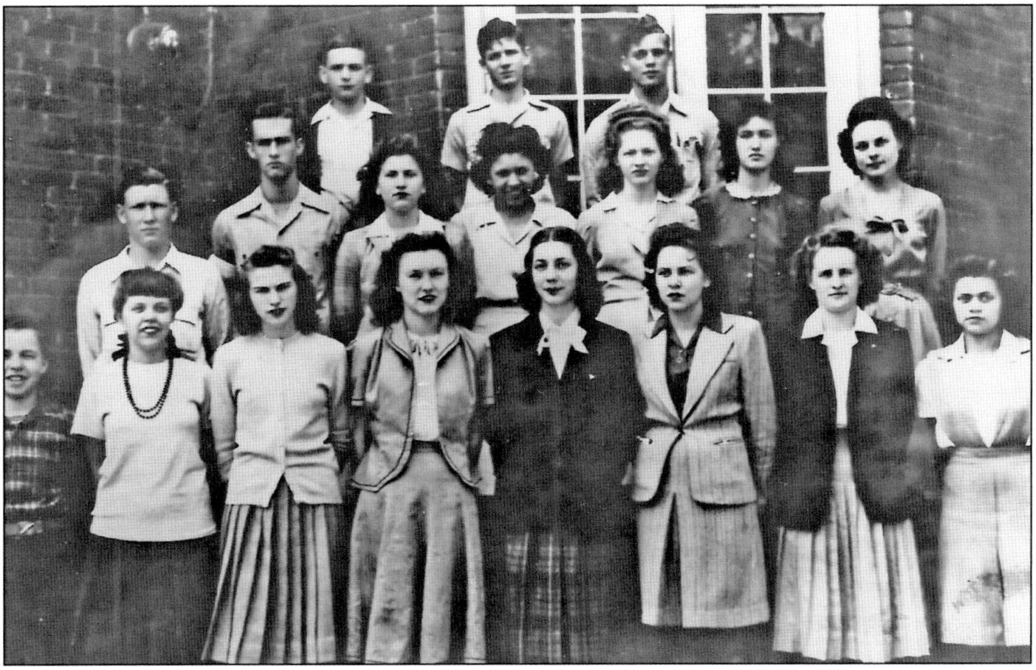

This Walland class is, from left to right, (first row) Bernie Mills, Bonnie Mills, Elizabeth Walker, Gladys Howard, Virginia Myers, unidentified, Ruby Ledbetter, and Jimmy Rogers; (second row) Bruce McCampbell, unidentified, Edna Patty, Lucille Williamson, Gaynell Wright, ? Waters, and Mabel Hill Reese: (third row) Otis Myers, Harold Myers, and R.M. Everett. (Courtesy of Earl Adams Jr., Inez McCauley Adams Collection.)

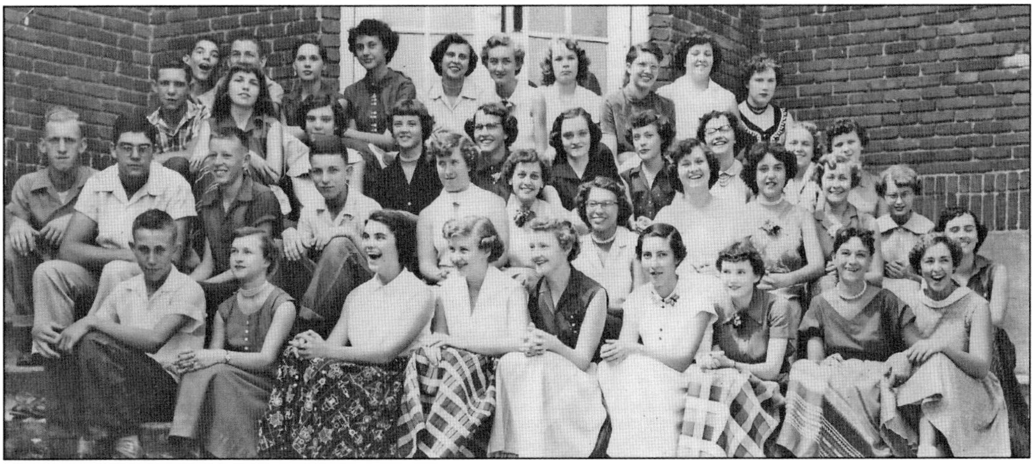

In 1955, the Walland Beta Club was, from left to right, (first row) John Caughron, Roberta Cable, Wanda Burns, Faye Everett, Velda Flynn, Evelyn Gillespie, Vivian Bible, Shirley Payne, and Eva Jo Ogle; (second row) Hubert McKinney, George Bales, Jerry McNeilly, Betty Waters, Louise Fancher, Bobbie Jean Martin, Evelyn Waters, Wilma Galyon, Sarah Lou Millsaps, Johnnie Mae Burns, and Delores Dalton; (third row) Ray Watson, Max Coulter, Janice Davis, Twila Wagner, Sue Cummings, Nora Kay Davis, Ruthie White, Cledith Millsaps, Sue Cummings, Vada Weakley, Jody Russell, and Jean Nichols; (fourth row) Charles Burns, Timmy Lowe, Thelma Barbra, Margaret Ford, Joann Coulter, Jewel Abbott, Joyce West, Elnor Perkins, and Reba Everett. (Courtesy of Missy Tipton Green.)

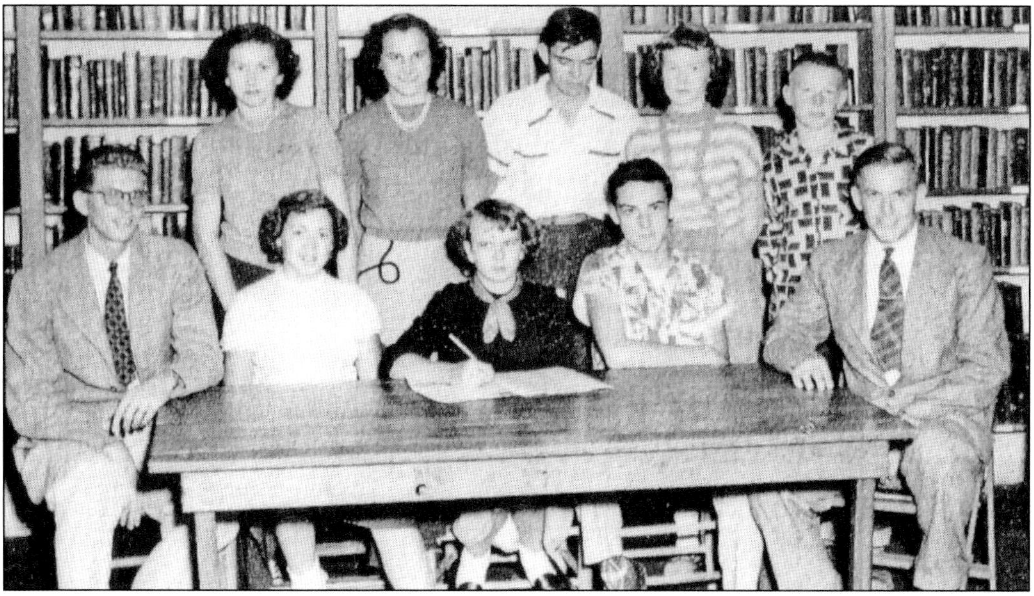

The 1953 Walland Student Council is, from left to right, (first row) Kenneth Trent, EvaJo Ogle, Helen Runion, Bill C. Martin, and J.D. Carpenter; (second row) Jean Lambert, Eva Russell, Lee Duck, Sue Cummings, and George Bales. (Courtesy of Missy Tipton Green.)

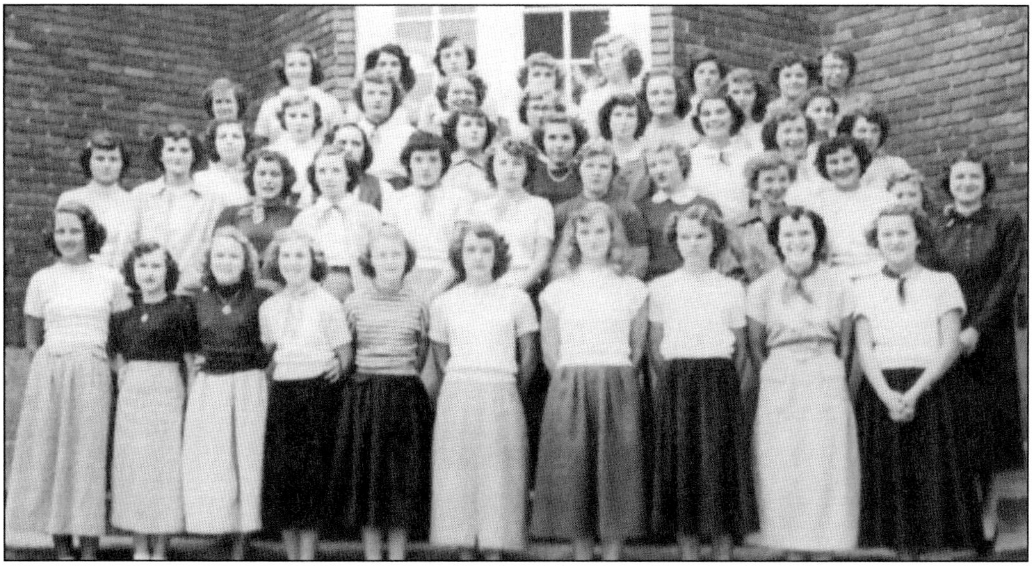

The Walland High School Future Homemakers of America (FHA) are, from left to right, (first row) Ruthie White, Roberta Cable, Joey Russell, Wilma Everett, Johnnie Burns, Imogene Teffeteller, Belle Sewell, Bess Cooper, Patsy Dixon, and Willa F. Keller; (second row) Sara L. Carroll, Helen Caldwell, Ida Kiser, Norman Brannum, Barbara Long, Barbara Morrison, Faye Everett, Velda Flynn, June Brackin, Glenda McCauley, Mary E. Tipton, and Mrs. Jimmie Eaves; (third row) Janice Davis, Vivian Wade, Barbara Howell, Mary Parrott, Maxine Sloan, Della M. Keller, Sara Millsaps, Ruthie Latham, Shirley Martin, Cledith Millsaps, Wanda Burns, Shirley Cloniger, Betty Garner, Flo Brewer, Louise Fancher, and Betty Turner; (fourth row) Betty Waters, Elnor Perkins, Wilma Galyon, Hope Mabes, Joy Hodge, Dorothy Jennings, Juanita Blevins, and Bobbie Martin. (Courtesy of Missy Tipton Green.)

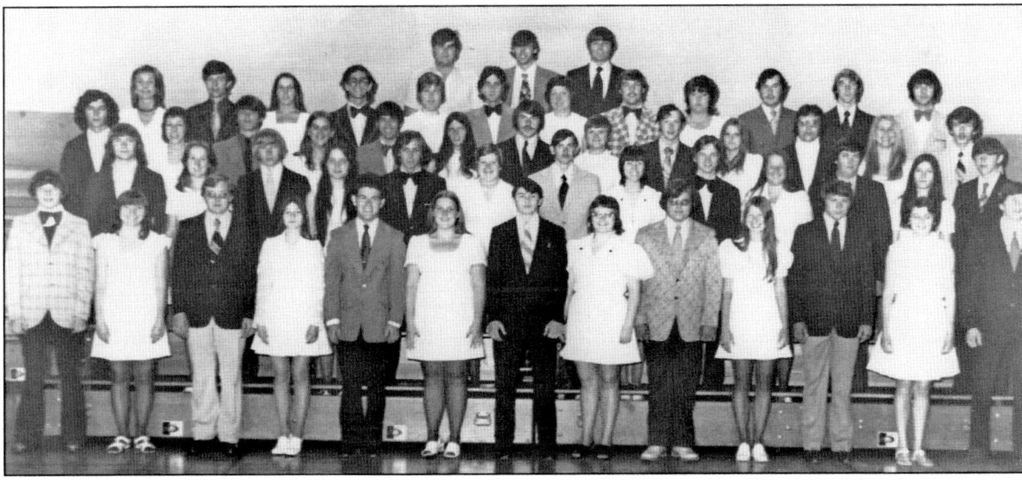

The Walland graduating class of 1974 is, from left to right, (first row) Robbie Kirkland, Janie Lowe, Joe Tipton, Ethel O'Dell, Aubrey Russell, Sylvia Martin, Allen Headrick, Cynthia Hatcher, Tony Adams, Shirley Roulette, Ricky Campbell, Janice Bell, and Phillip Potter; (second row) Danny Hutsell, Carolyn Robertson, Mike Hatcher, Joyce Oliver, Jay White, Pat Riddle, Mike Cable, Kathy Potter, Trent Teffeteller, Vickie Strickland, Dale Garner, Janet Lawson, and Wade Nuchols; (third row) Steve Cooper, Connie Martin, Tommy Thomason, Debbie Graham, Dwight Waters, Carrie Alexander, Jackie Gregory, Marilyn Whitehead, Don Carr, Linda Robertson, Steve Martin, Libby Ford, and Dane Cooper; (fourth row) Barbara Sauls, Kenneth Branton, Cindy Martin, Richard Mogridge, Pam Law, Steve Law, Micki McKinsey, Mike Law, Linda Wolfe, Jim Gourley, Keith Frye, and Robbie Robertson; (fifth row) Lee McKinney, Danny Burns, and Kevin Barton. (Courtesy of Earl Adams Jr., Inez McCauley Adams Collection.)

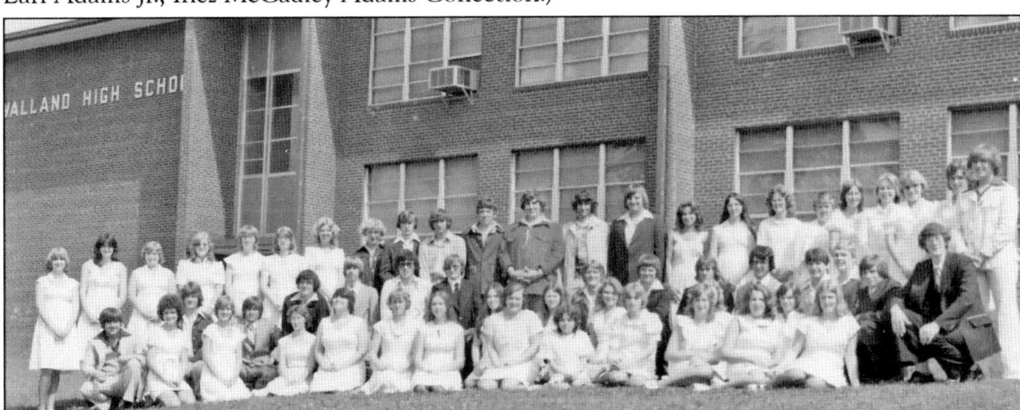

The last class of Walland High School graduated in 1977. From left to right are (first row) Cathy Adams, Macheala Inman, MeMe Payne, Debbie Hall, Mary Watson, Patsy Huskey, Aleene Burnett, Pam Hindman, Regina Brewer, Libby Reagan, Karen Renfro, Becky Turnmjire, Debbie Dillingham, Glenda Garner, Betsy McKinsey, and Kim Roberts; (second row) Ricky Keller, Jackie Hurst, Malcolm Inman, Cleve Miles, Steve Cannon, Terry Effler, Donnie Campbell, Dennis Whitehead, Jimmy Owens, Tony Gregory, Johnny Sweet, Tim Ivens, Scott Law, Alan Walker, and Alan Dillingham; (third row) Teresa Myers, Debbie Keller, Pam Campbell, Wanda Coulter, Debbie Russell, Missy Tipton, Cindy Stephens, Chuck Tipton, Steve Headrick, Ricky Nichols, Brad Conway, Brian Myers, Kent Stephens, Tim Ledbetter, Debbie Holbert, Vicky Teffeteller, Lisa McCauley, Vanessa Moss, Debbie Miller, Donna Pangle, Brenda Whitehead, Carol Nuchols, and Ricky Trentham. (Courtesy of Missy Tipton Green.)

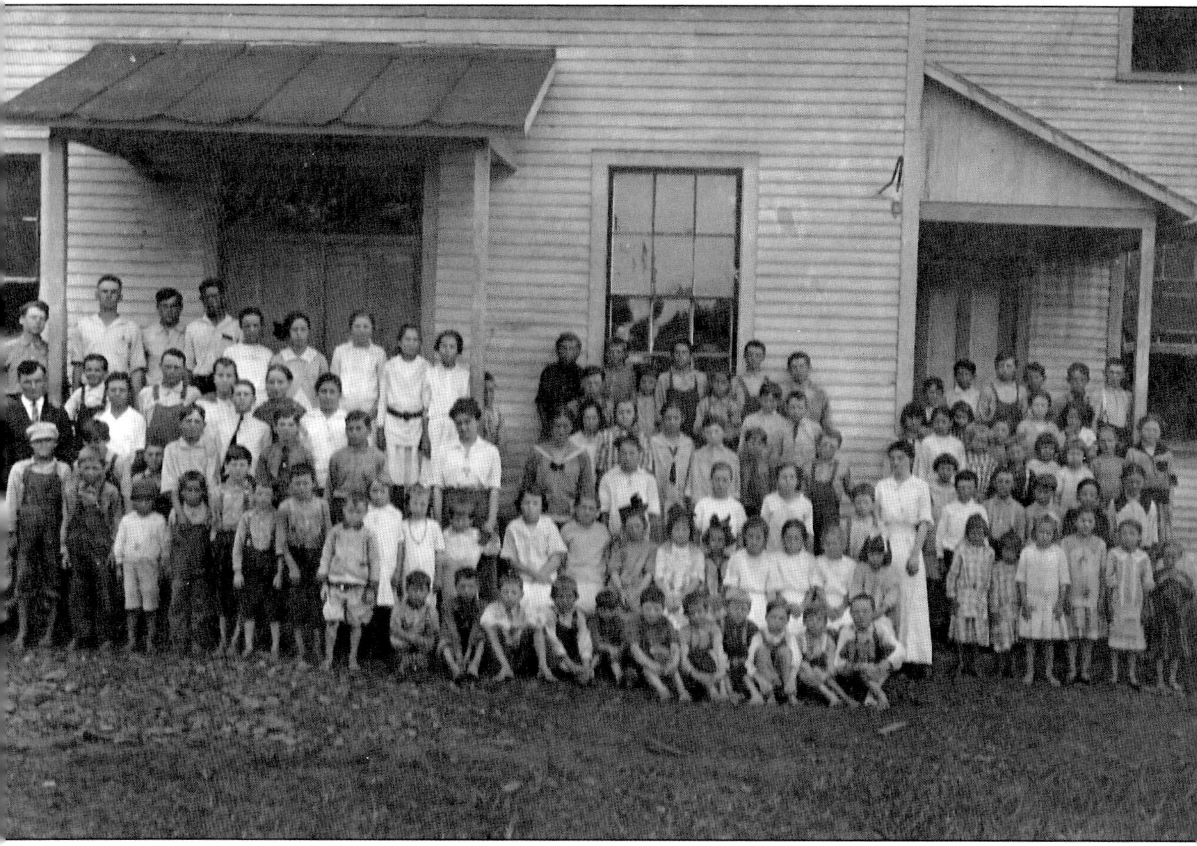

Walland School was built in 1916 by Schlosser Leather for employees' children and local children to attend. Pictured in the left column, beginning with the top row, are Richard Greene, Charlie Everett, Hugh Greene, John Everett, Mayme Kilpatrick, Della Harbison, Abbie Gillespie, Annabell Gillespie, Maggie Walker, ? Hurst, George D. Roberts (teacher), John Bible, Arthur Ruble, Huse Martin, Maggie Fagg, Kenneth Greene, Frankie Burns, Marjorie Blazer, Sam Harbison, Earl Blazer, Bill Hurst, Arthur Hancox, Roy Greene, Charlie Simerly, Howard Gamble, Fred Martin, Bob Walker, George Cagle, Lawrence Cagle, Clyde Martin, Wade Martin, Ruth Martin, Lois Long, A.J. Fisher Jr., Nell Howard Lamon (teacher). In the second column, beginning with the top row, are Ross Bible, Burnett Greene, Harold Bird, Levi Farmer, Mike Farmer, Willie Boring, unidentified, Roy Chaney, Ernest Thomas, Ralph Walker, Kathryn Gillespie, Edna Chaney, Belle Anthony, Raymond Thomas, Elmer Hancox, Lawrence Whitehead, Alice Hurst, Grace Martin, Ellen Stillwell, unidentified, James Stillwell, Norma Singleton Smith (teacher), Sarah Hurst, Lizzie Hurst, Bonnie Cagle, Dorothy Fisher, Aleene Blazer, Bertha Kilpatrick, Agnes Fagg, Edith Roulette, Crysta Walker. In the right column, from top left, are Jerome Thomas, Charles Henry Walker, Leonard Boring, Brian Walker, Charlie Cagle, Bob Law, four unidentified, Pauline Walker, Margaret Sands, Lillie Stillwell, Joe Chaney, Charlotte Fisher, Margaret Jane Hurst, Annabell Burns, Beulah Hurst, Mae Brewer, Gardill Noe, James Law, Fred Bird, unidentified, Louisa Mitchell, Verna Walker, Evelyn Walker, Maude Gillespie, Bertie Greene, Audrine Walker, and Mayme Whitehead. Seated on the ground in front are Arthur Farmer, Ed Fagg, Raymond Walker, Jess Roulette, Henry Hatcher, Hardie Gillespie, Leonard Whitehead, Robert Chaney, ? Boring, ? Boring, and Walt Hurst. (Courtesy of Missy Tipton Green.)

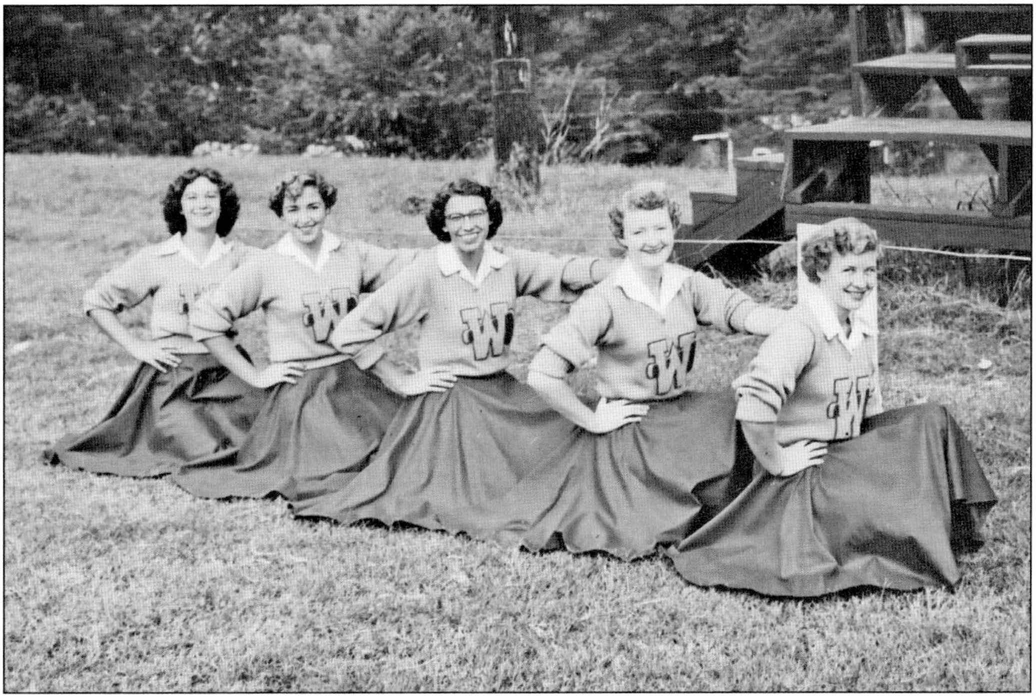

Pictured in 1955, from left to right, are Walland cheerleaders Shirley Payne, Eva Jo Ogle, Bobbie Jean Martin, Velda Flynn, and Faye Everett. (Courtesy of Missy Tipton Green.)

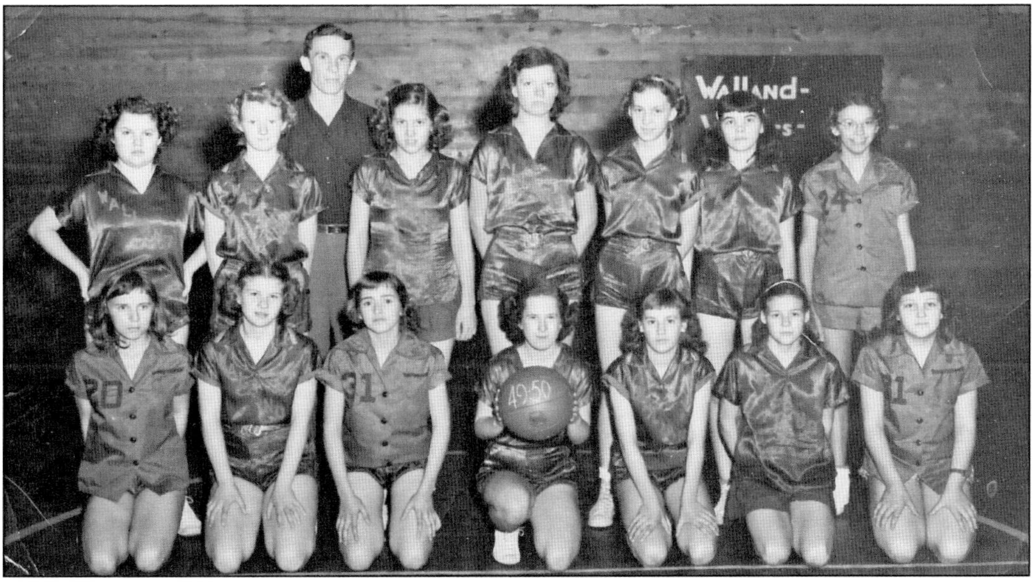

The Walland girls' basketball team of 1949–1950 is, from left to right, (first row) Vivian Wade, Faye Everett, Eva Ogle, Betty Waters, Shirley Fife, Birdia Hatcher, and Elnor Perkins; (second row) Flo Brewer, Velda Flynn, coach Ray Lillard, Joyce Myers, Ruth Gredig, Hope Mabes, Wanda Burns, and Bobbie Jean Martin. (Courtesy of Missy Tipton Green.)

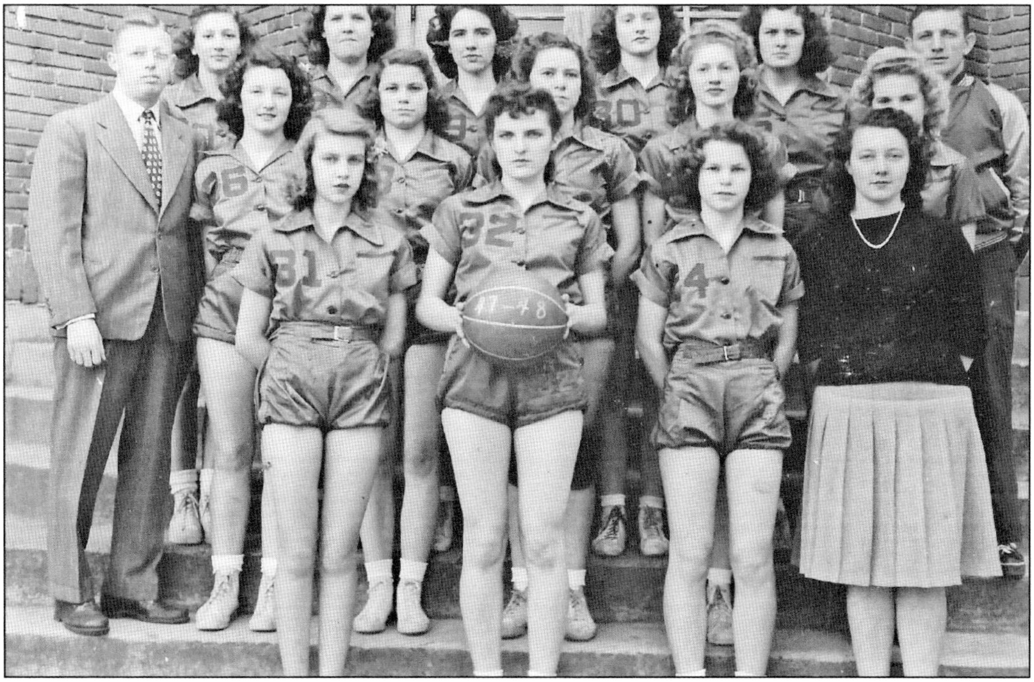

The 1947–1948 Walland High School girls' basketball team, from left to right, are (first row) Betty June Inman, Sara Waters, June Abbott, and Edna Roberts Whaley; (second row) coach Ben Cunningham, Joan Roberts, Reba Abbott, Sue Ogle, Gaynell Wright, and Jarvis Holland; (third row) Nita Ogle, Anna Mae Waters, Aileene Myers, Delite Wright, Ruby Joe Williams, and coach Ken Stinnett. (Courtesy of Missy Tipton Green and Paulette Ledbetter.)

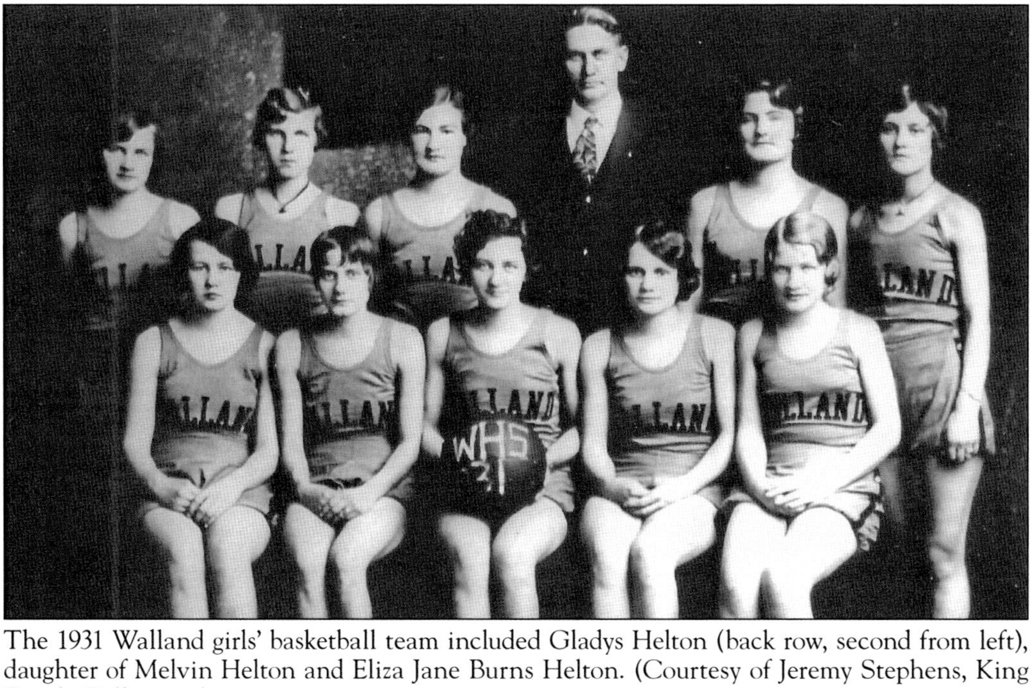

The 1931 Walland girls' basketball team included Gladys Helton (back row, second from left), daughter of Melvin Helton and Eliza Jane Burns Helton. (Courtesy of Jeremy Stephens, King Family Collection.)

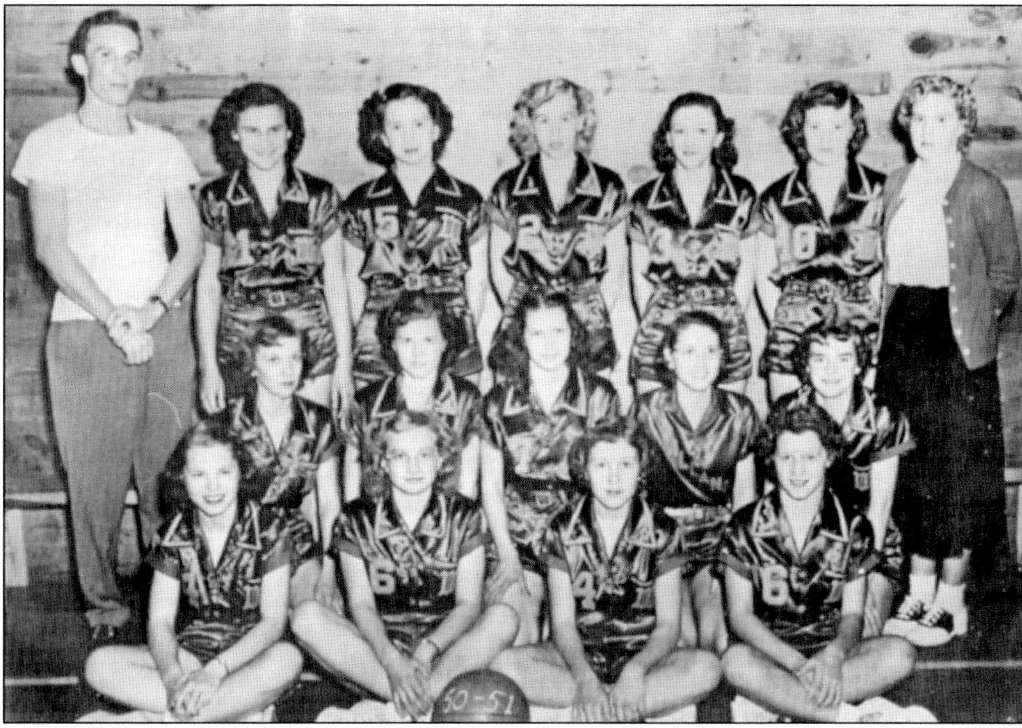

The Walland girls' basketball team is, from left to right (first row) June Abbott, Hazel Mogridge, Mae Ogle, and Winnie Gregory; (second row) Betty June Inman, Sue Duck, Bueonas Ayers, Virginia Roberts, and Vonnie Flynn; (third row) Eva Lee Russell, Jean Lambert, Sue Bales, Nita Ogle, and Nancy Latham. The coach was Ray Lillard, and the manager was Jarvis Holland. (Courtesy of Missy Tipton Green and Paulette Ledbetter.)

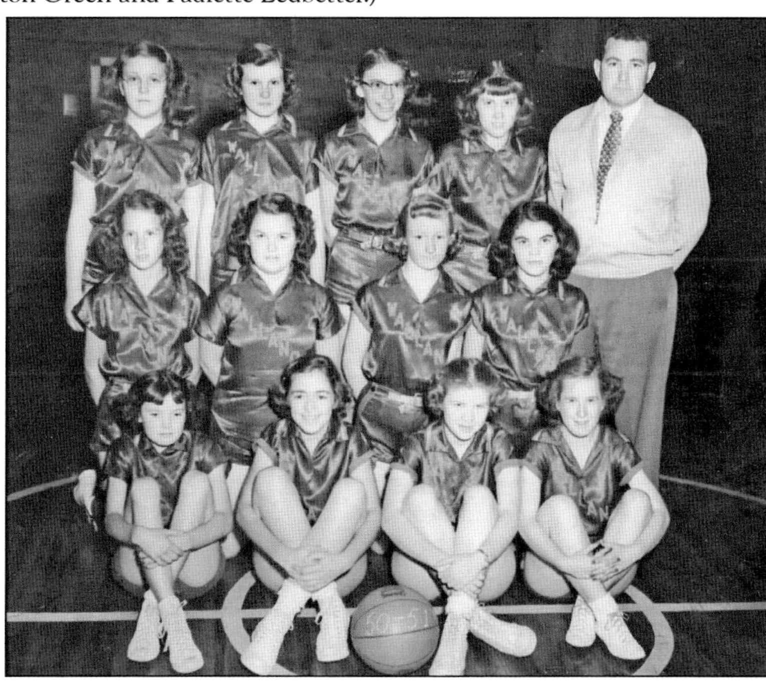

The 1950–1951 Walland girls' basketball team is, from left to right, (first row) Vivian Bible, Eva Ogle, Faye Everett, and Betty Waters; (second row) Ruthie White, Flo Brewer, Velda Flynn, and Wanda Burns; (third row) Elnor Perkins, Betty Magill, Bobbie Jean Martin, Joyce West, and coach A.J. Wilson. (Courtesy of Missy Tipton Green.)

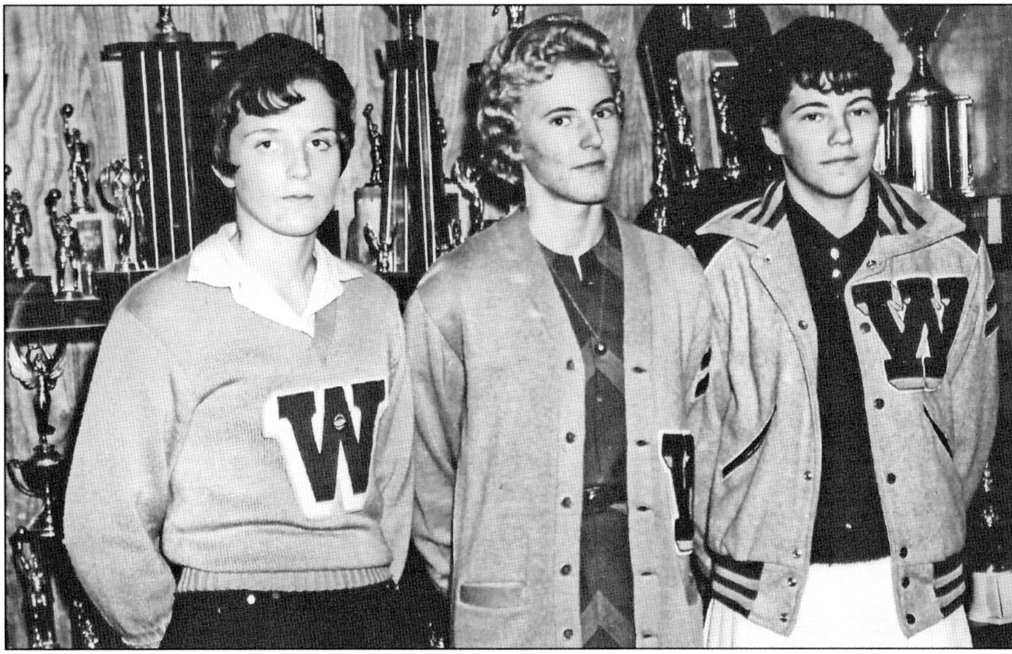

The 1962 Walland girls' basketball team was first runner-up in the state championship. From left to right are Viola Powell, Charlotte McNeilly, and Shirley White. This team was coached by A.J. Wilson, who twice led the team to 36 wins and 3 losses, in 1962 and 1963, and played in the state championship games both years, ending as first runners-up. (Courtesy of Mike White.)

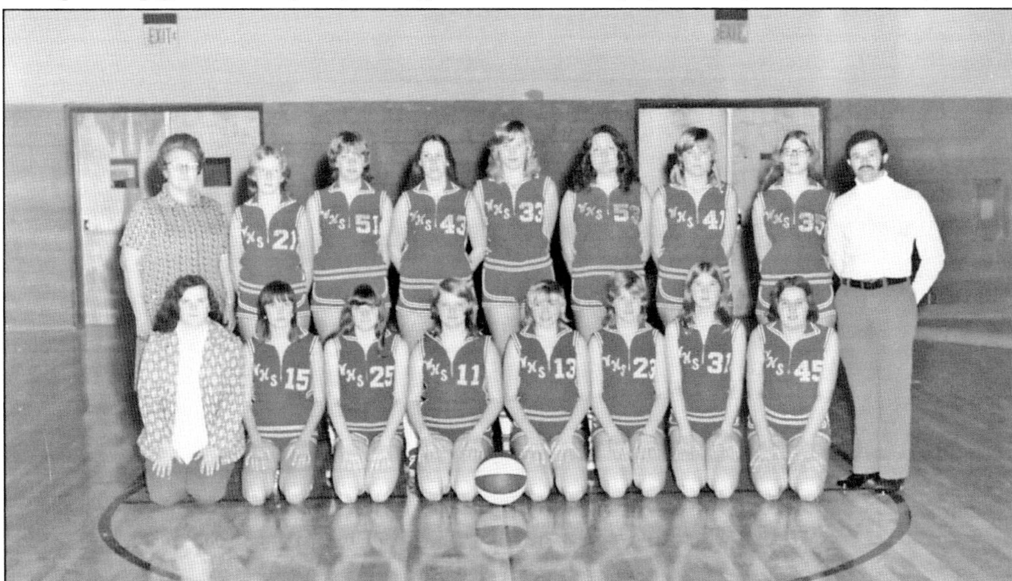

The 1973–1974 Walland girls' basketball team is, from left to right, (first row) manager Aileene Burnette, Kathy Walker, Yvonne Martin, Kim Roberts, Sheila Potter, Glenda Garner, Missy Tipton, and Betsy McKinsey; (second row) sponsor Gladys King, Debbie Russell, Vicki McKinsey, Cindy Martin, Jacque Braun, Micki McKinsey, Jeanne Braun, Darlene Whitener, and coach Ed Bales. (Courtesy of Missy Tipton Green.)

Doyle (left), Mary Jane (center), and Horace Stephens (right), children of James Lee Stephens and Oma Lucy Helton Stephens, graduated from Walland High School, where they were active in sports. (Courtesy of Jeremy Stephens, King Family Collection.)

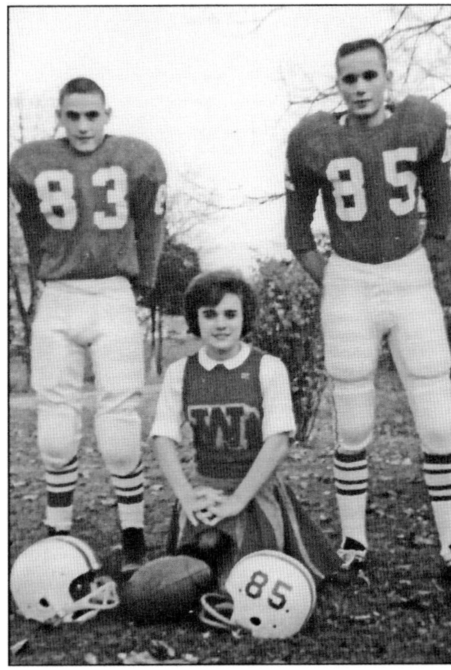

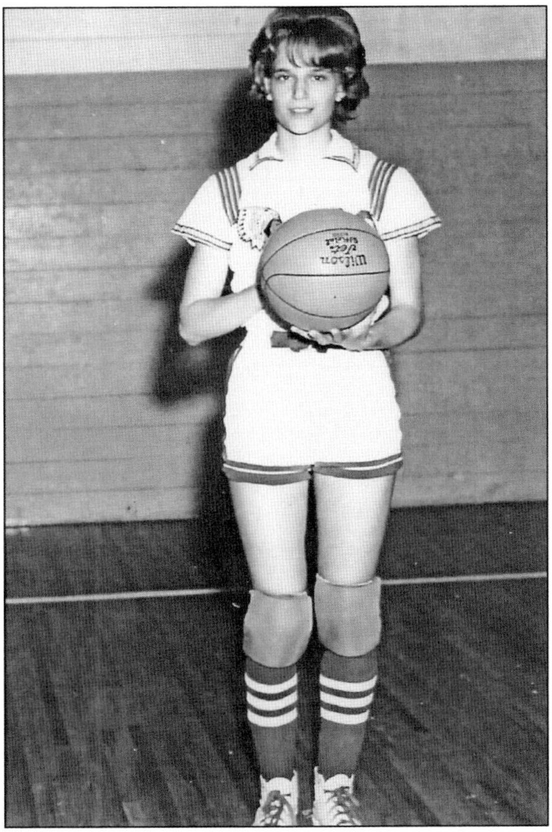

Pictured is Walland basketball player Rolena King, daughter of Rocklan King and Gladys Helton King. (Courtesy of Jeremy Stephens King Family Collection.)

Shirley Ledbetter, daughter of Ernest Max Ledbetter and Dorothy Juanita Ogle Ledbetter, graduated from Walland High School in 1965. (Courtesy of Shirley Ledbetter Martin.)

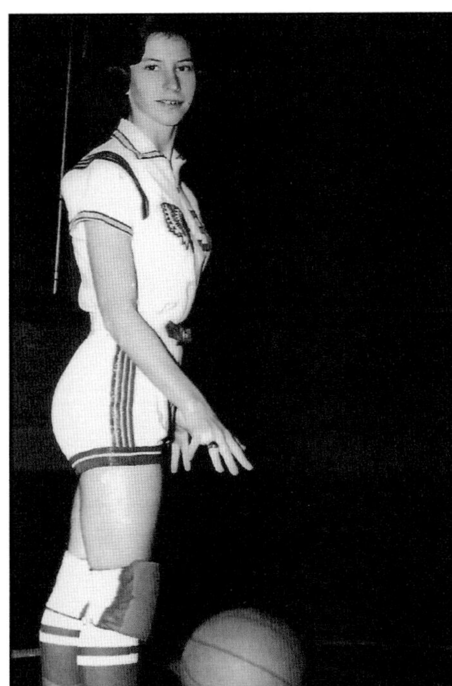

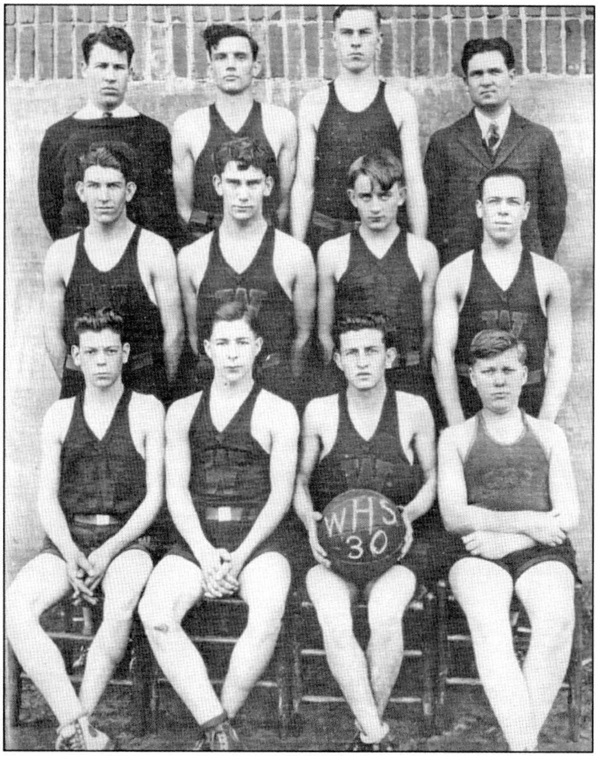

The 1930 Walland boys' basketball team is, from left to right, (first row) Harry George Walker, Sam Lane, Noah Tipton, and Charlie Millsaps; (second row) Chester Burns, Frank Headrick, Wade Clark, and Jim Thomas; (third row) coach George Ballard, Jim Clark, Ernest Tipton, and George Dillingham, principal. (Courtesy of Earl Adams Jr., Inez McCauley Adams Collection.)

The Walland boys' basketball team is, from left to right, (first row) Hugh Tipton, Robert Maxey, Robert Williams, J.D. Burchfield, and Richard Everett; (second row) Darrell Coulter, D.C. Hall, L.M. Rogers, coach J.A. Maxey, and A.J. Davis. (Courtesy of Missy Tipton Green and Paulette Ledbetter.)

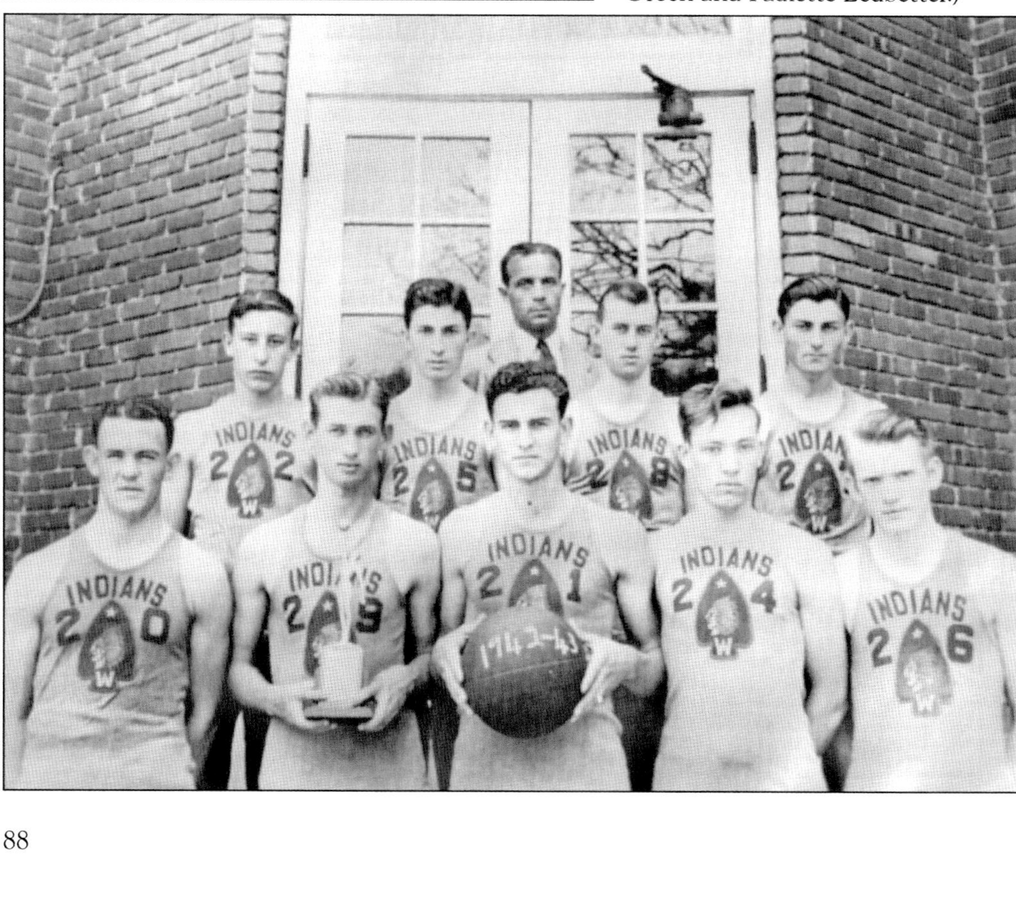

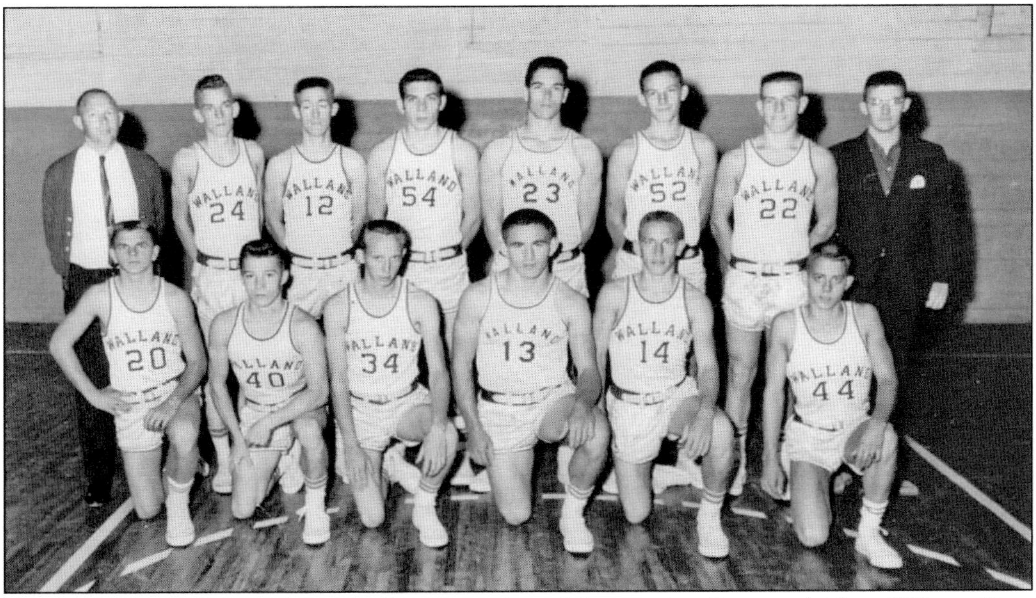

The 1965 Walland boys' basketball team is, from left to right, (first row) Chris White, Gary Teffeteller, Monte Stephens, Benny Dalton, David Caughron, and Larry Hodge; (second row) coach Lenville Powell, Ricky Hinchman, Jackie Vaughn, Chester Caldwell, James McKinney, Ronald Caldwell, Louie Eggers, and manager Buddy Walker. (Courtesy of Missy Tipton Green and Paulette Ledbetter.)

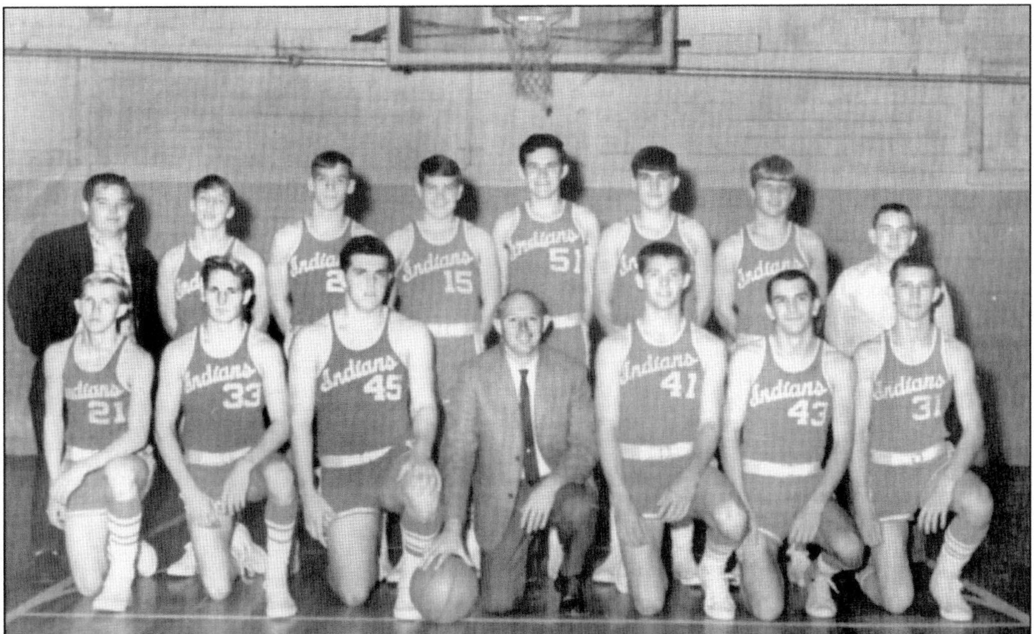

The 1968–1969 Walland boys' basketball team is, from left to right, (first row) Roger Teffeteller, David Hutsell, Roger Williamson, coach Lenville Powell, Danny Hutsell, David Conner, and David Braun; (second row) Eddie Kirkland, Mike Martin, Edward Hill, Allen Martin, Fred White, Doug Teffeteller, Darrell Hurst, and Jim Sloan. (Courtesy of Missy Tipton Green and Paulette Ledbetter.)

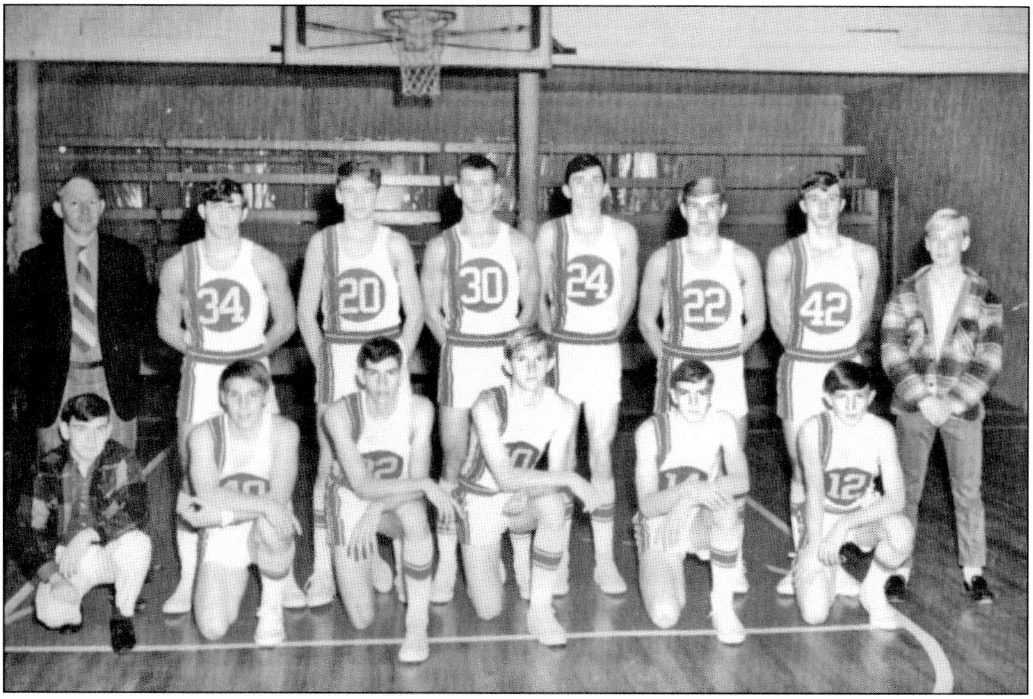

The 1970–1971 Walland boys' basketball team is, from left to right, (first row) Jim Sloan, Mike Martin, Junior McCulloch, Roger Teffeteller, Terry Myers, and Trent Teffeteller; (second row) coach Lenville Powell, Kent Merriman, Robbie Everett, David Braun, Mike Headrick, Allen Martin, Steve Wolfe, and manager Charles Stott. (Courtesy of Missy Tipton Green and Paulette Ledbetter.)

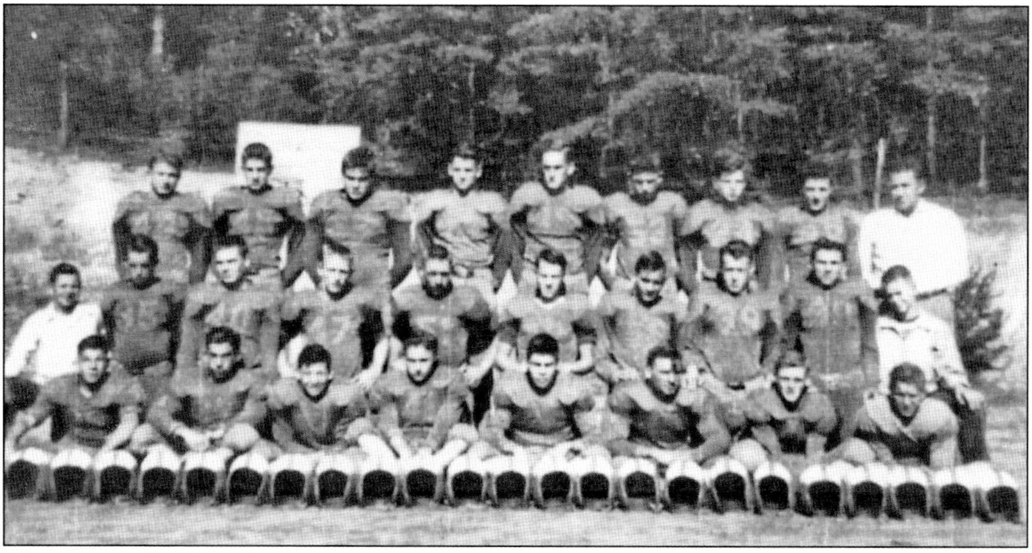

The 1952 Walland football team is, from left to right, (first row) Bobby Everett, Leroy Roberson, Wayne Everett, Sammy Compton, Vernon Everett, Johnny Bible, Larry Wilson, and John Edward Russell; (second row) manager Ralph Wilhoite, Donald Lowe, David Myers, Bob Cagle, Bruce Brackin, Walter Martin, Bill Joe Fancher, Arthur Dotson, Wade Headrick, and manager Bill Patty; (third row) Edgar Cloniger, Joe Payne, J.H. Swift, Clifford Wilburn, Cecil Herron, Jimmy Hitch, Gene Patty, Ray Hurst, and coach A.J. Wilson. (Courtesy of Missy Tipton Green.)

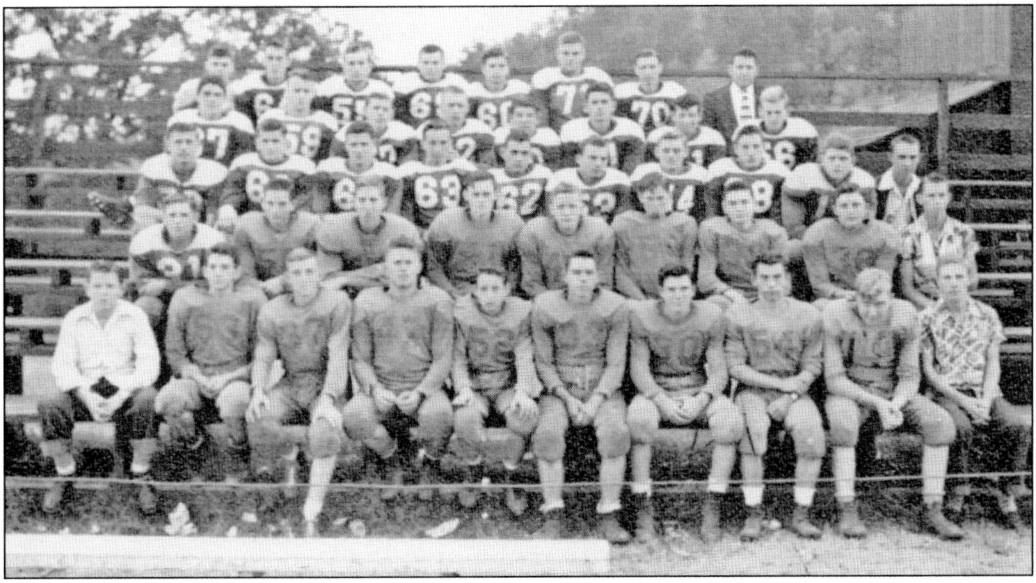

The 1953 Walland football team is, from left to right, (first row) manager Jimmy Payne, Robert Brown, John Gregory, Don Dotson, Charles Schlangen, Fred R. Headrick, Lee R. Roberson, Jerry Campbell, Lowell Gregory, and unidentified; (second row) Max Coulter, Marshall Powell, Fred Millsaps, Willard Henry, John Russell, Billy Lowe, R.L. Grindstaff, Billy Caldwell, and Don Lowe; (third row) Gene Duck, Joe Payne, Ray Hurst, Bobby Hall, Bill Fancher, John Bible, Larry Wilson, John Kiser, Ralph Boring, and Wayne Gregory; (fourth row) Hubert McKinney, Arthur Dotson, Jimmy Davis, Bruce Brackin, Bob Everett, Jimmy Hitch, Wayne Everett, and Clarence Story Jr.; (fifth row) Vernon Everett, Cecil Hearon, J.T. Anthony, David Myers, Gene Patty, J.H. Swift, Jimmy Gregory, and coach A.J. Wilson. (Courtesy of Missy Tipton Green.)

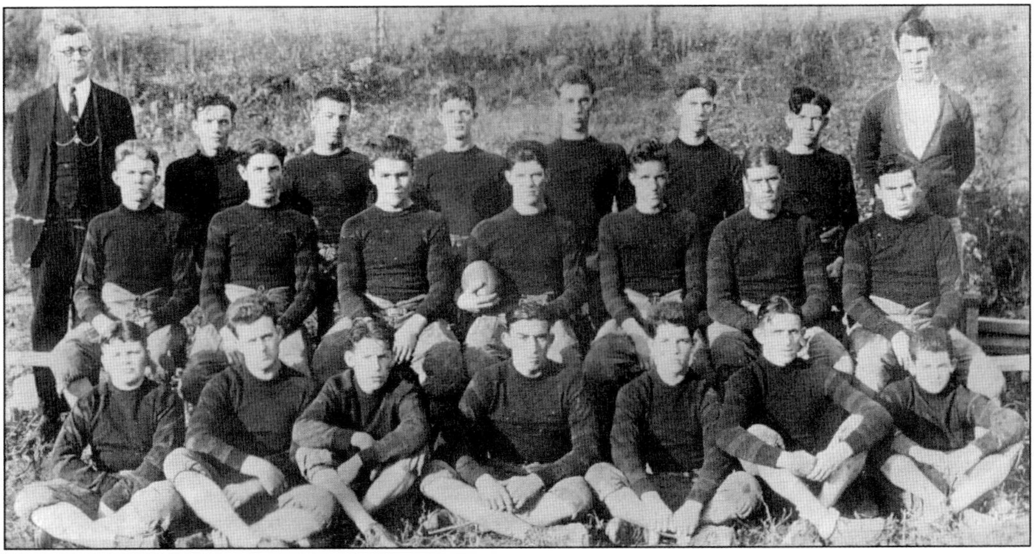

Pictured are members of the Early Walland football team that went by the nickname "Leathernecks." Their school colors were orange and blue. In later years, the nickname was changed to "Indians" and the school colors changed to red and gray. The early Walland School was a consolidation of nearby schools, Waters of East Miller's Cove, Caughron, Garland, and Webb of West Miller's Cove. (Courtesy of Missy Tipton Green and Paulette Ledbetter.)

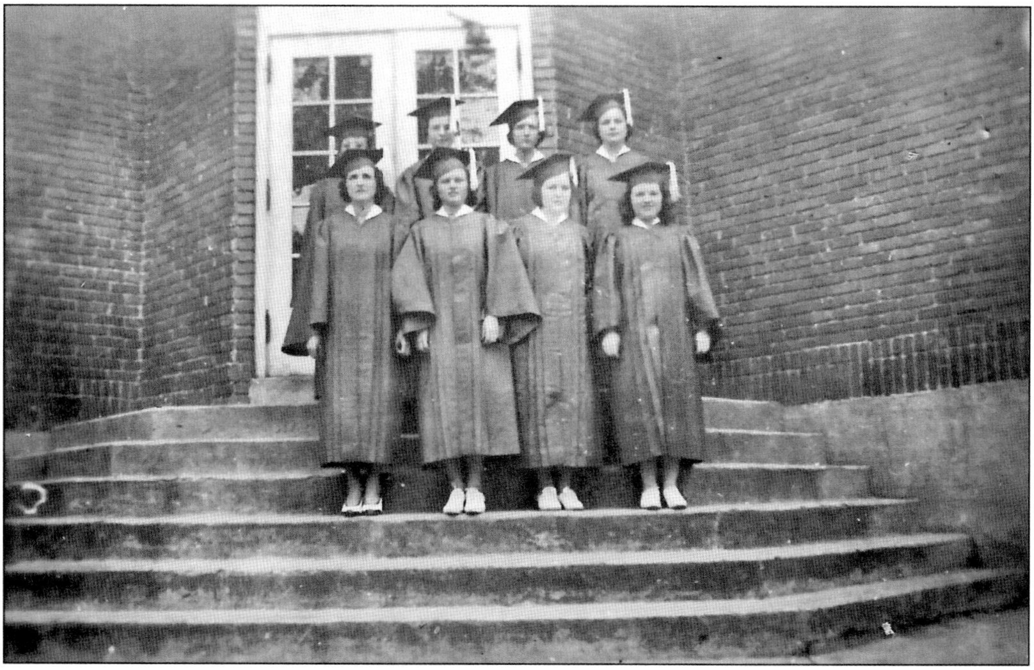

Pictured is the graduating class of Walland High School in 1939. This was the year that the deadliest conflict in human history, World War II, started. Many local young men would go to war before graduating high school. (Courtesy of Paul Roberts.)

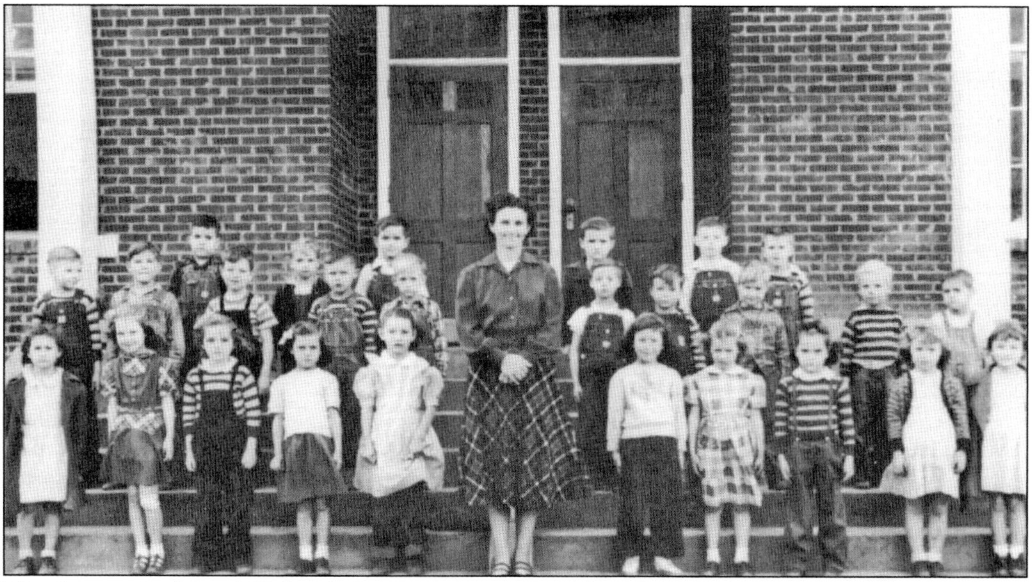

The first-grade class of Walland Elementary in 1950 is, from left to right, (first row) Joyce Jenkins, Louise Cameron, Charlene Medlin, Wilma Hatcher, Joyce Everett, Margaret Waters, Virginia Hurst, Janie Headrick, Carol Gredig, and Wilma Herron; (second row) Glenn Myers, Roy Roberts, Steven Patty, Lawrence Adams, Billy Ledbetter, Burl Tallent, Lester Gregory, David Reno, Eugene Yearout, and Rodger Weakley; (third row) Tommy Headrick, Madison Inman, Jimmy Hill, Glen Hatcher, Mitchell Moles, and J.W. Nichols. The teacher is unidentified. (Courtesy of Missy Tipton Green.)

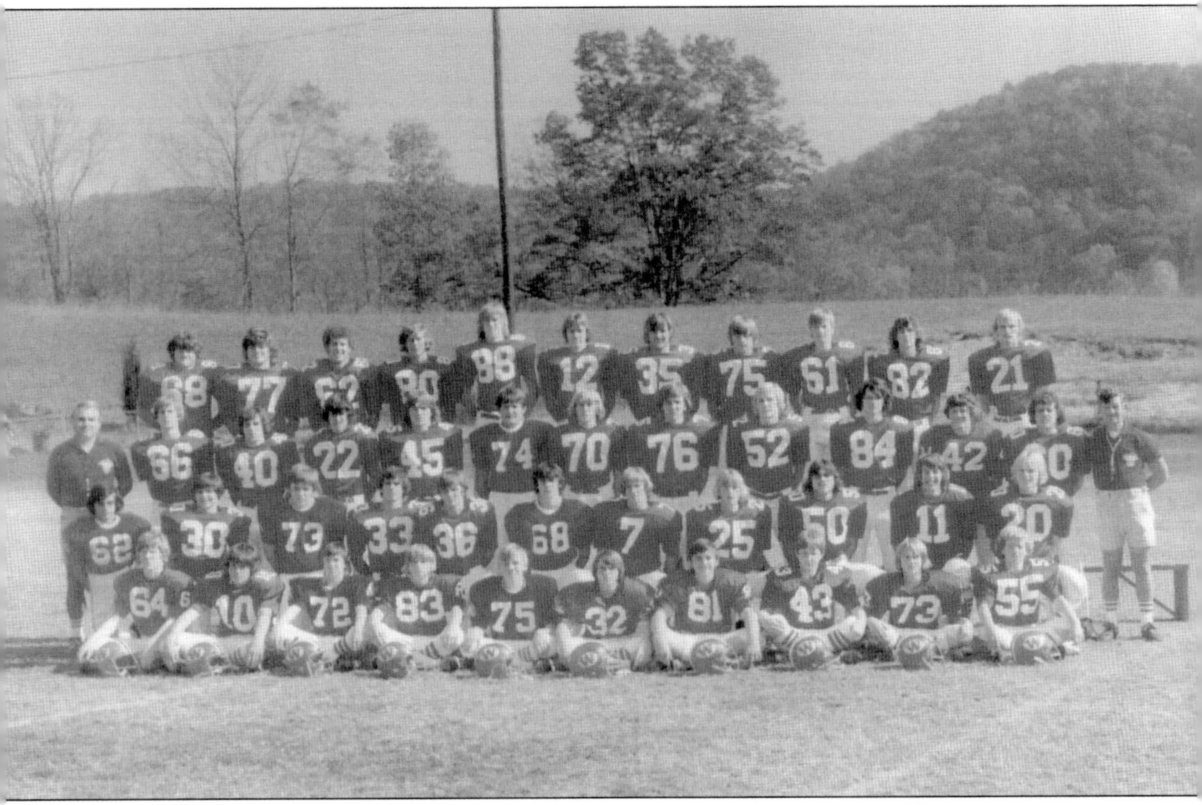

On November 27, 1975, before a standing-room-only crowd of 2,331 in Murfreesboro, Tennessee, the Walland Indians football team won the Class A State Championship. The Indians beat a powerful White House in a 22-6 victory, giving Blount County their first A Division state championship. Walland played this game under a size disadvantage, with White House being bigger and apparently stronger. The Walland defense held White House scoreless until the Indian offense could get points on the scoreboard. The Walland offense scored late in the second quarter and continued until Walland won its first state championship. Under the leadership of coach Jack Renfro and assistant coach Wayne Everett, the Indians completed the 1975 season 13-0. Pictured from left to right are (first row) Tim Tipton, David Powell, Lonnie Burns, David Everett, Phillip Row, Lance White, Roger Suttles, Mike McKinsey, Phillip Flynn, and Bobby Miller; (second row) Wayne Cooper, Tim Ivens, Tony Suttles, Kent Roberts, Kevin Renfro, Jim Patty, Marty Kimsey, Lynn Freeny, Randall Everett, Danny Compton, Bobby Everett, and Tommy Reagan; (third row) coach Jack Renfro, Jim Patty, Gary Coulter, Kent Stephens, Mike Vittetoe, Steve McDonald, Steve Green, Brad Conway, Scott Law, Alan Stephens, Steve Compton, Kenny Tucker, and assistant coach Wayne Everett; (fourth row) David Compton, Jeff Campbell, Mike Caughron, Mike Stewart, Tony Gregory, Tim Ledbetter, Jimmy Ledbetter, Danny Hobbs, Phillip Matthews, and Jacky Teffeteller. (Courtesy of Wayne Everett.)

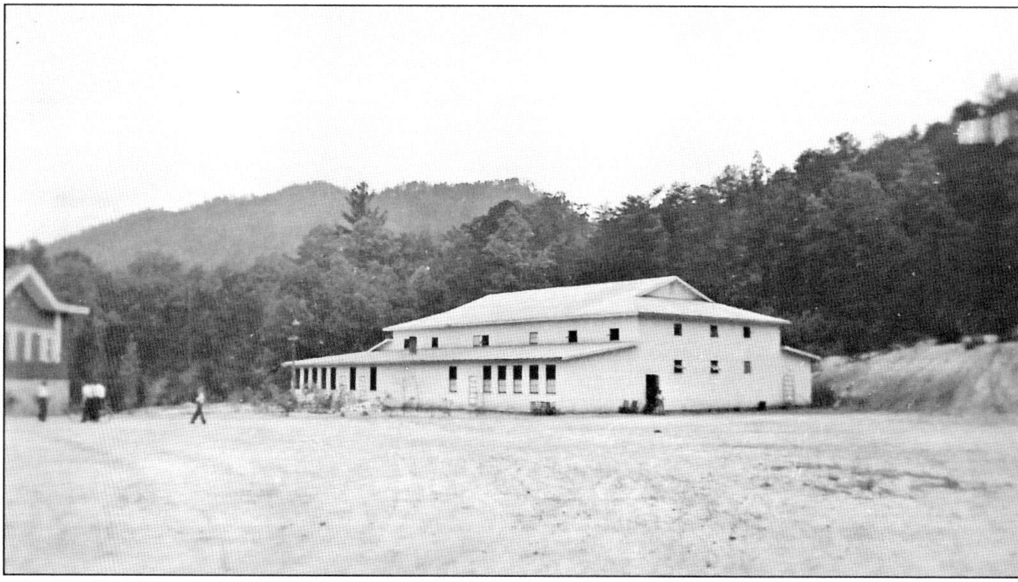

The Walland gymnasium was once a building of the Schlosser Tannery. This gym was used by the basketball teams to practice and play games. In 1973, a new gymnasium replaced this building. (Courtesy of Paul Roberts.)

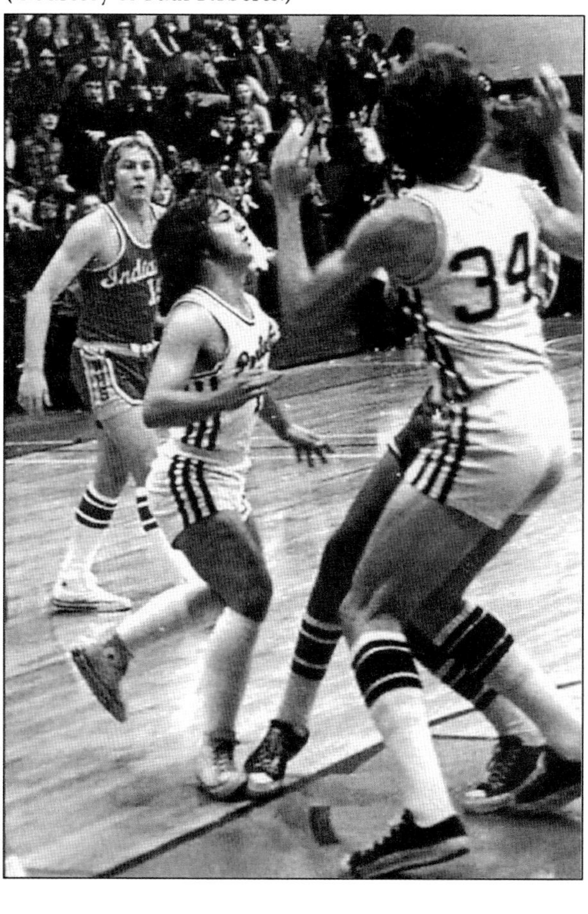

Walland High School played rival Porter High School, with Eddie Vittetoe (number 15, far left) for Walland involved in the play. Walland and Porter were rivals in every sport they played against each other. This photograph was taken in the 1975–1976 season for the Walland Indians. (Courtesy of Eddie Vittetoe.)

Four

Schlosser Leather Company

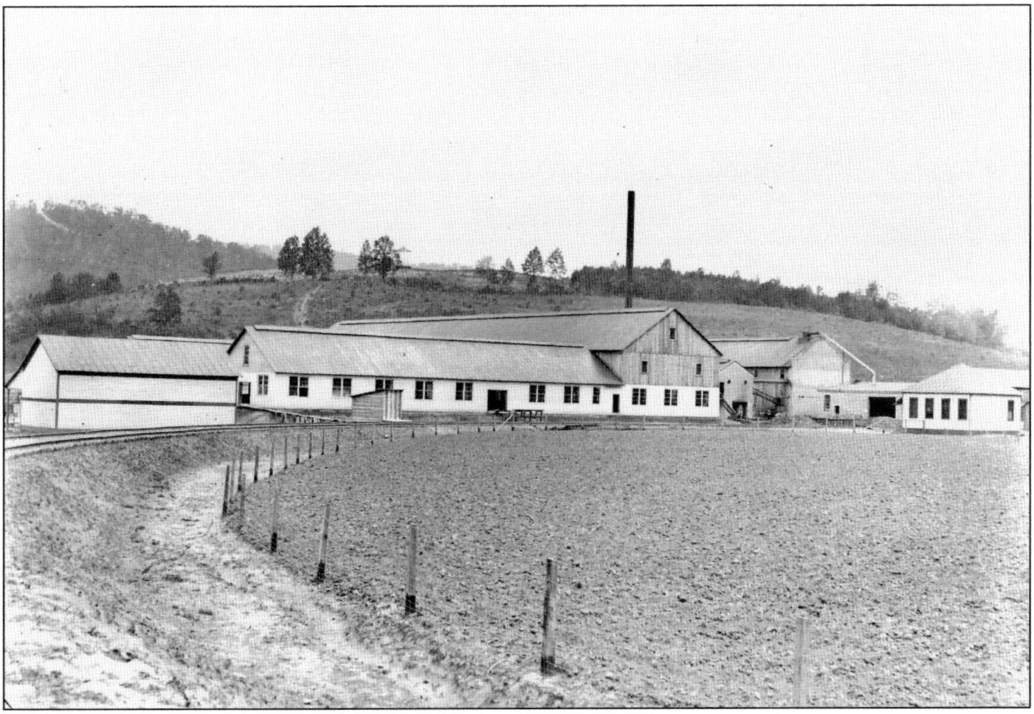

In May 1901, Schlosser Leather Company was chartered to tan hides and manufacture leathers. Josias Stutt Gamble sold a tract of 223 acres on the northeast side of Little River to the Schlosser Leather Company, and the construction of the tannery began in Miller's Cove. The construction was led by John W. "J.W." Fisher. His son A.J. "Jack" Fisher was the superintendent of the tannery. (Courtesy of Blount County Library, Adele McKenzie Collection.)

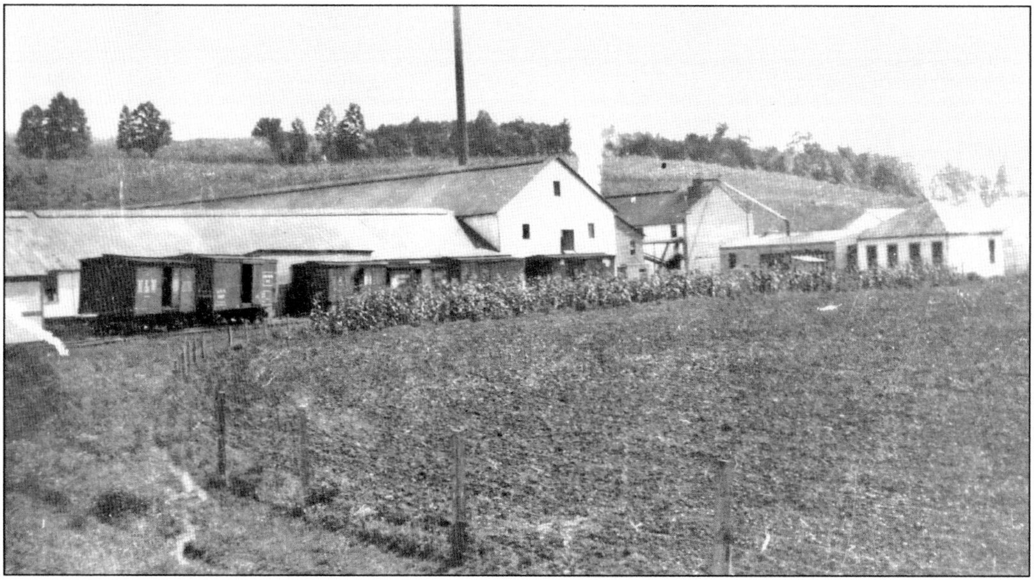

After choosing Miller's Cove for the tannery, the England and Walton Leather Company needed great amounts of tanbark from the uncut forests of the Little River valley but wanted somebody else to do the logging. It is said that John W. "J.W." Fisher persuaded a group of Midwestern investors to form Little River Lumber Company with a successful Pennsylvania lumberman, W.B. Townsend, as the managing partner. (Courtesy of Earl Adams Jr., Inez McCauley Adams Collection.)

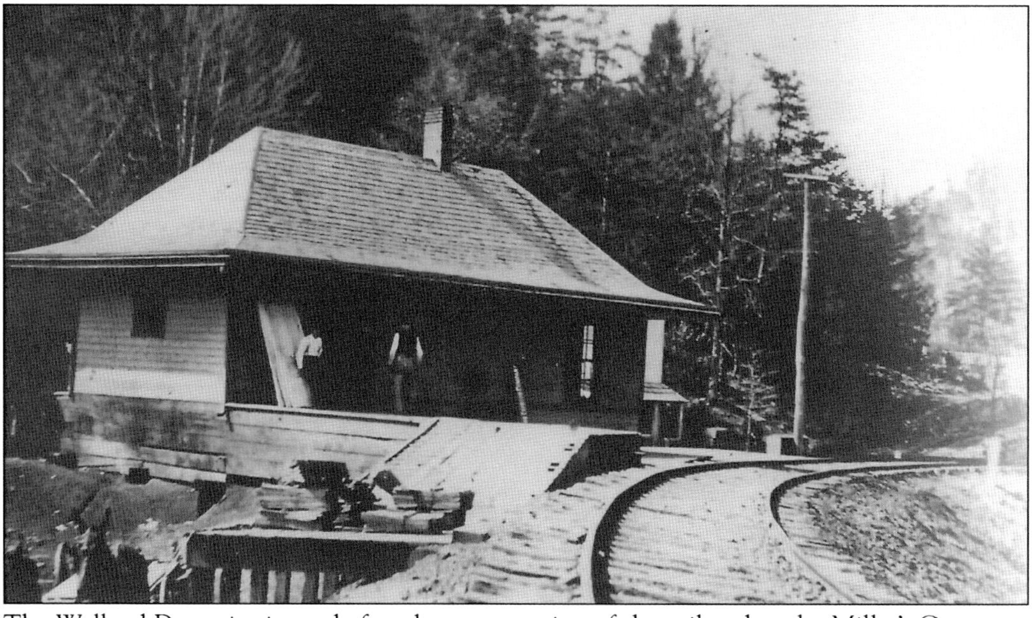

The Walland Depot is pictured after the construction of the railroad to the Miller's Cove area and the site of Schlosser Tannery. Under the supervision of John W. Fisher, the Schlosser Tannery grew into a power plant, hotel, village, and dam. This was the first major industry in Blount County. It employed the largest number of people and had the largest payroll in Blount County before the coming of ALCOA. A new name was given to this village, after two chief investors of the tannery, Walton and England, making the new name Walland. (Courtesy of Earl Adams Jr., Inez McCauley Adams Collection.)

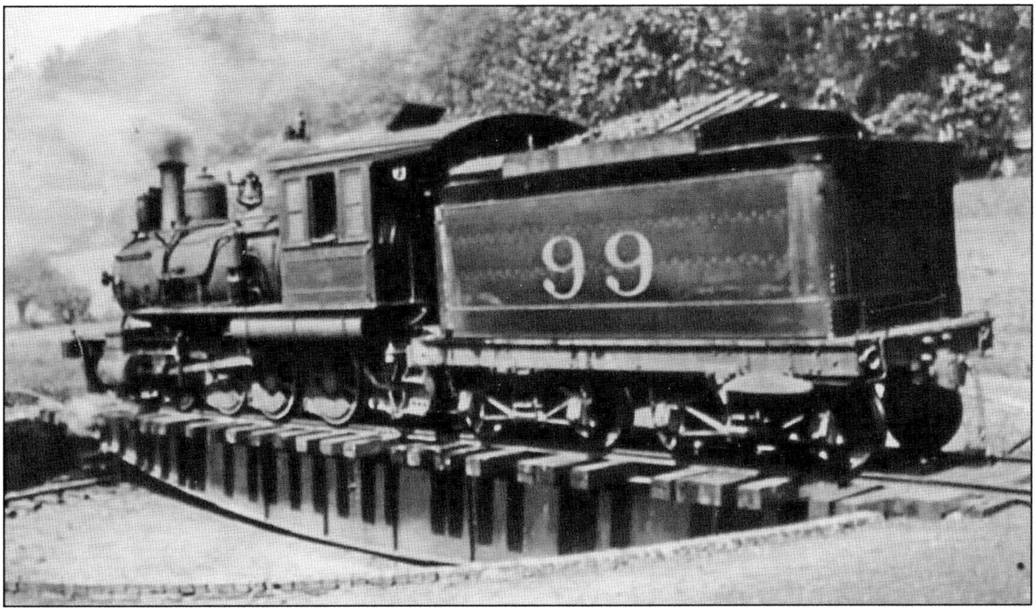

This turntable was at the depot where the Southern & Augusta Railway and the Little River Railroad met. The turntable enabled engines to turn around without having to be backed to their closet destination. The great iron horse began coming from Maryville to Walland on December 21, 1901. (Courtesy of Missy Tipton Green and Paulette Ledbetter.)

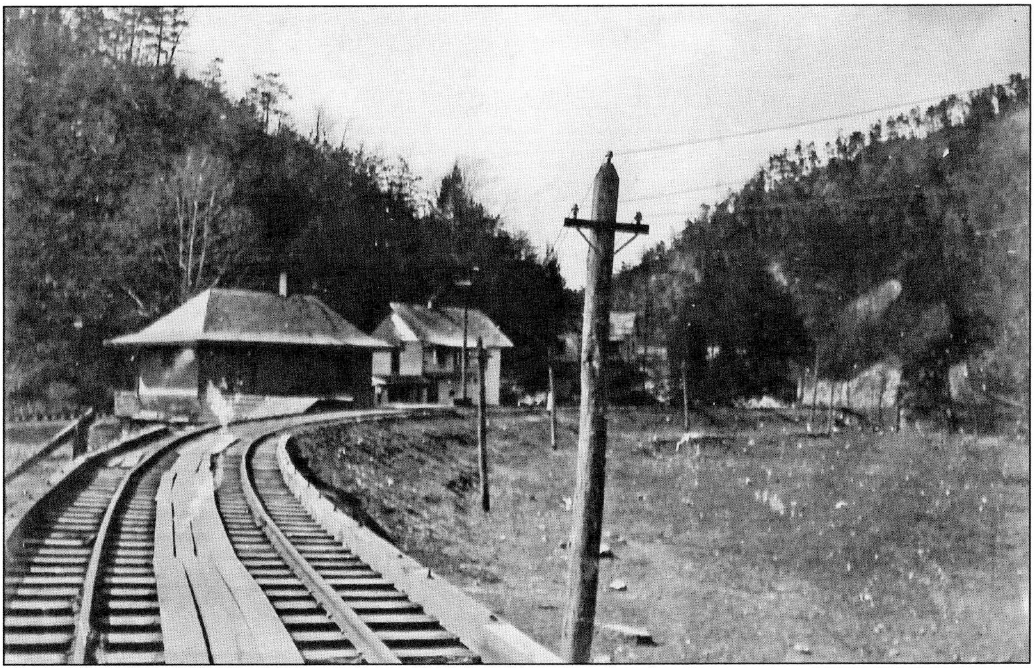

Around 1900, John W. "J.W." Fisher tried to persuade the Southern Railway to extend its line from Maryville to Miller's Cove. After the tannery was up and running and bringing in hides imported from Argentina, Southern Railway became more assured that the railroad might be profitable. Southern bought the tannery's connector in 1902 and tried to buy Little River Railroad's connector also but was told it was not for sale. (Courtesy of A.J. Fisher Collection.)

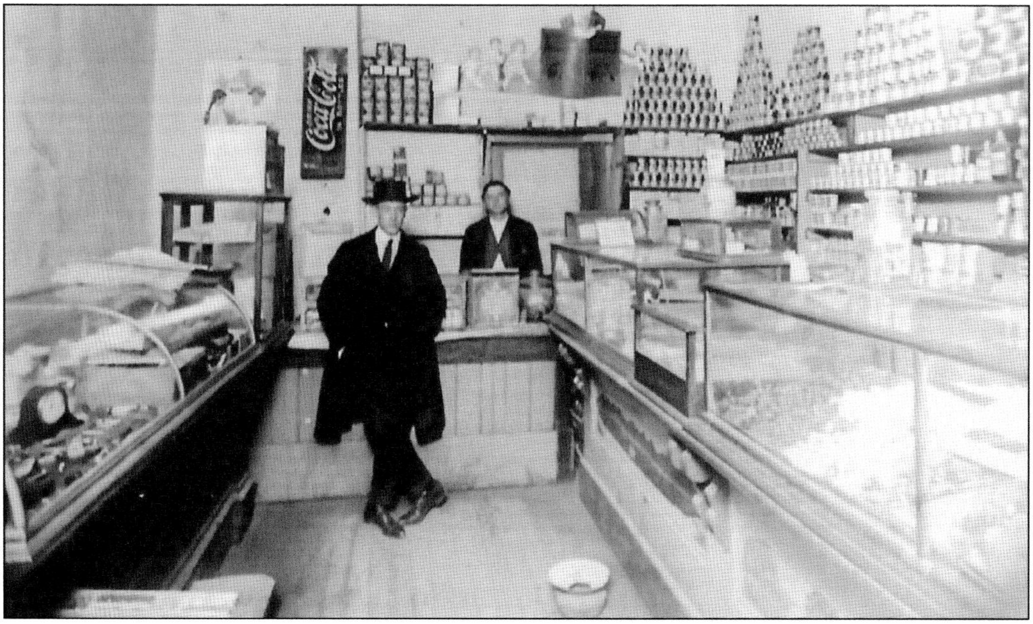

In most company towns of this era, a company store would be built where the company employees felt compelled to shop. England and Walton did build a store but rented it to private merchants. Pictured is the Walland store with J.J. Myers inside of the store. (Courtesy of Blount County Library, J.J, Myers Collection.)

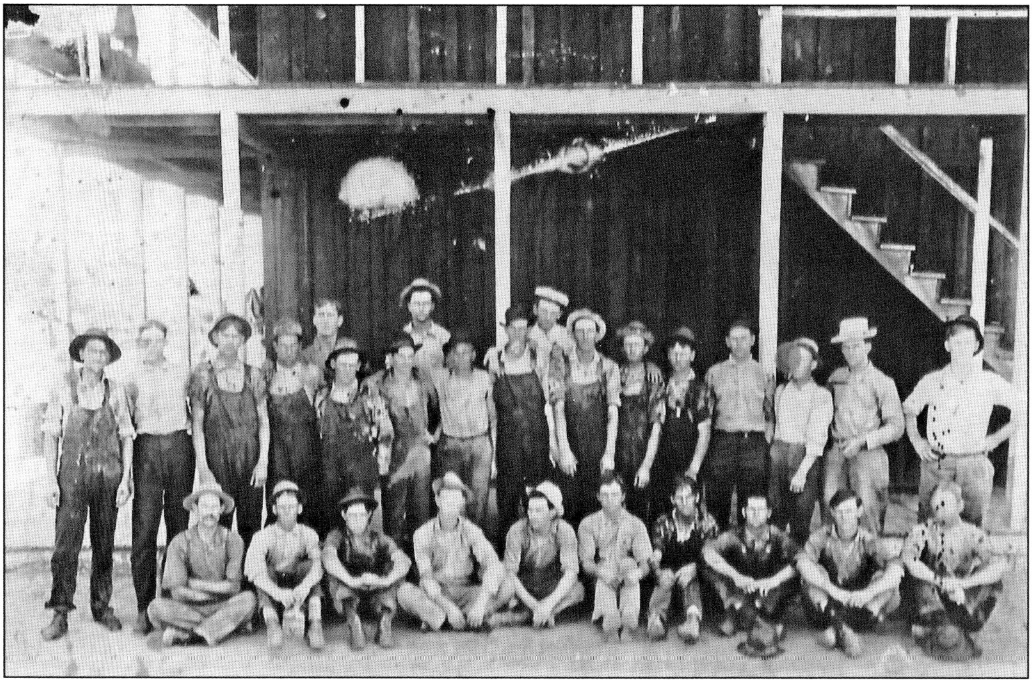

The base pay for most workers of the tannery was $2.20 per day, and the tannery employed about 250 men. The tannery workers had a washroom with hot showers and one sit-down bathtub, and they were obligated to clean what they had used when they were finished. This allowed the men to go home clean in the evening. (Courtesy of Missy Tipton Green.)

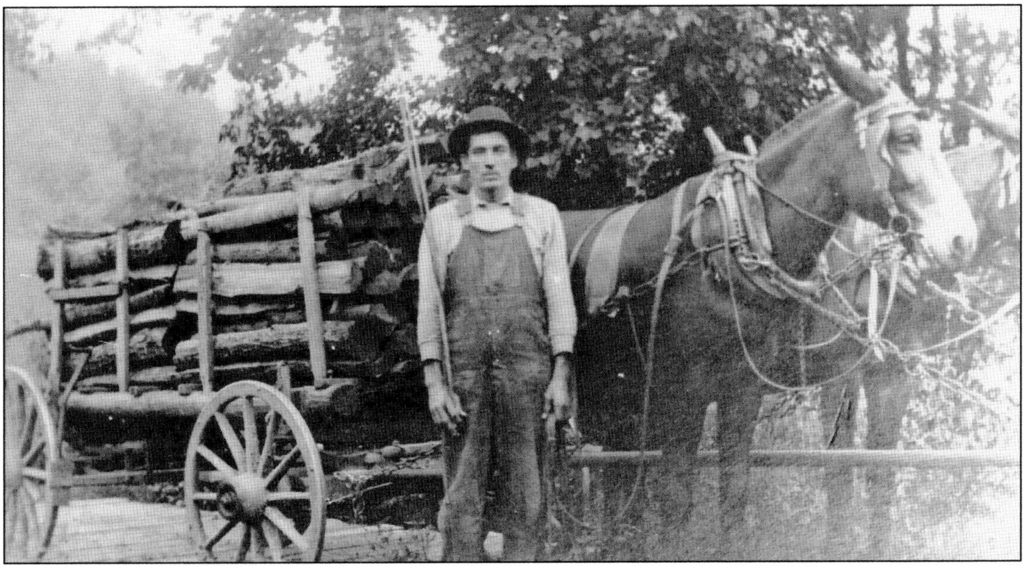

Bob Thompson is pictured with a load of tanbark for the tannery. Tanbark is the bark of certain kinds of trees, usually oak and hemlock. Life in a tannery town was tough, and the work was hard manual labor. (Courtesy of Earl Adams Jr., Inez McCauley Adams Collection.)

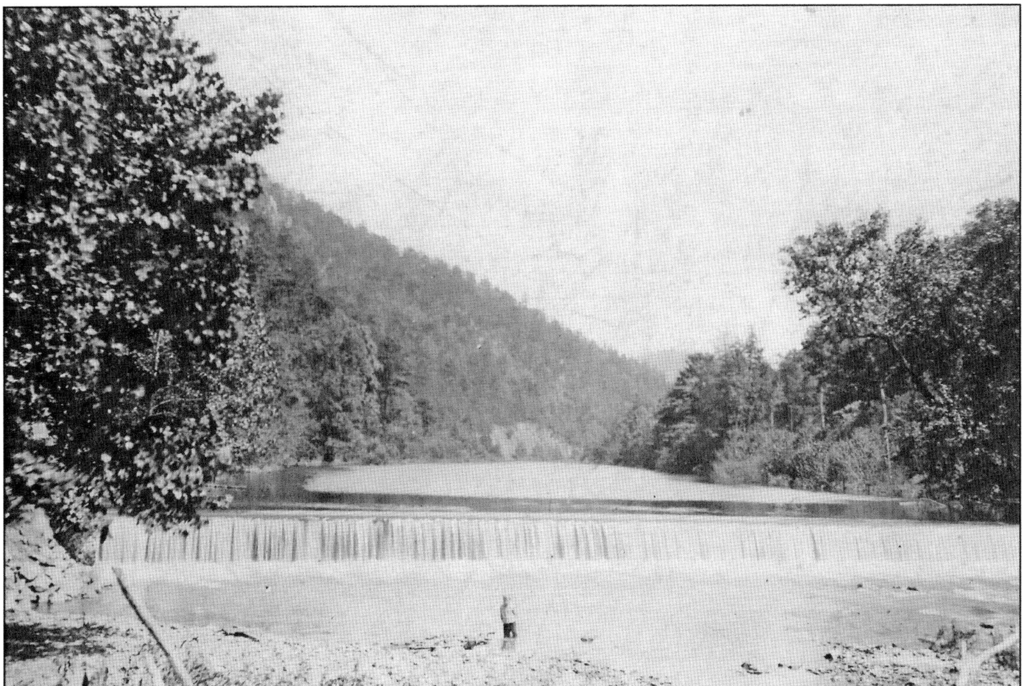

Walland Power Dam as built by the Schlosser Tannery in 1909 to provide power to the tannery and the Walland community. It also made electricity possible for the residents of Walland. The residents of Walland made their little community as self-supporting as possible. Everybody depended on their own land to make a living, except perhaps millers, blacksmiths, or workers in the iron forges. Although they had to work themselves on their own farms, also. (Courtesy of Earl Adams Jr., Inez McCauley Collection.)

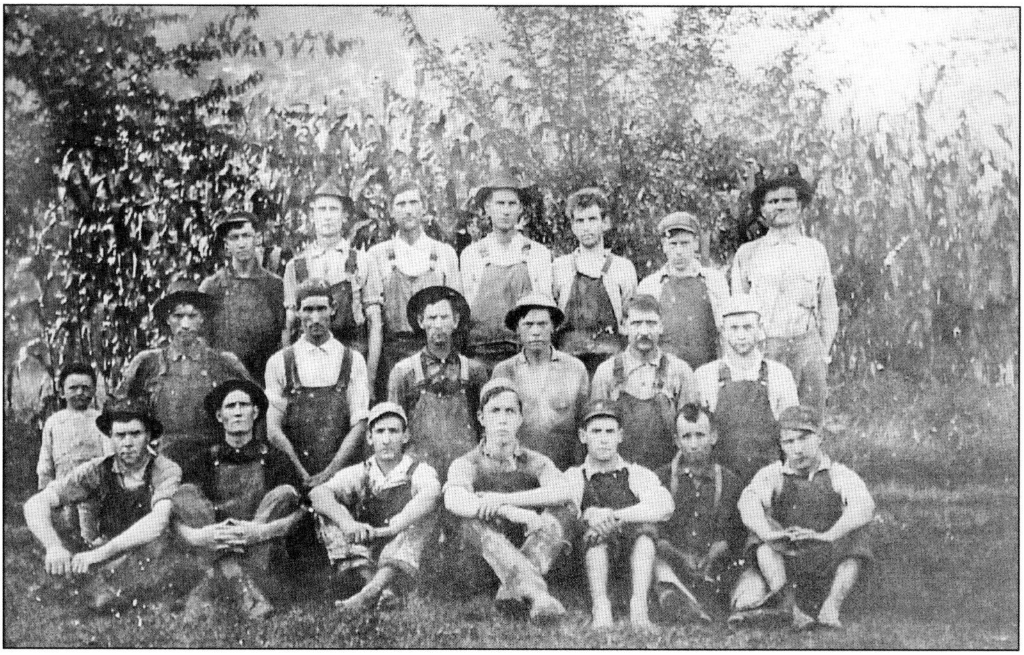

The beam house was the first step in the tanning process. Here, hides were soaked, limed, unhaired, scudded, fleshed, delimed, bated, drenched, and pickled. From left to right are (first row) George Wilson, Joe Gossett, Jim Everett, Tom Hurst, Clarence Hancock, Oscar Frazier, and Roy Henry; (second row) John Chaney, Brownlow Christopher, Pete Henry, John Christopher, Pleas Hurst, Sim Hurst, and Parrott Wilson; (third row) Austin Christopher, John Law, Sam Henry, Agee Hancock, Ervin Burns, Harve Wilson, and Henry Chaney. (Courtesy of Linda Christopher Baker.)

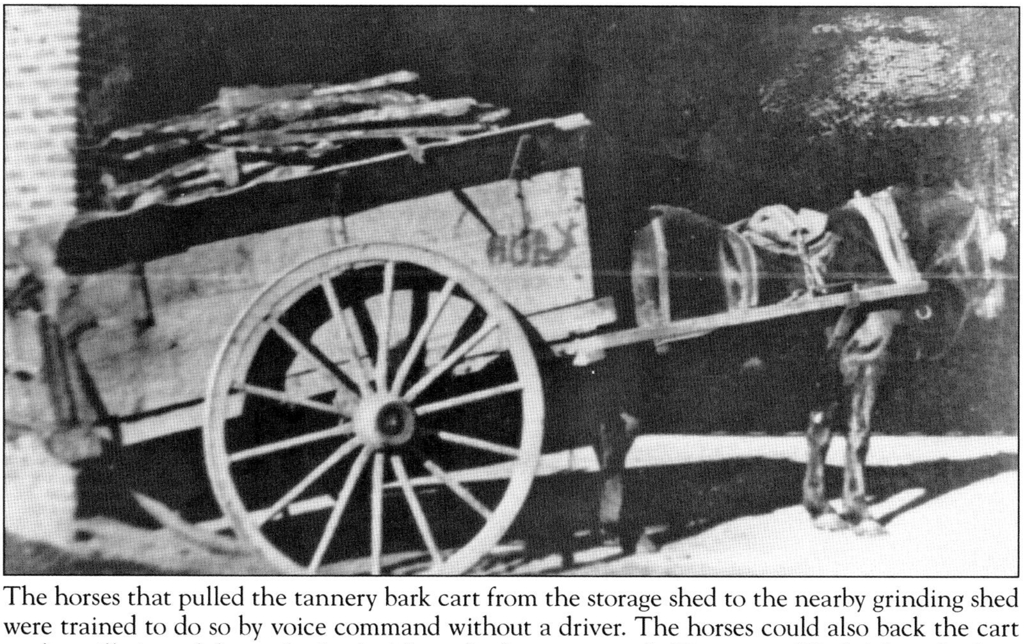

The horses that pulled the tannery bark cart from the storage shed to the nearby grinding shed were trained to do so by voice command without a driver. The horses could also back the cart to the mill pit and dump the load without further command. (Courtesy of Earl Adams Jr., Inez McCauley Adams Collection.)

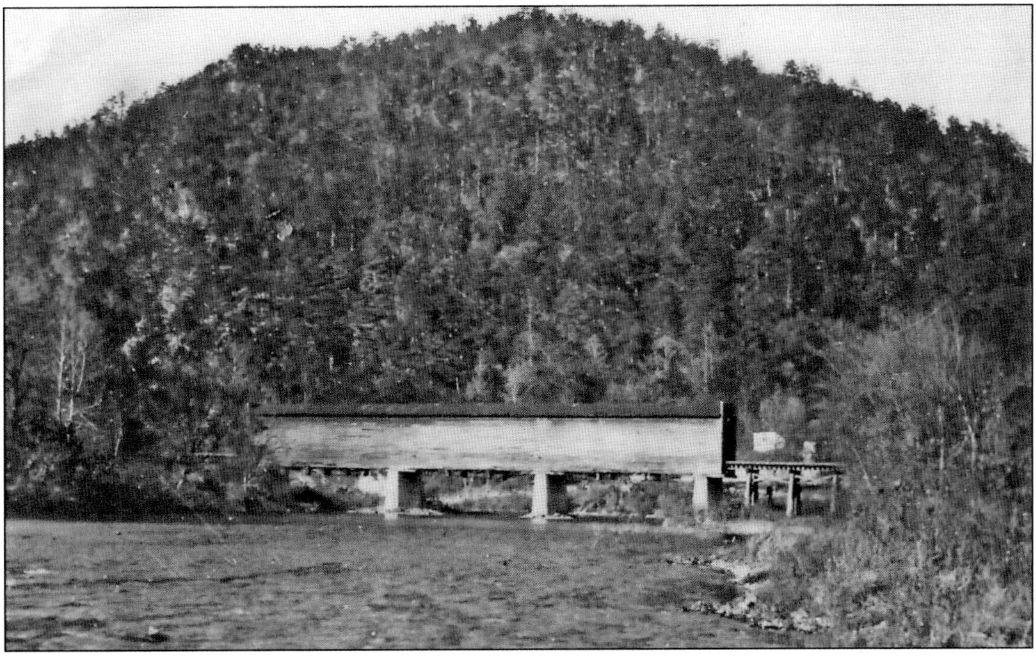

Walland's covered bridge was the only bridge across Little River for many years. This bridge included a pedestrian walkway. The first train engine crossed the bridge on December 21, 1901, with Johnny McCampbell as the engineer and John Donelson as the fireman. The railroad bridge was dismantled around 1940. (Courtesy of Earl Adams Jr., Inez McCauley Adams Collection.)

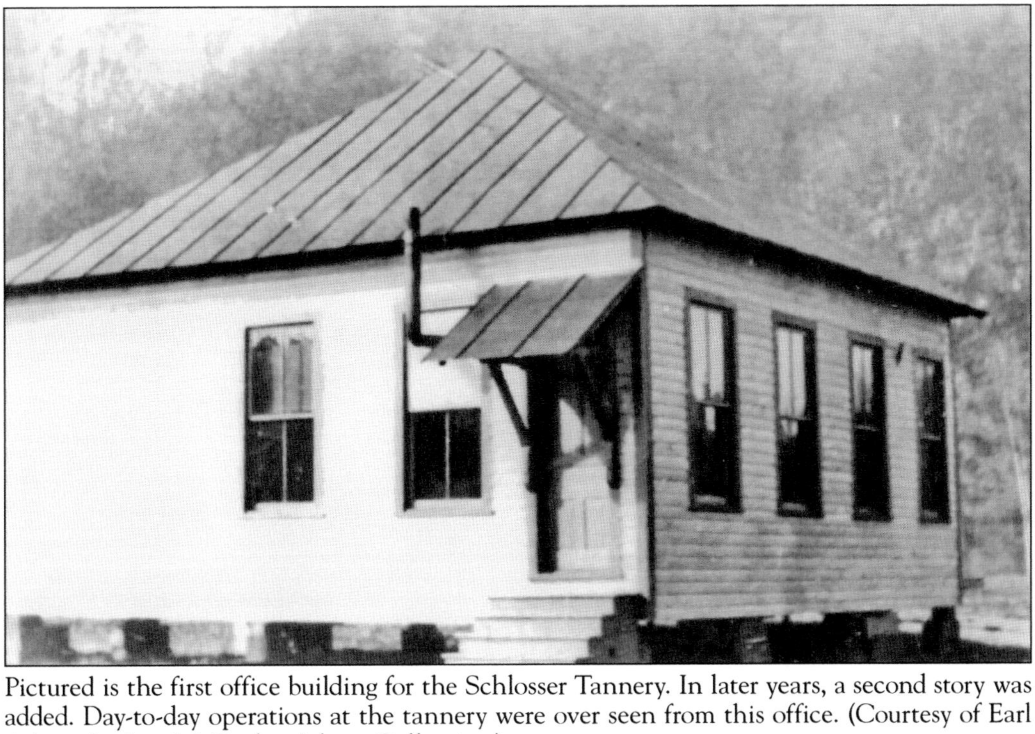

Pictured is the first office building for the Schlosser Tannery. In later years, a second story was added. Day-to-day operations at the tannery were over seen from this office. (Courtesy of Earl Adams Jr., Inez McCauley Adams Collection.)

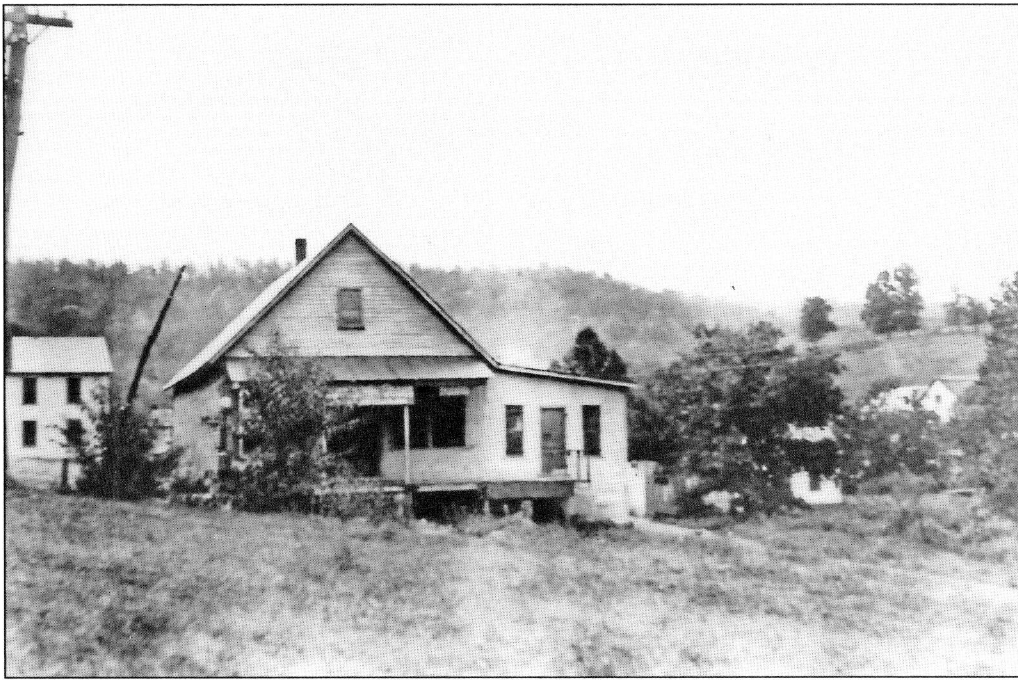

The Schlosser Leather Company did not issue scrip, which is temporary money used as an advance against payday that could only be used at a company store. On payday, most employees would go to the company store and purchase items with the money they had earned. (Courtesy of Earl Adams Jr., Inez McCauley Adams Collection.)

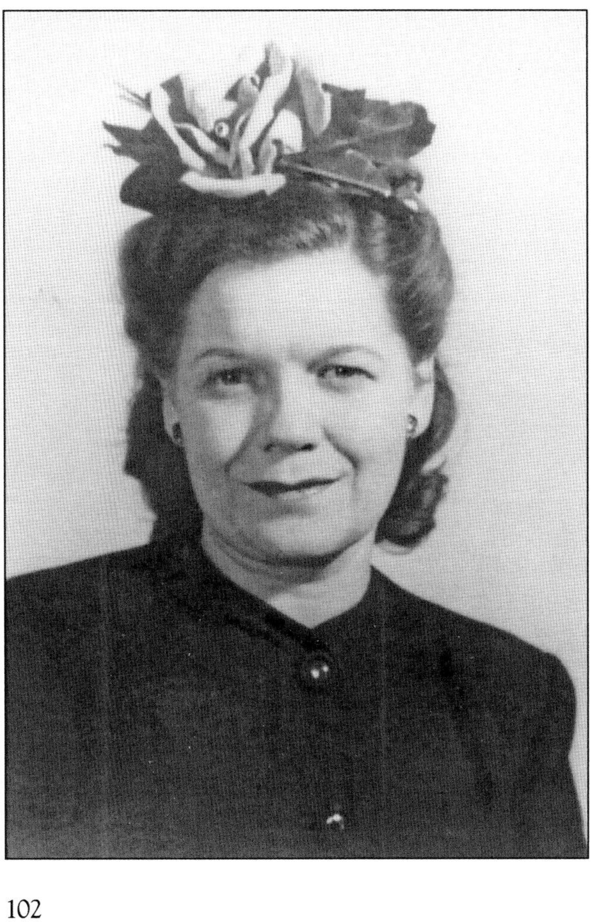

A.J. "Jack" Fisher ran the tannery as superintendent from its beginning in 1901 until it was sold to A.W. Lawrence Leather Company in 1922. Pictured at left is Dorothy Marlott Fisher, daughter of A.J. and Rachel Fisher. (Courtesy of A.J. Fisher Collection.)

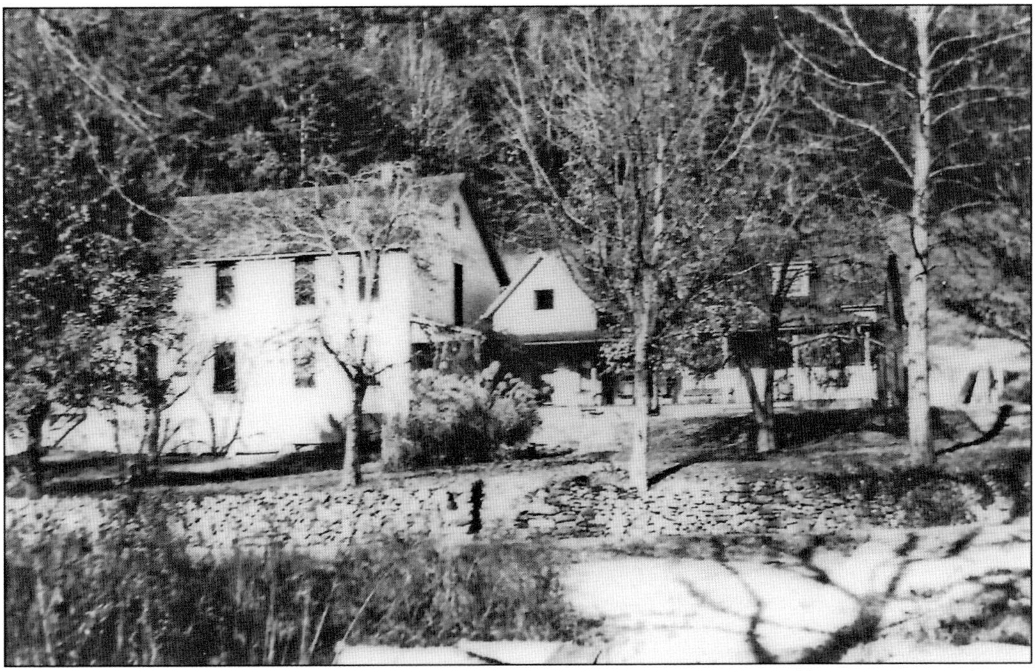

A parcel of land near a mineral spring at the mouth of Reed's Creek in Miller's Cove was chosen for the site of a five-room cottage. This cottage would accommodate out-of-town officials visiting the tannery. In 1904, the 10-room Chilhowee Inn was built to accommodate more guests. Teachers also boarded at the inn while teaching at the Walland School. Chilhowee Inn was famous for fine food and was a popular weekend resort. (Courtesy of Earl Adams Jr., Inez McCauley Adams Collection.)

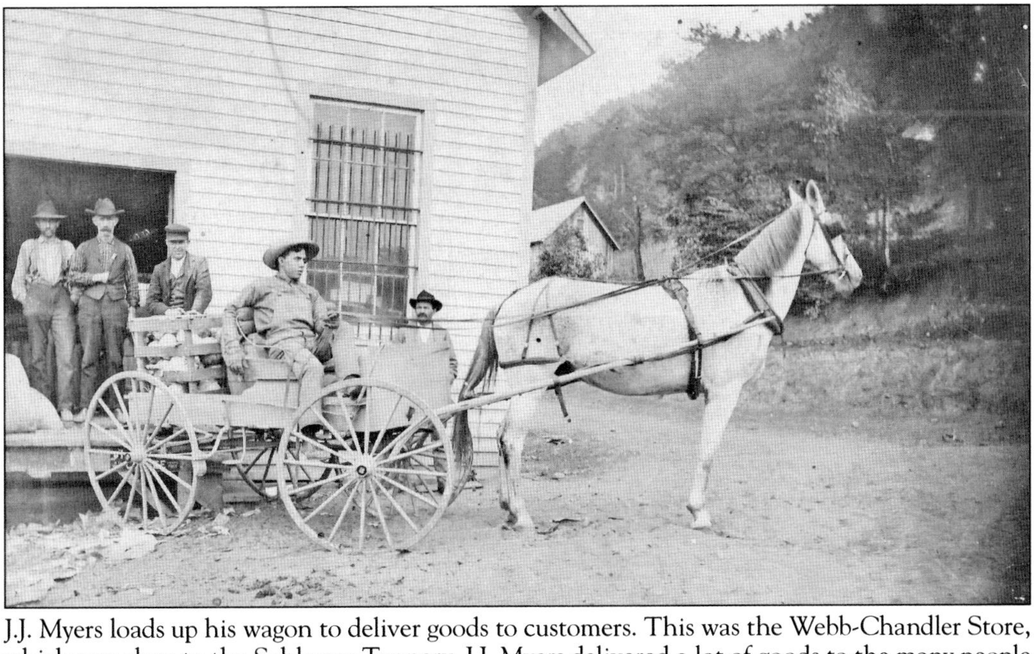

J.J. Myers loads up his wagon to deliver goods to customers. This was the Webb-Chandler Store, which was close to the Schlosser Tannery. J.J. Myers delivered a lot of goods to the many people of the community. (Courtesy of Blount County Library, J.J. "Beef" Myers Collection.)

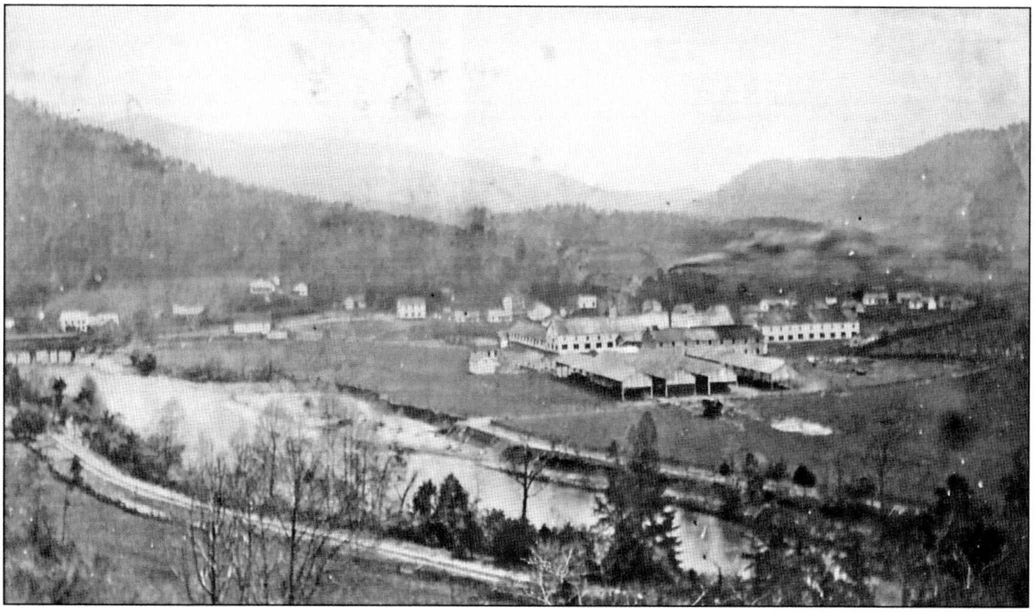

The England and Walton Leather Company of Philadelphia, Pennsylvania, sent John W. "J.W." Fisher to East Tennessee to look for suitable land to build a tannery. Fisher started his search about 1893. The site had to be accessible to a railroad or river and have access to endless rows of trees, the bark of which was used in the tanning process. Local water of a certain quality was also necessary to the tanning chemistry. Fisher found all of the things needed in the Miller's Cove area. (Courtesy of Blount County Library, J.J. "Beef" Myers Collection.)

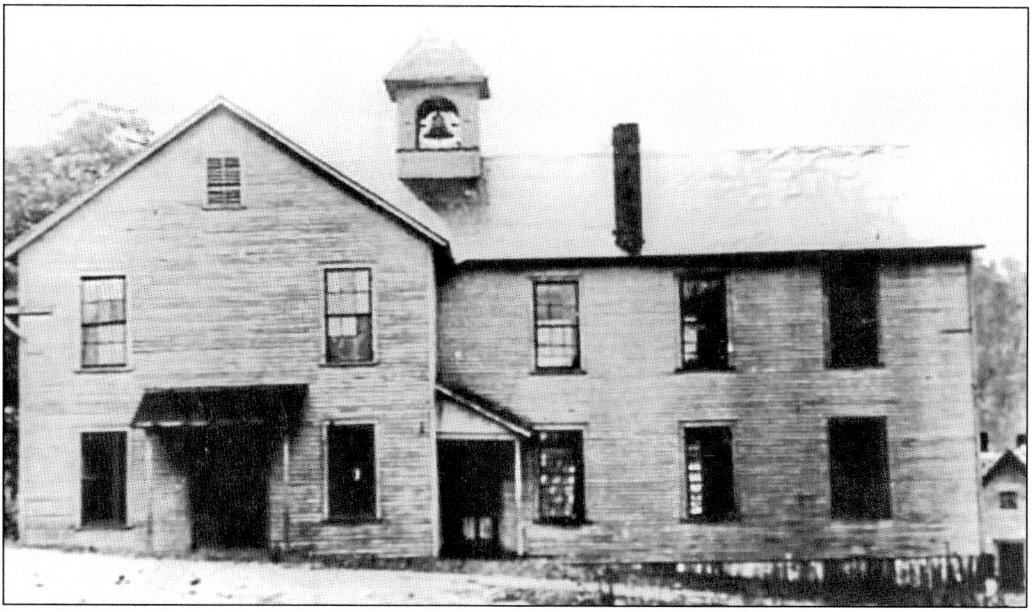

Tannery superintendent A.J. Fisher's wife, Rachel, persuaded the England and Walton Company to provide the money for the longer school year and to double teachers' salaries. Blount County in the first years provided funds for six months of school, with $50 a month pay for the teachers. The school started as a one-room schoolhouse that was completed in January 1902. (Courtesy of Earl Adams Jr., Inez McCauley Adams Collection.)

Five

Rocky Branch

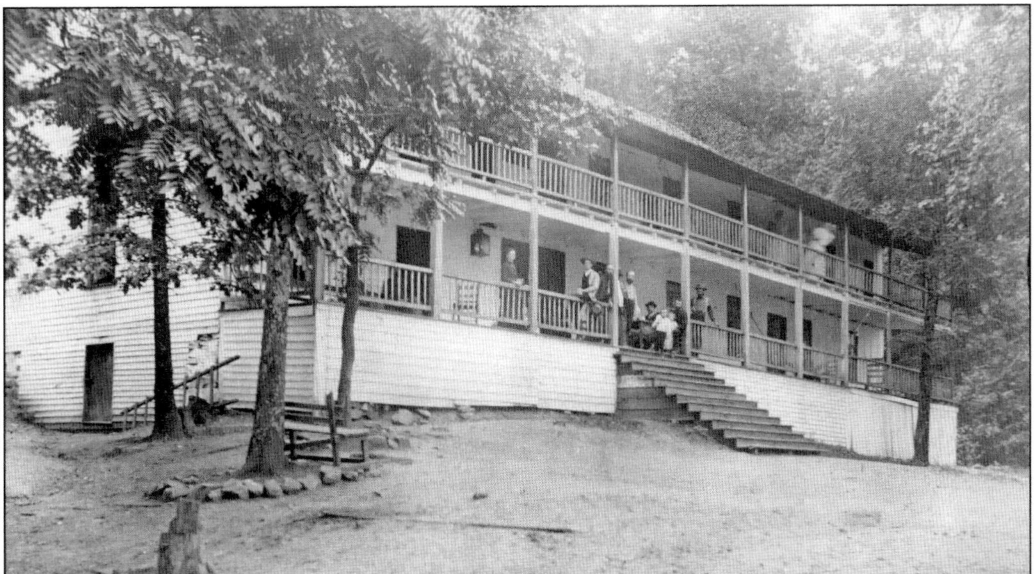

Mount Nebo Hotel was built and operated for a number of years by Alexander Kennedy. It opened its doors on June 2, 1877. The hotel occupied 200 acres on the north side of Chilhowee Mountain one mile west of Little River, a site formerly known as Gillespy Mineral Springs. Kennedy had a large family and many friends, and this was a getaway place for them to spend quality time and business time together. As with many early watering places, hotels and inns, there was medicinal springs here. They were known as Walker Spring and Yellow Spring. In 1887, the hotel was sold to David Jones. Mary Wilson purchased the hotel in 1887 and ran a successful business in the summer months, and she was followed by various owners until 1937. Sam Ogle bought the hotel around 1920 so he could cut the timber in the surrounding areas. He ran the lumber mill until 1937. (Courtesy of University of Tennessee, Knoxville Library, Special Collections, W.C. Cochran Collection.)

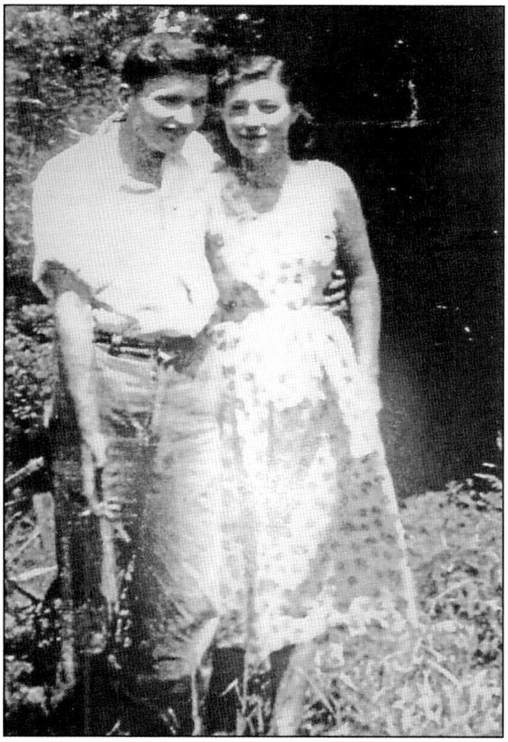

Edward Pink Proffitt was born in 1931, and Juanita Ruth Morgan was born in 1935. Pink grew up on Nebo Mountain, and Ruth spent her early years in Oak Ridge. She moved to Mount Nebo with her parents in 1940 when they were hired to be caretakers of the inn. Pink was out squirrel hunting one day and got thirsty. He went to the spring, and he met Juanita, the sweetest and prettiest young woman he had ever seen. It did not take long for Pink to pop the big question, and they were married on June 6, 1951. The rural milkman gave them a ride around Nebo Loop, honking and shouting congratulations the whole way. (Courtesy of Patsy Proffitt Coppenger.)

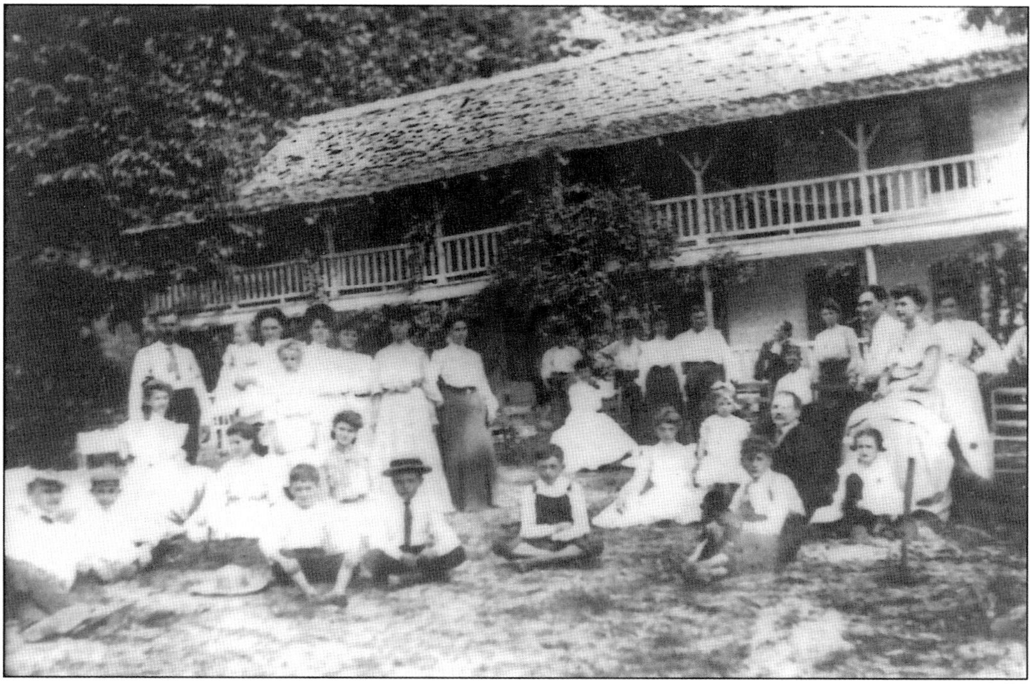

In 1884, John H. Morton sold 50 acres formerly known as the McGinley or Millsaps tract to John and Susan Miller. The land was about three miles west of the Mount Nebo Hotel's springs at the foot of Chilhowee Mountains. A 24-room hotel called Melrose Springs was built next to the Millsaps tanyard. (Courtesy of Earl Adams Jr., Inez McCauley Adams Collection.)

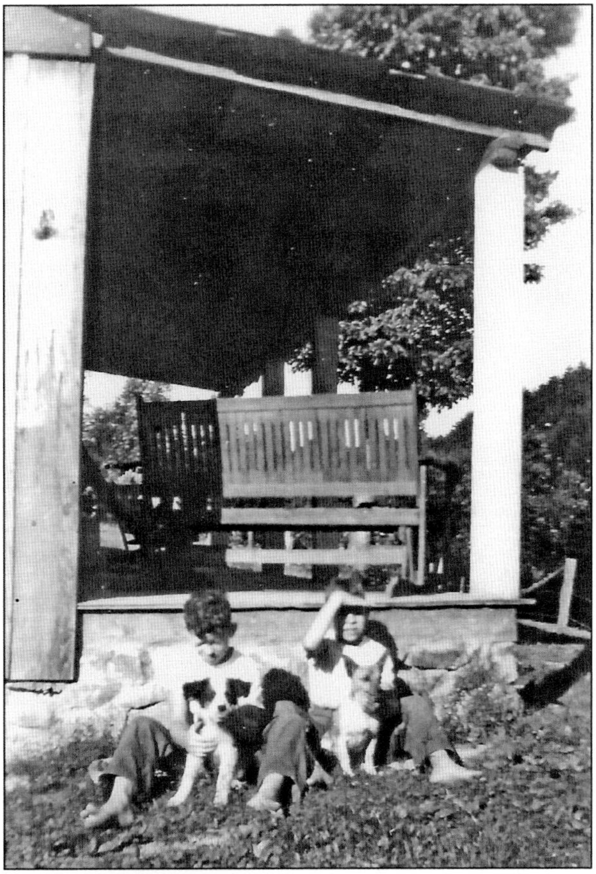

Wayne Everett (left) and Bobby Everett (right) are sons of James "Jay" Everett and Mary Jane Latham Everett. Jay Everett was born on July 25, 1910, to Sampson Everett and Mary Morrison Everett. (Courtesy of Wayne Everett.)

Fred Henry Gossett of Rocky Branch enlisted on September 24, 1934. Fred was born on August 8, 1916, to Joe Gossett and Myrtle Henry Gossett. The Korean War started on June 25, 1950, and ended on July 27, 1953. Fred Gossett was killed on October 21, 1952, while in the Korean War. He is buried at Rocky Branch Missionary Baptist Church Cemetery. (Courtesy of Missy Tipton Green.)

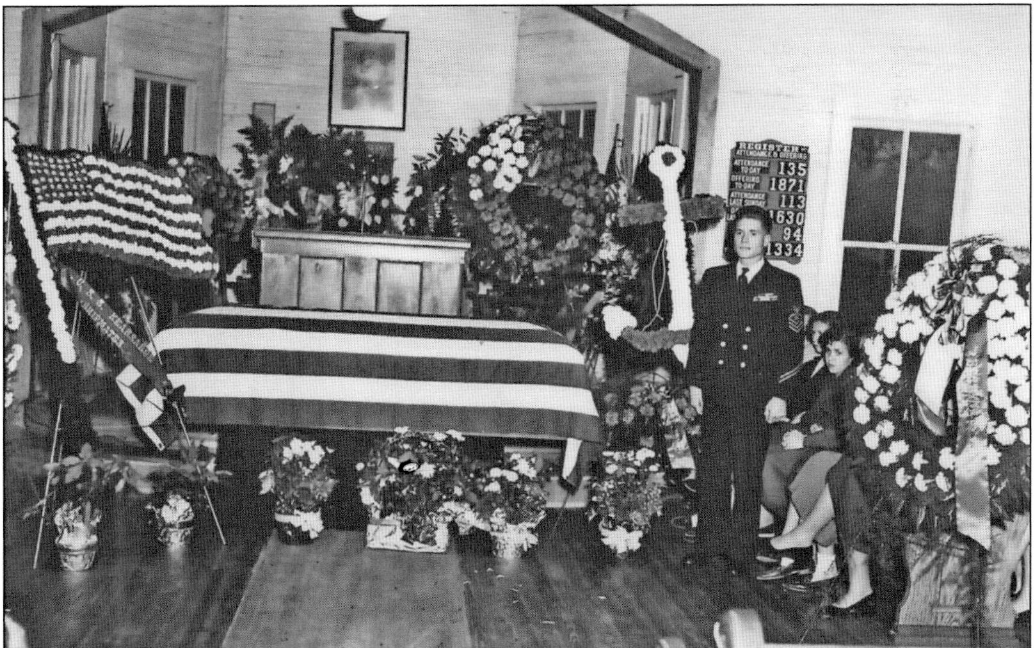

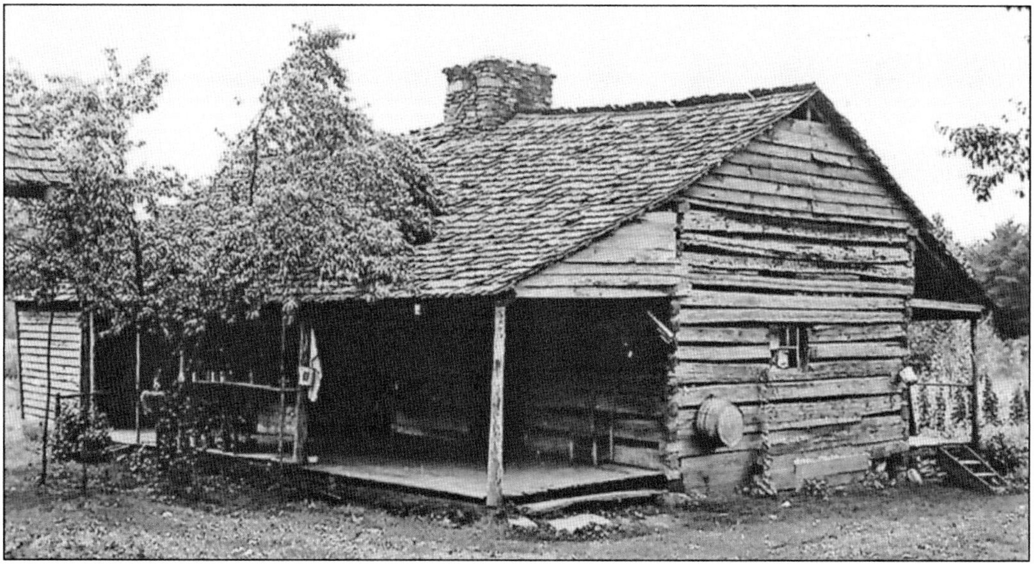

Burley, Pliney, and Alzenia Everett were all born and raised in this dogtrot log house. Some theories say that the dogtrot house originated in the Appalachian Mountains. This style of house consisted of two log cabins connected by a breezeway or "dogtrot" all under a common roof. Usually one of the cabins would be used for cooking and dining and the other one used for sleeping space. Chimneys would be located at each gable end of the house. Most dogtrot houses would also have full-width porches on both sides. (Courtesy of Missy Tipton Green.)

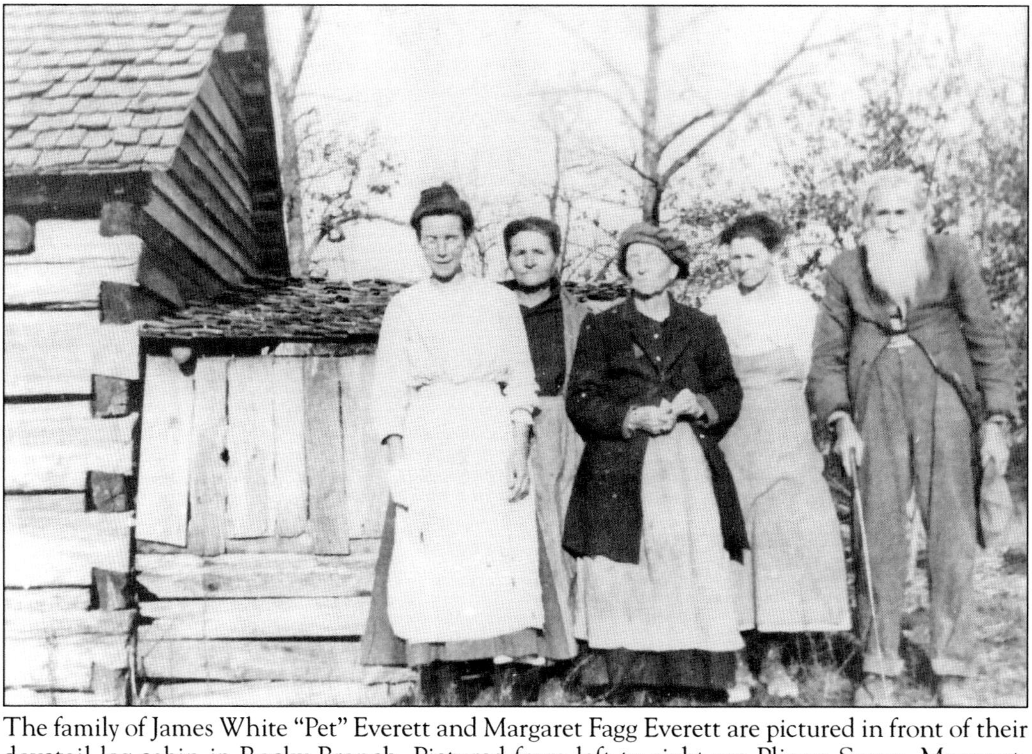

The family of James White "Pet" Everett and Margaret Fagg Everett are pictured in front of their dovetail log cabin in Rocky Branch. Pictured from left to right are Pliney, Susan, Margaret, Alzenia, and James Everett. (Courtesy of Missy Tipton Green.)

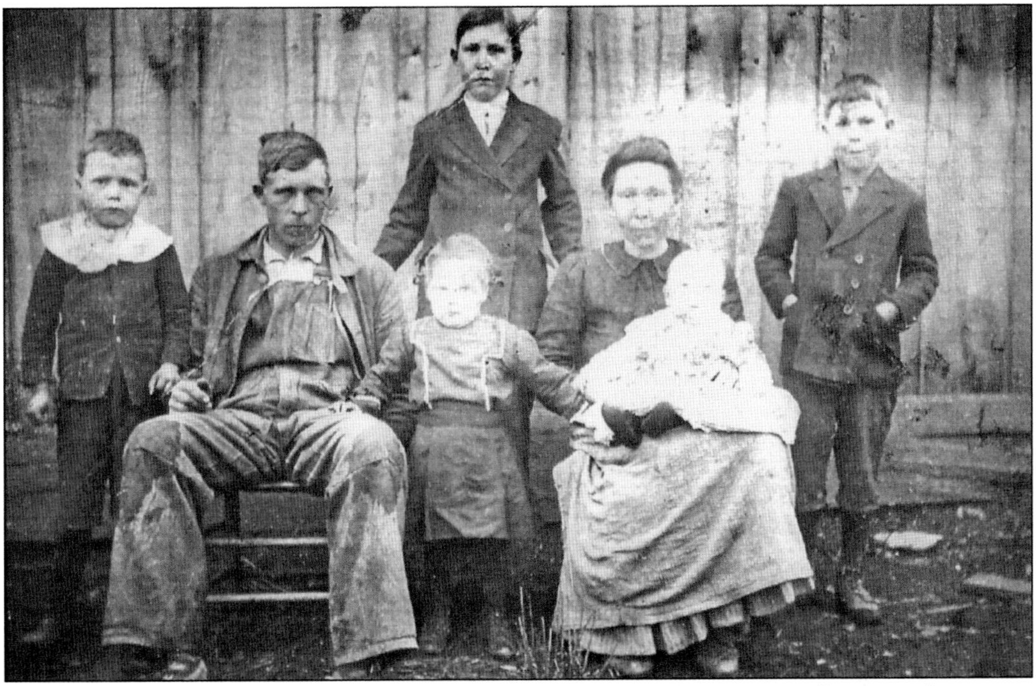

The William Thomas "Will" Martin family is, from left to right, Tom, Will, Mattie (center, in skirt), Huse (behind Mattie), Margaret Ann "Mattie" Ogle Martin holding Bill, and Sam. Will was born on March 24, 1885, to Thomas "Tom" Martin and Agnes Caldonia Burchfield. Mattie was the daughter of Samuel Houston Ogle and Nancy Jane Fagg Ogle. (Courtesy of Barbara Martin Sloan.)

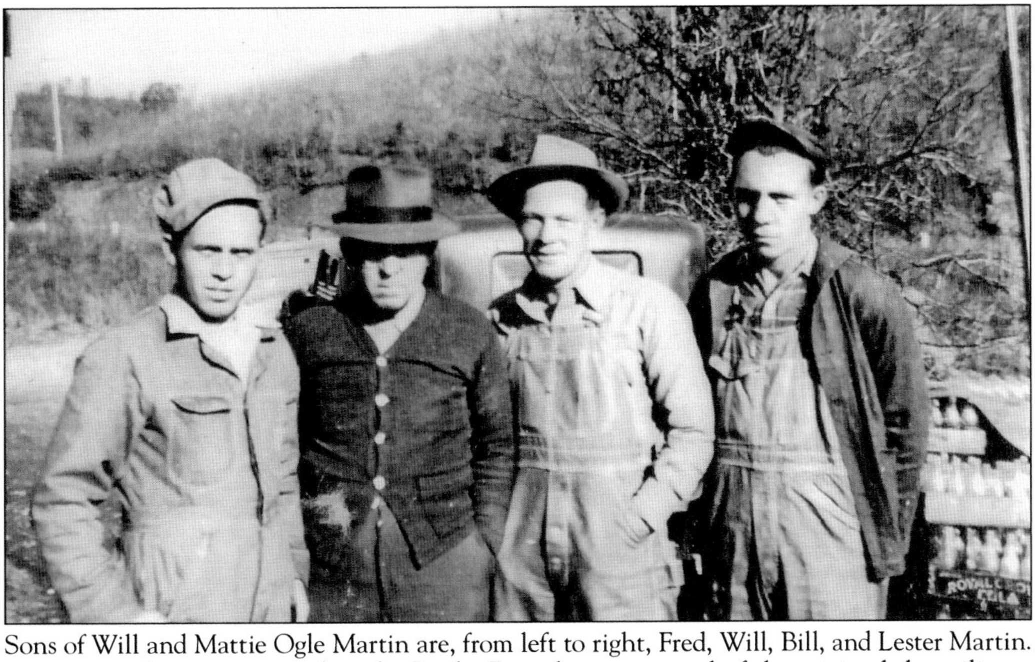

Sons of Will and Mattie Ogle Martin are, from left to right, Fred, Will, Bill, and Lester Martin. The Martin boys were raised in the Rocky Branch area; several of them joined the military. (Courtesy of Barbara Martin Sloan.)

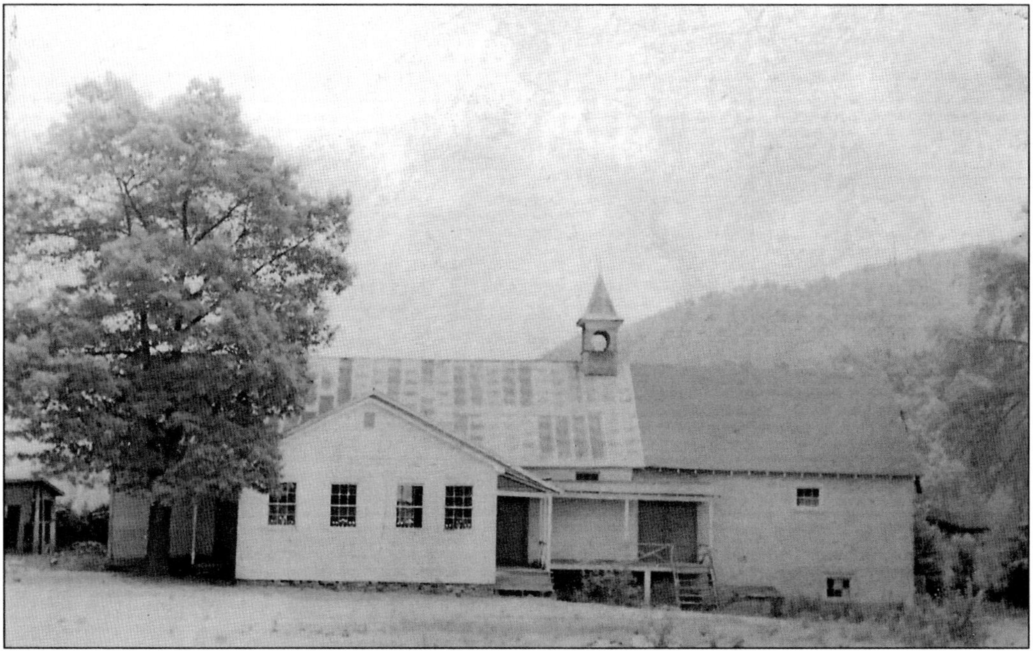

About 1888–1889, the home of Fate Everett was vacant. Mary Wilson, who ran the Nebo Hotel along with her husband, helped in getting the Everett house for the Rocky Branch children to have as a school building. The name Rocky Branch came from the type of stream that crossed the road nearby. (Courtesy of Bill and Joan Vansickle Sloan.)

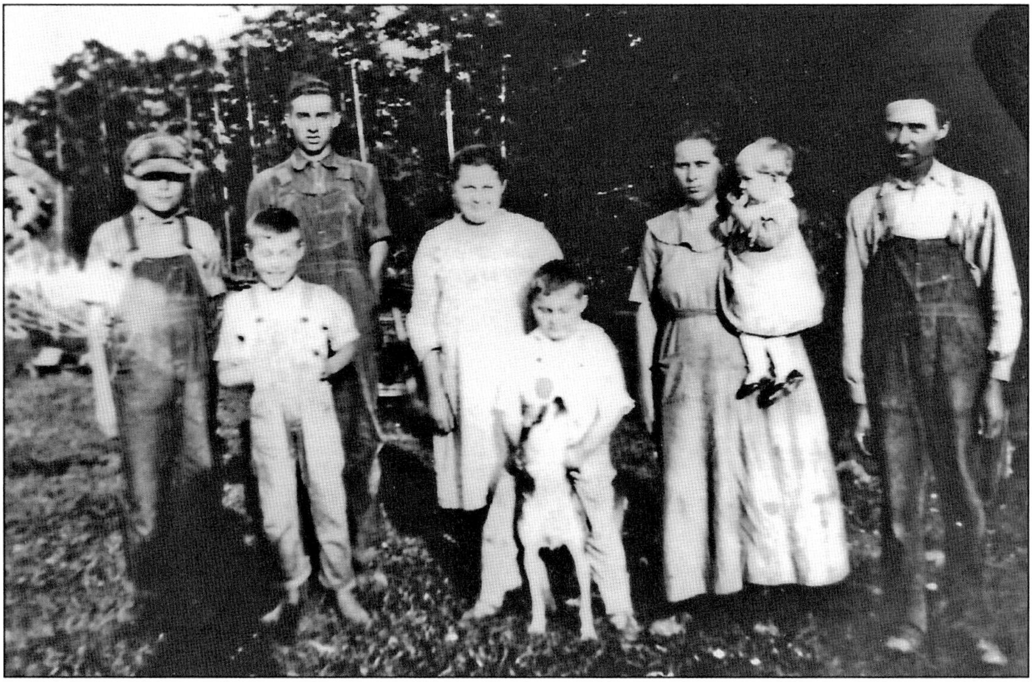

Moses Millsaps and Ida Garner Millsaps are pictured with children (from left to right) John, Elmer, Charles, Mae, and George with his dog. The Millsaps resided in Rocky Branch. Moses was a farmer who owned approximately 40 acres. (Courtesy of Bill and Joan Vansickle Sloan.)

From left to right are Lester, Chester, and Huse Martin, sons of Will and Mattie Ogle Martin. They are the grandsons of Tom Martin and Agnes Caldonia Burchfield Martin and Sam Houston Ogle and Nancy Jane Fagg Ogle, all of Rocky Branch. (Courtesy of Barbara Martin Sloan.)

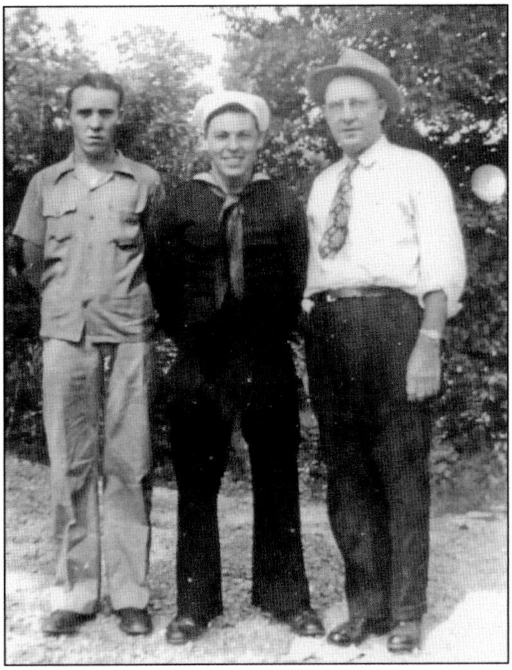

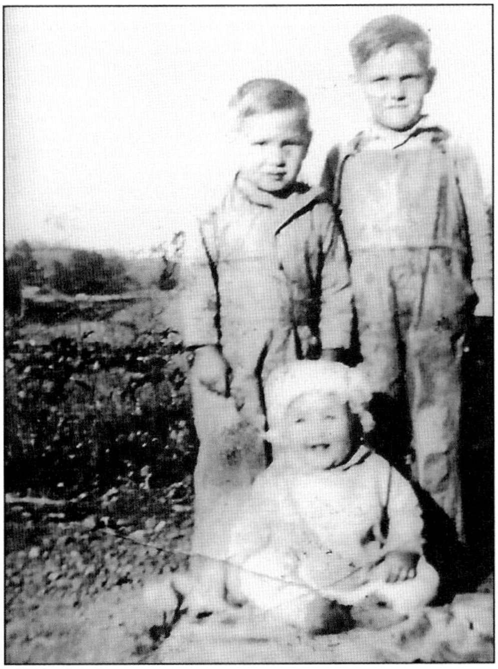

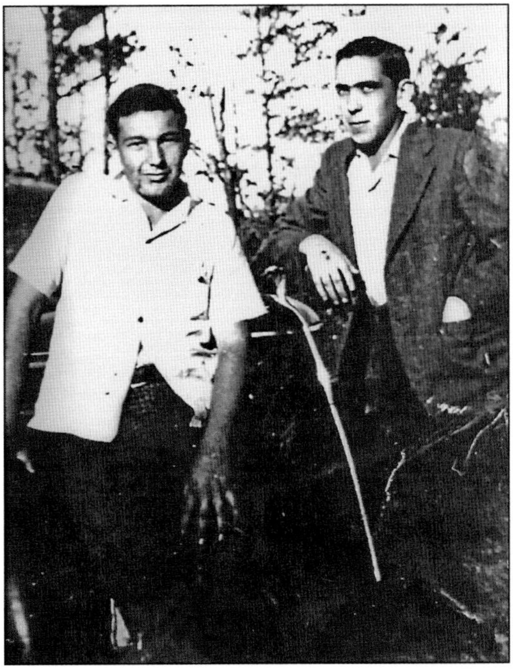

Mamie and Joe Sloan grew up and raised their seven children in the rural area at the foothills of the Great Smoky Mountains in Walland, Tennessee. Pictured at left are three of their children about 1936–1937. In front is daughter Lora Maxine, with sons Clifford Rex in the center and William Elmer Sloan on the right. James "Muncie" Sloan and Charles Houston Sloan (pictured right) were also sons of Mamie and Joe. James was also known as "Howard," and Charles was also known as "Turk" and "Louie." If these names were spoken around the community, everyone knew whom they were speaking of. (Courtesy of Bill and Joan Vansickle Sloan.)

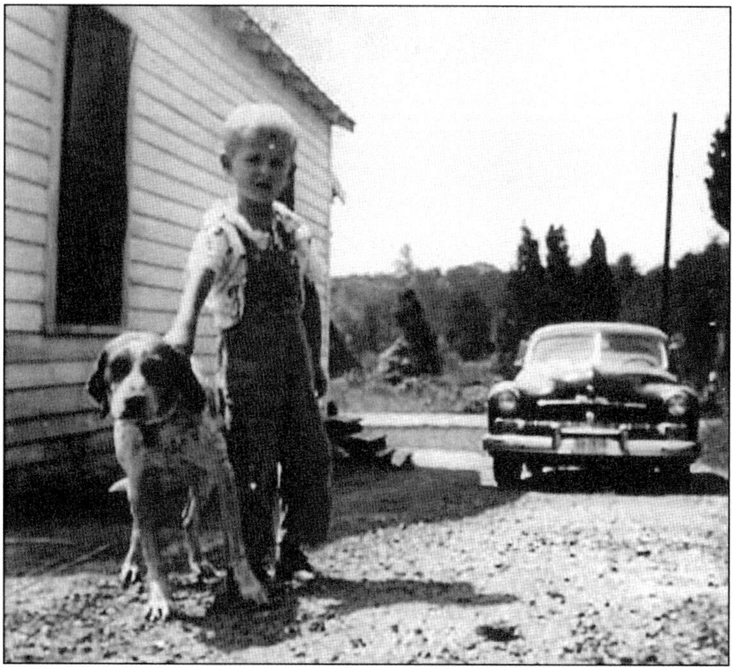

Every good hunter had to have a good hunting dog to go with him. Kenneth Baker and Butterhead look like they are getting ready to head out on a hunt. The dogs were usually as excited to go as the hunter was. (Courtesy of Linda Christopher Baker.)

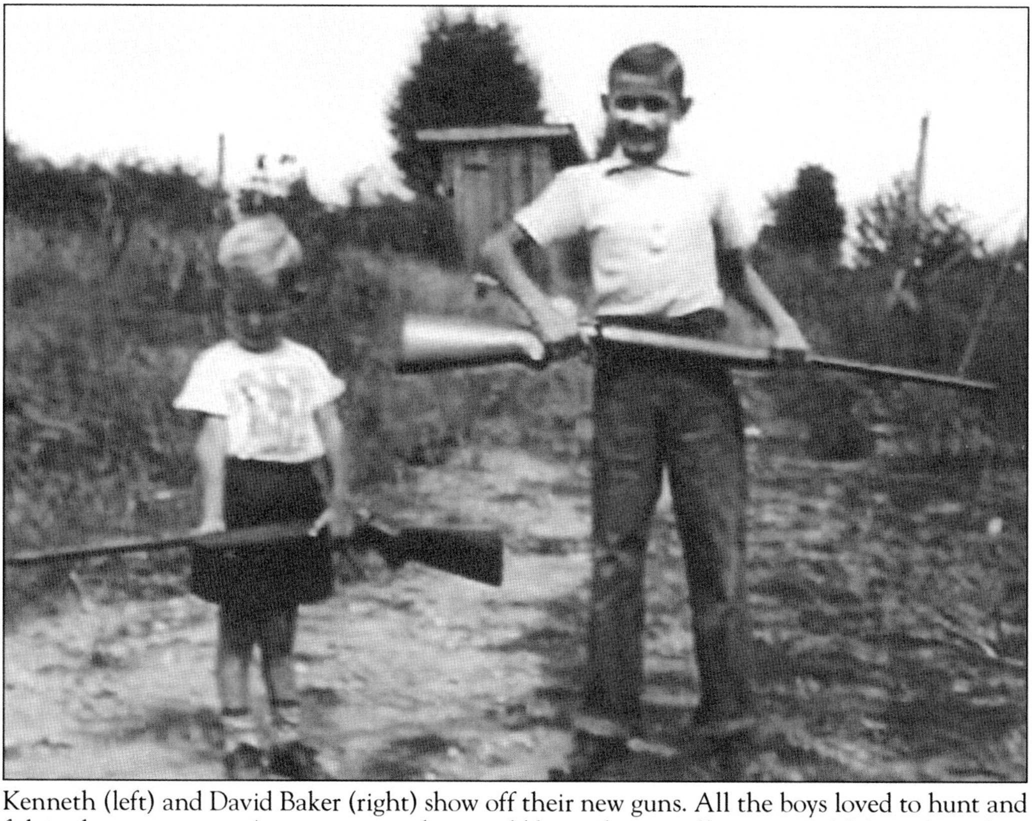

Kenneth (left) and David Baker (right) show off their new guns. All the boys loved to hunt and fish in their spare time. At a young age, they would learn the arts of hunting and fishing from their fathers, older brothers, or maybe even a grandfather. (Courtesy of Linda Christopher Baker.)

Samuel "Sam" Houston Ogle was born on June 11, 1865, to Will Ogle and Rebecca Lane Ogle; he married Nancy Jane Fagg Ogle. Sam raised his family in the Rocky Branch community in Walland. (Courtesy of Bill and Joan Vansickle Sloan.)

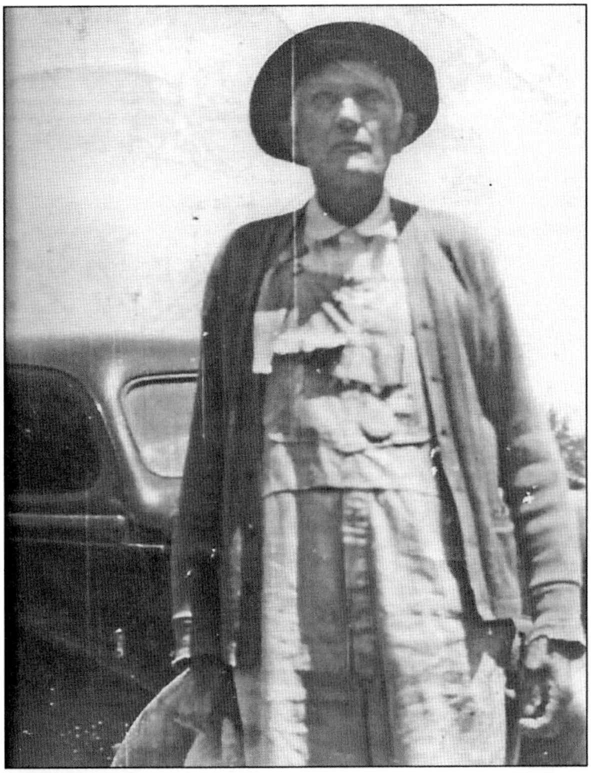

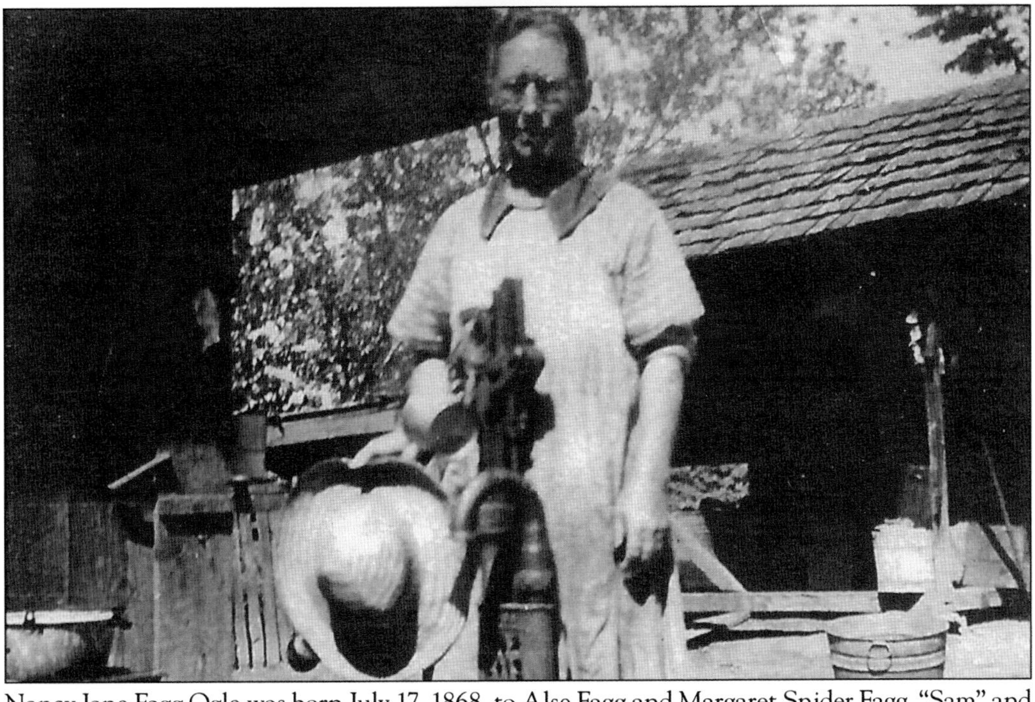

Nancy Jane Fagg Ogle was born July 17, 1868, to Alse Fagg and Margaret Snider Fagg. "Sam" and Nancy were parents of 11 children: Margaret, Mary, Bill, Alse, John, Abe, Jack, Martha, Mamie, Myrtle, and Minnie. (Courtesy of Bill and Joan Vansickle Sloan.)

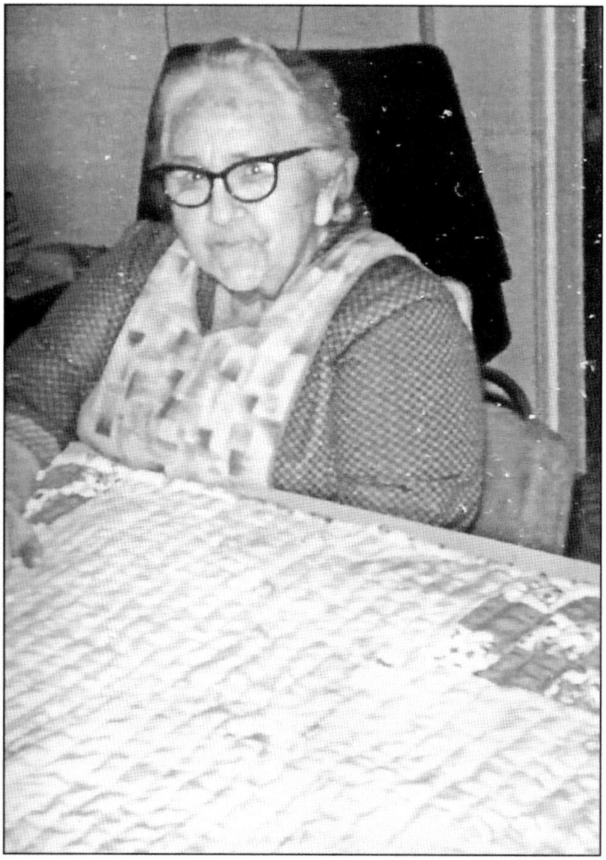

Mamie Ogle Sloan was known to be a great quilter. It took a lot of tedious work, but she greatly enjoyed it. Women and girls would often gather together for a quilting bee. (Courtesy of Bill and Joan Vansickle Sloan.)

Mamie Alice Ogle was born on April 16, 1905, to Samuel "Sam" Ogle and Nancy Jane Fagg Ogle. She married Joe Abslum Sloan on August 10, 1921, and seven children were born to them. (Courtesy of Bill and Joan Vansickle Sloan.)

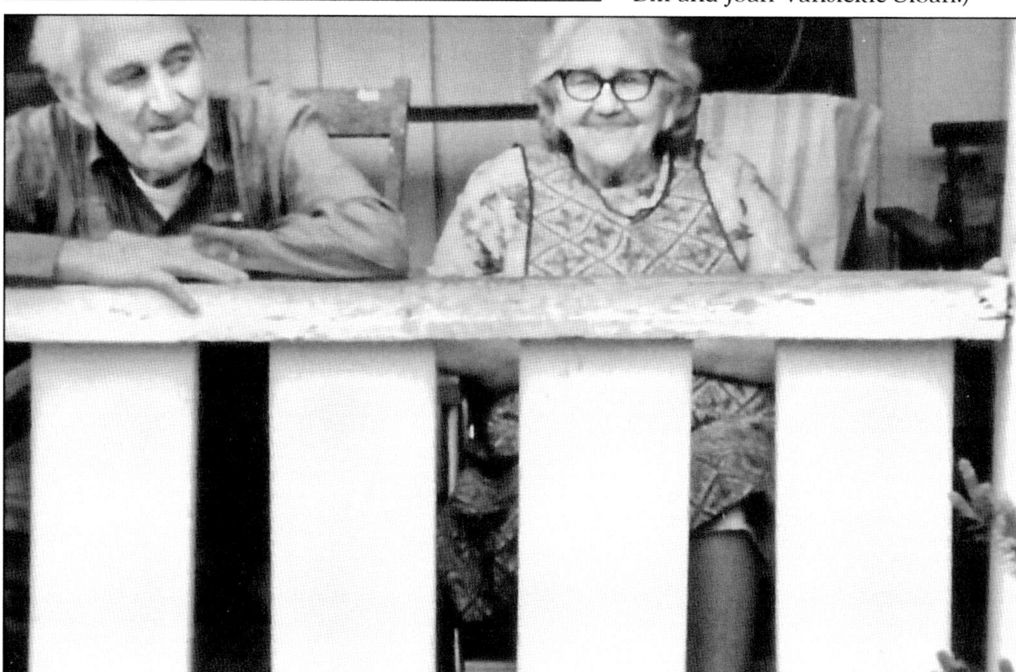

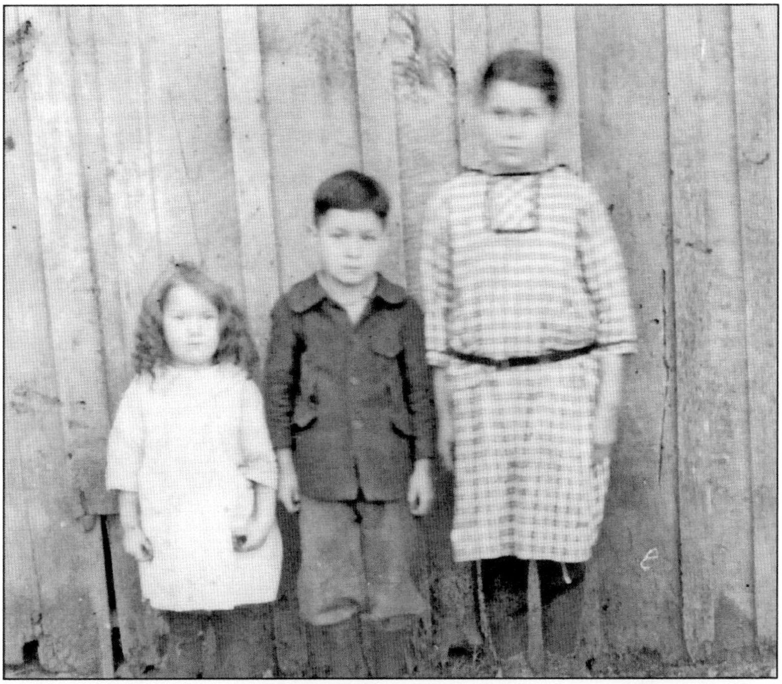

Children of Daley Lawson and Annie Walker Lawson are, from left to right, Ruth, born on March 26, 1921; Earl, born on December 18, 1918; and Oma, born on September 9, 1915. (Courtesy of Paulette Ledbetter.)

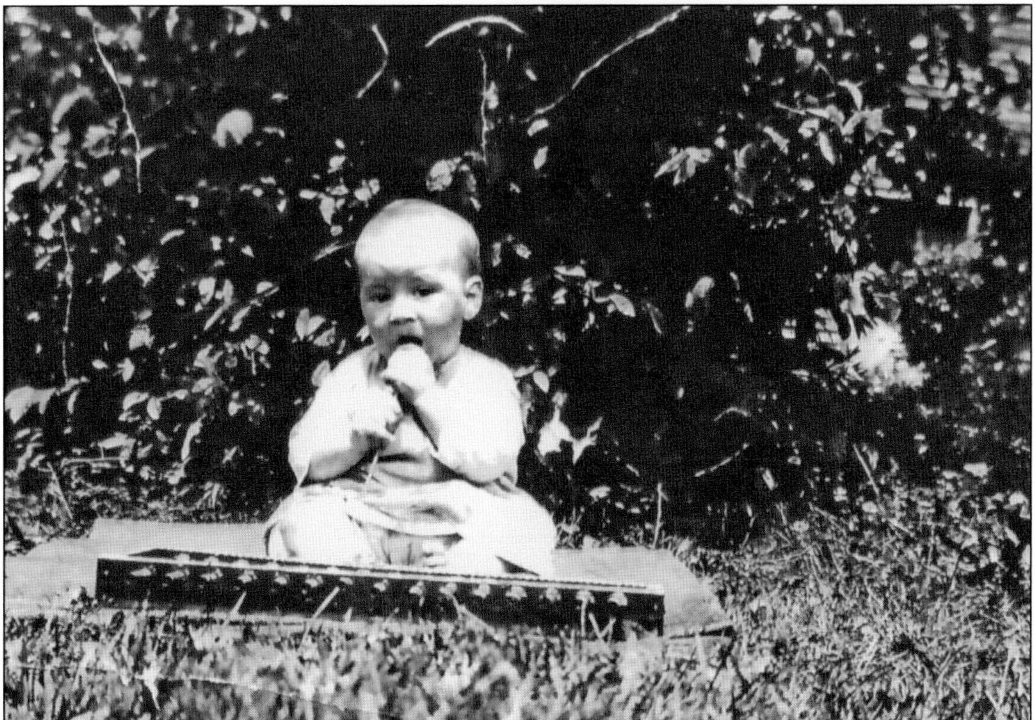

During the Great Depression, people became homeless, and many were scared and hungry. Bread lines and soup kitchens opened to feed the hungry. Sheridan Lawson was born before the start of the Depression on September 22, 1926, to Daley and Annie Walker Lawson. (Courtesy of Paulette Ledbetter.)

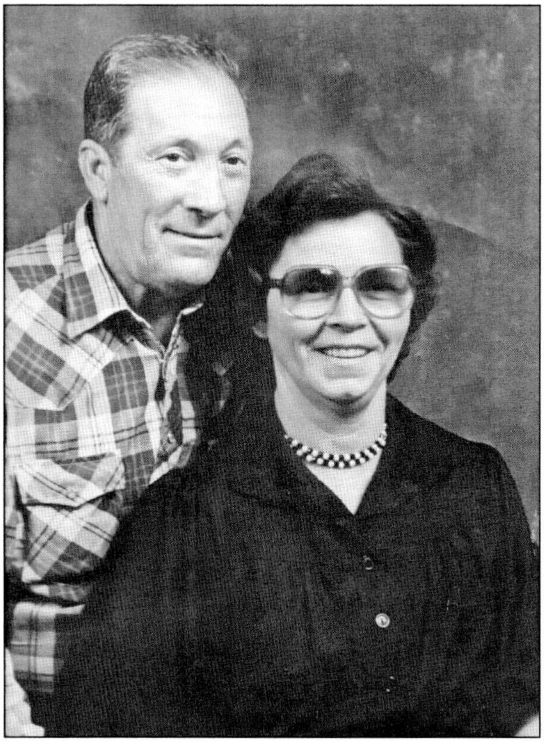

Sheridan Lawson was born on September 22, 1926, to Dally Lawson and Annie Walker Lawson of Wears Valley, Tennessee. Juanita Effler Lawson was born on July 25, 1928 to Harrison Effler and Daisy Morris Effler of Townsend, Tennessee. Sheridan and Juanita were married on June 17, 1944, with five girls and two boys born to their union; one son died young. Like most families of that time, the Lawsons had a garden to supplement food for their large family. After the ground was prepared, Sheridan would lay off the rows while Juanita cut the seed potatoes for planting. At least two eyes were needed on each cutting of the potato to be planted. After planting the potatoes, extra dirt was put around each, making a hill. Sheridan's girls' basketball team and coach helped plant the garden. The next items planted were onion sets and cabbage. This planting took place before the warm weather of spring arrived. (Both, courtesy of Paulette Lawson Ledbetter.)

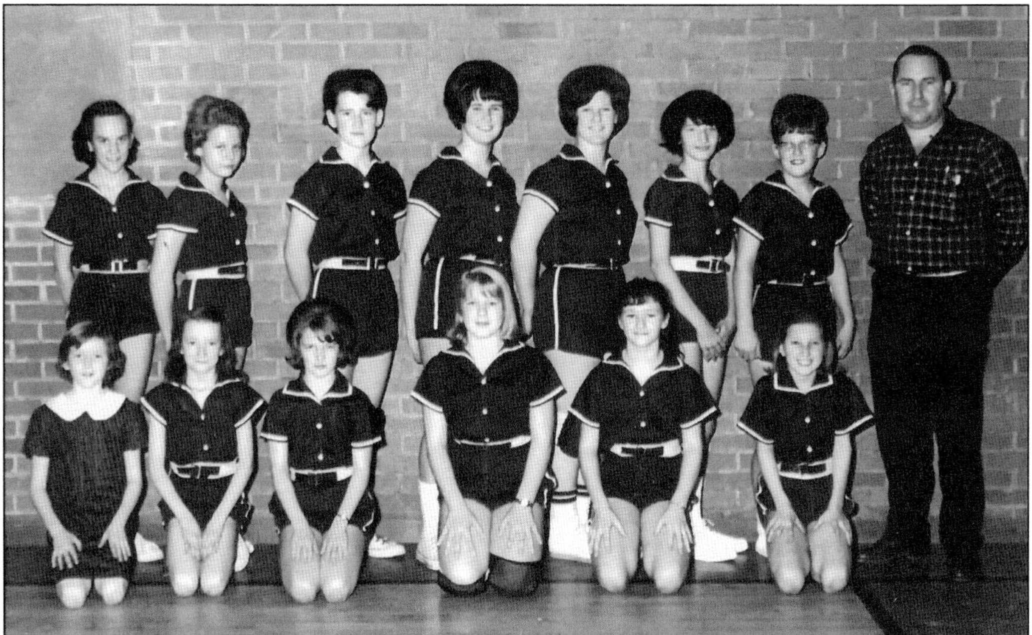

Members of the Rocky Branch girls' basketball team are pictured here. From left to right are (first row) Ginger Lawson, Darlene Cooper, Elaine Whitehead, Linda Fagg, Pam Cooper, and Kathy Proffitt; (second row) Gail Flanagan, Faye Graham, Jeannie Abbott, Carrie Henry, Rita Law, Linda Proffitt, Brenda Proffitt, and coach Gene Sloan. (Courtesy of Missy Tipton Green and Paulette Ledbetter.)

Six

Peery's Mill and Cold Springs Area

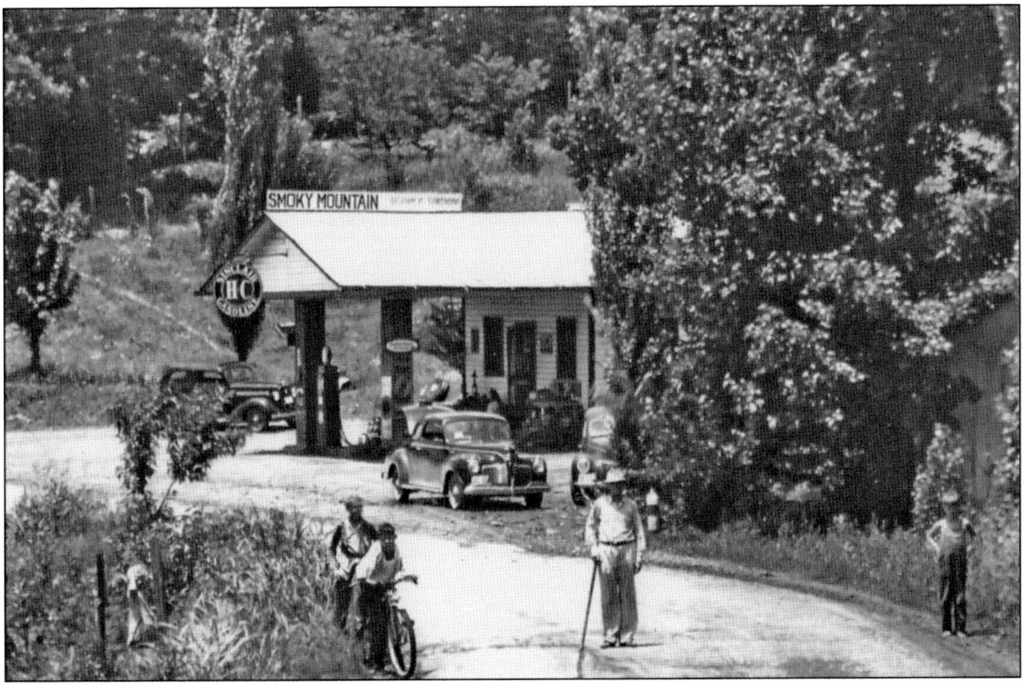

The Smoky Mountain Service Station on Old Walland Highway was built by Jack Gamble. This Sinclair station was one of the very few stations of the area; it also housed a small store. Pictured are Sandra Gamble (left), Stut Ridings (on bike in front), Jimmy Gamble (on bike in back), and Jimmy Coulter (right). (Courtesy of Carolyn Gamble Sloan.)

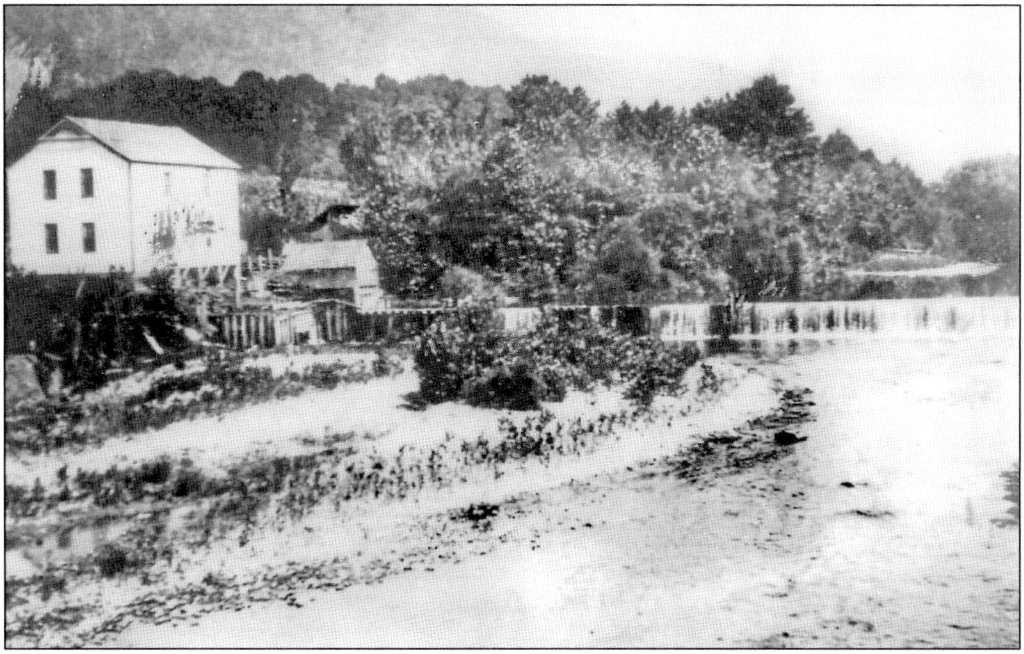

In 1841, Samuel Henry petitioned the legislature for permission to build a dam across Little River in Blount County. This permission was necessary because Little River had been declared navigable to Tuckaleechee by an act of 1801. The gristmill was built in 1842 and ran under the name Sam Henry and Sons. The mill changed hands and after August 25, 1886, ran under the name of Newbert's Mill, owned by John G. Newbert. It was sold to Scale Amerine in 1842, and Bud Hitch bought it in 1906. A few years later, it was owned by Hitch, William Wynn "Squire" Peery Sr., and Ira Peery. Within a few years, the Peerys bought out Hitch and ran the mill as Peery Brothers and Little River Mills. The Peery brothers also owned the Peery Brothers Store in Maryville. Ira Peery operated the store, and Squire Peery operated the gristmill. (Above, courtesy of Earl Adams Jr., Inez McCauley Adams Collection; below, courtesy of Missy Tipton Green.)

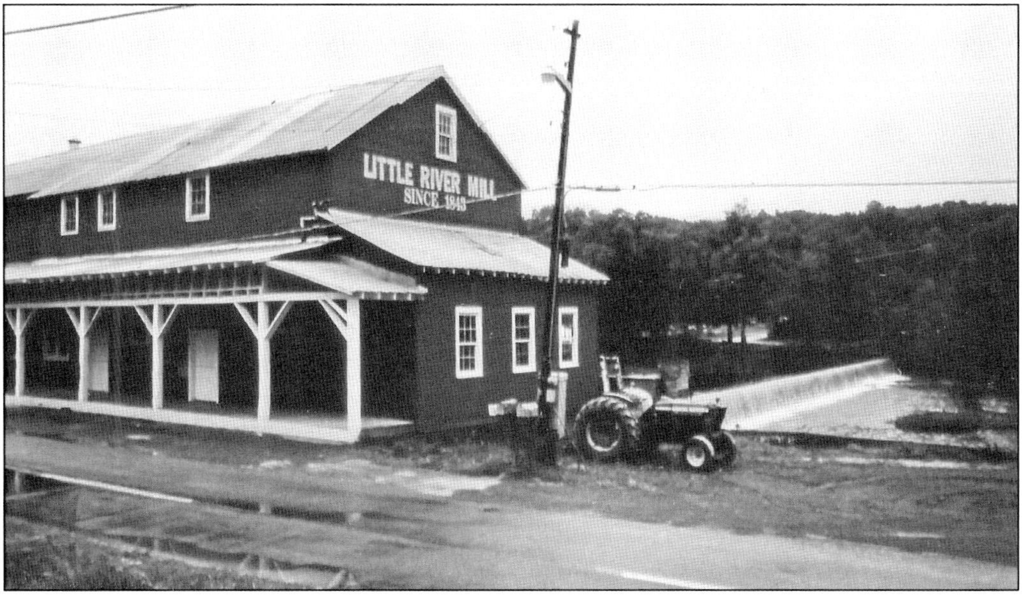

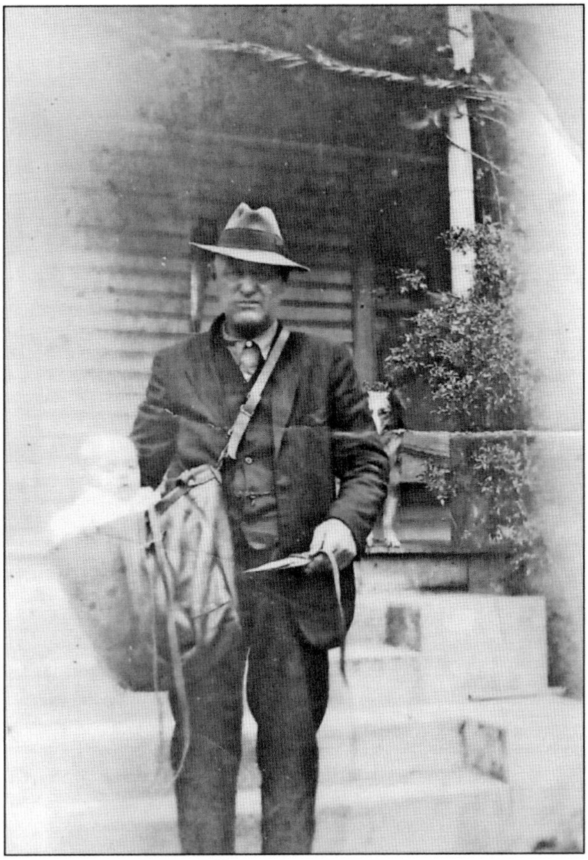

James Thomas "Jack" Gamble was born on July 22, 1870, on Little River near the Peerys' mill. In 1897, Jack married Frances McKeldry "Fannie" Walker, born on March 15, 1878, to Andrew J. Walker and Rachel Kinnamon Walker. (Courtesy of Carolyn Gamble Sloan.)

Jack Gamble built this house on Little River in 1915 for his family. Jack and Fannie Gamble had five children that grew to adulthood: Joseph Leonard, James Howard, Blanche, Aleene Walker and Mary Elma. (Courtesy of Earl Adams Jr., Inez McCauley Adams Collection.)

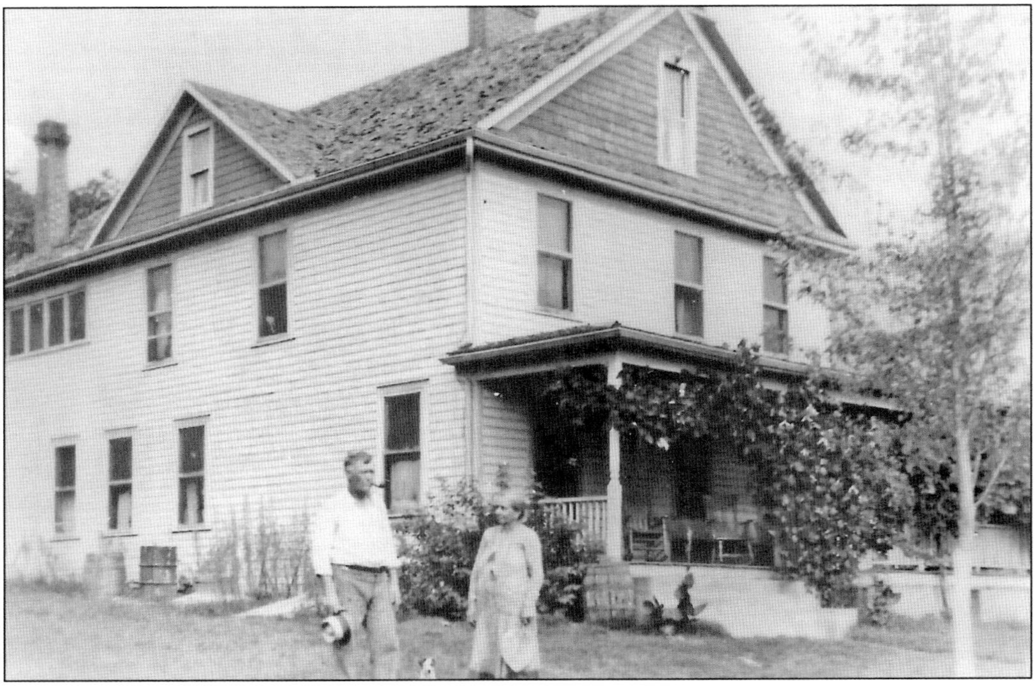

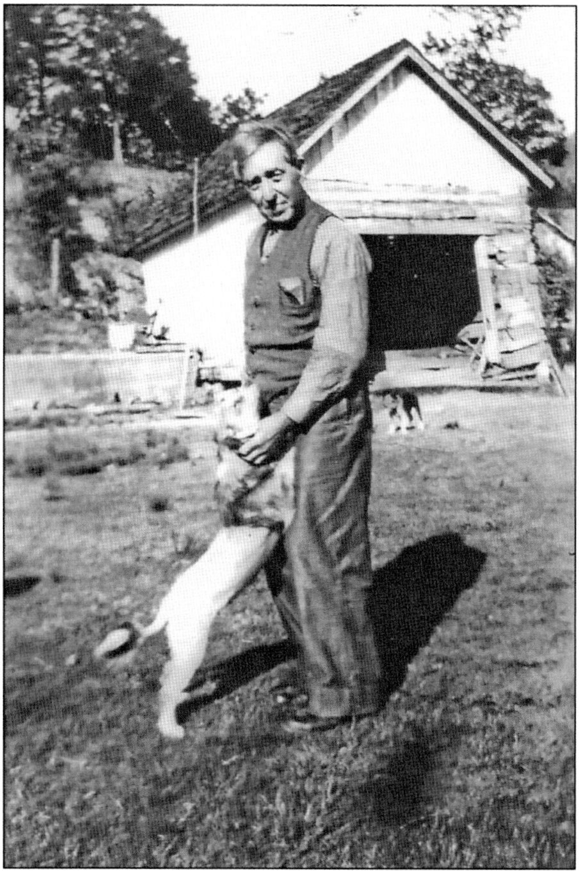

Andrew Pleasant "A.J." Walker was the son of Pleasant Walker and Fannie McKendry Perry Walker. He married Rachel T. Kinnamon on June 7, 1877. A.J. and Rachel's daughter, Fannie, married Jack Gamble, who lived on Little River in the Walland area. (Courtesy of Carolyn Gamble Sloan.)

Walker's Chapel was a Methodist church founded in 1843 by Little River on what is known today as Old Walland Highway. This church was named in honor of the man who gave the land for the church building, Samuel Walker. Eleven people placed their membership at the Walker's Chapel because there was no Methodist church in Miller's Cove. (Courtesy of Carolyn Gamble Sloan.)

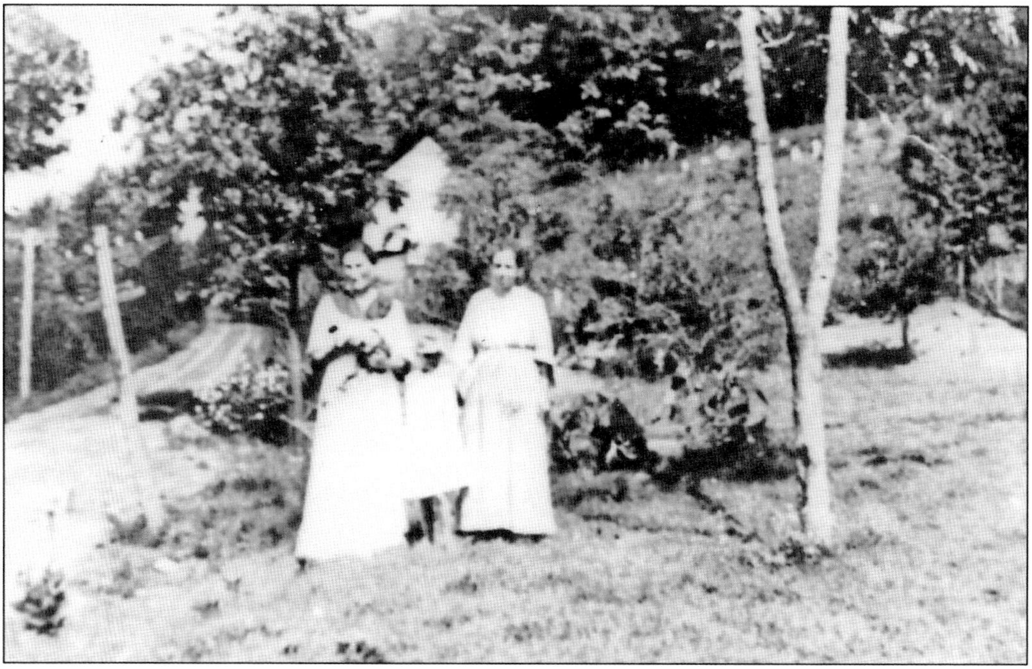

Austin Christopher Jr. married Ruth Hatcher on March 10, 1949. Austin was born on May 13, 1927, to Austin Christopher Sr. and Martha Ogle Christopher. Ruth was born on September 27, 1928, to William Oscar Hatcher and Margaret Kathern Wilson Hatcher. Pictured are Austin Jr. holding son David and Ruth holding daughter Linda. (Courtesy of Linda Christopher Baker.)

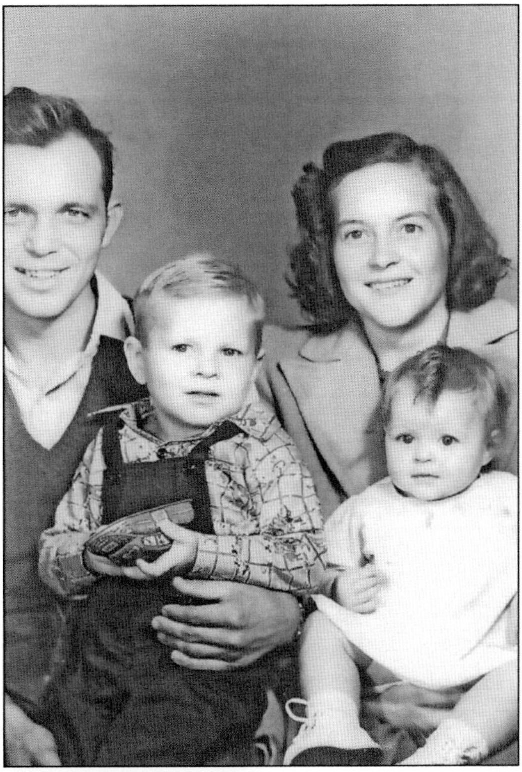

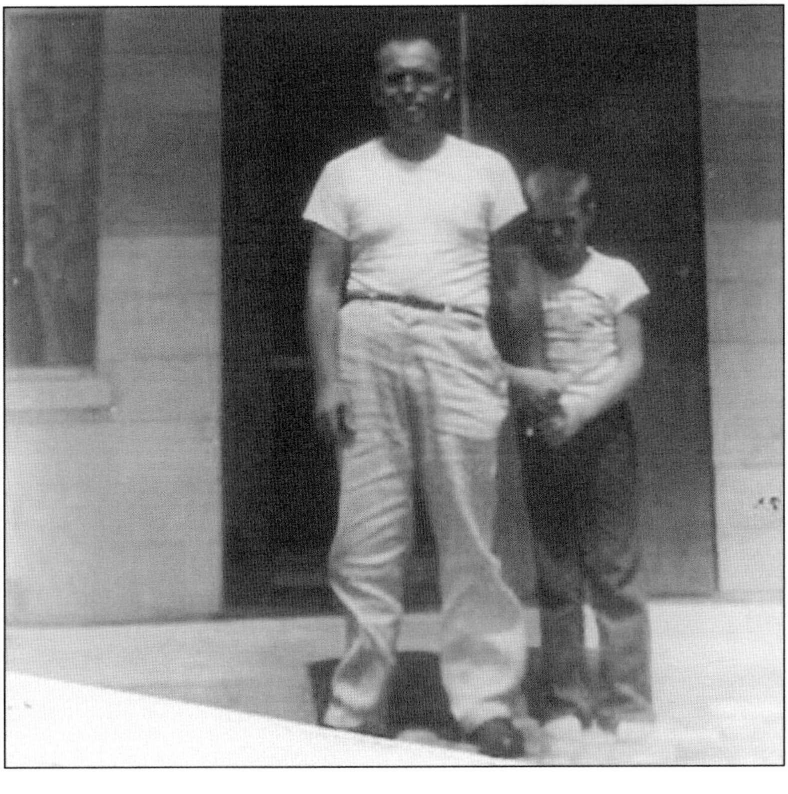

Austin Christopher Jr. and his son, David, are pictured at Christopher's Grocery in Cold Springs. Austin Jr. built this store in the fall of 1958 after the death of his father, Austin Sr., in May 1958. Austin's mother, Martha Ogle Christopher, ran the store until April 1961. Austin Jr. and his wife, Ruth Christopher, ran the store until 1964. (Courtesy of Linda Christopher Baker.)

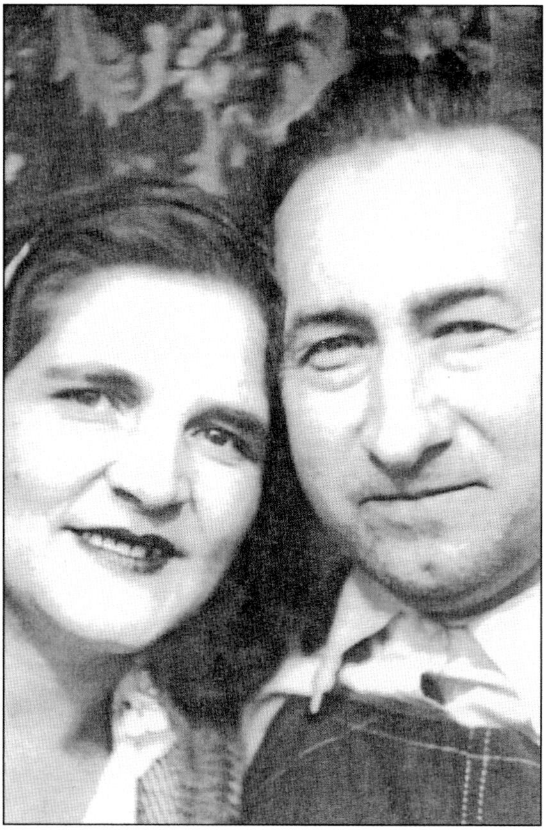

Wiley Dempsey Compton and Rosa Mable Compton lived in the Cold Springs area of Walland. Wiley was born on May 4, 1895, in Sevier County, Tennessee, to Samuel Lincoln Compton and Mary Elizabeth Reagan Compton. Rosa was born on February 18, 1905, to Jepthey Culbertson Compton and Elsie Frye Compton. (Courtesy of Mable Compton Whitehead.)

Wiley Dempsey Compton and Rosa Mable Compton's children are, from left to right, Sam, Mable, and Woody. The children walked to the nearby Cold Springs Elementary School and went on to attend Walland High School. (Courtesy of Mable Compton Whitehead.)

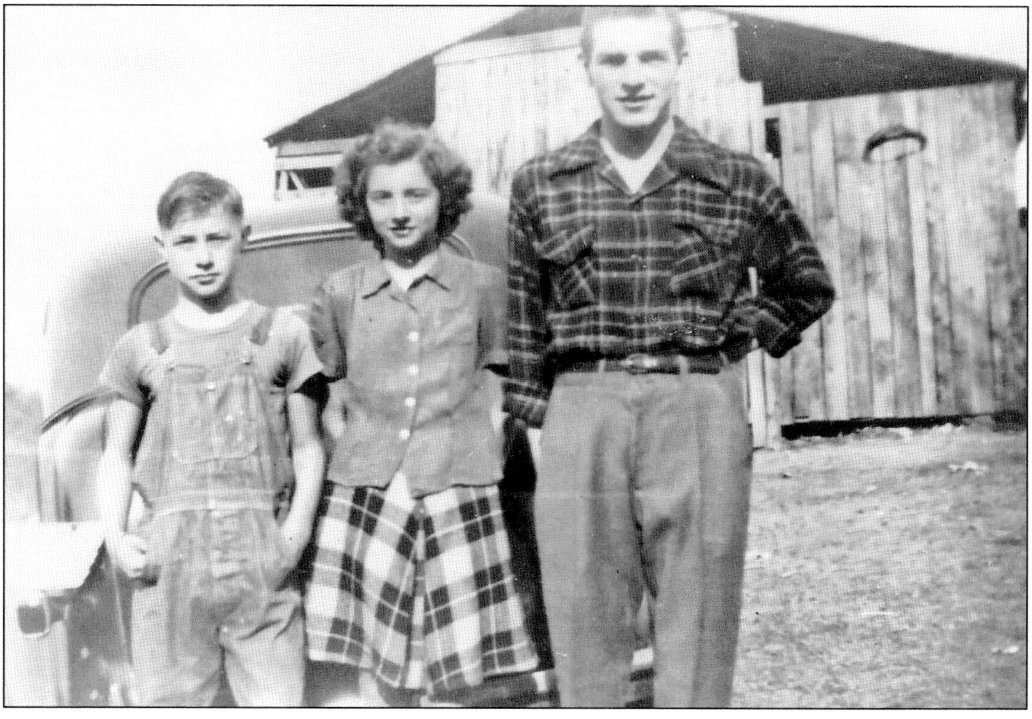

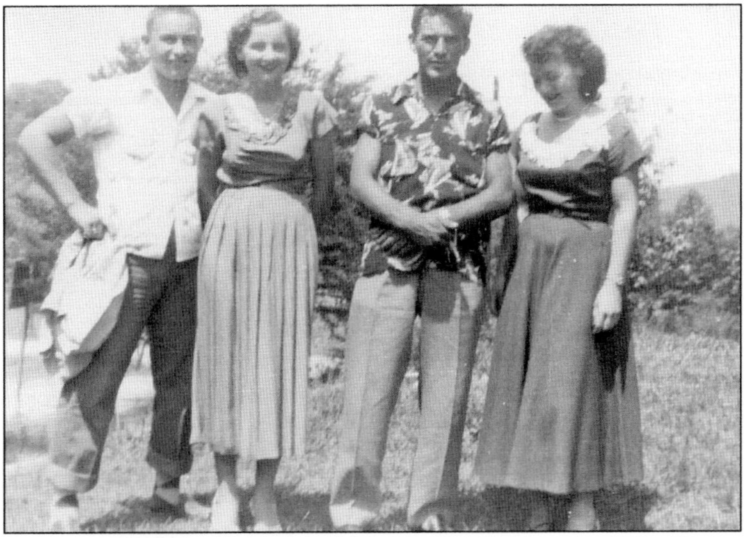

Pictured from left to right are Samuel Jepthey Compton, Willa Mae Compton, Woodrow Murphy Compton, and Mable Compton, the children of Wiley Dempsey Compton and Rosa Mable Compton of Cold Springs. (Courtesy of Mable Compton Whitehead.)

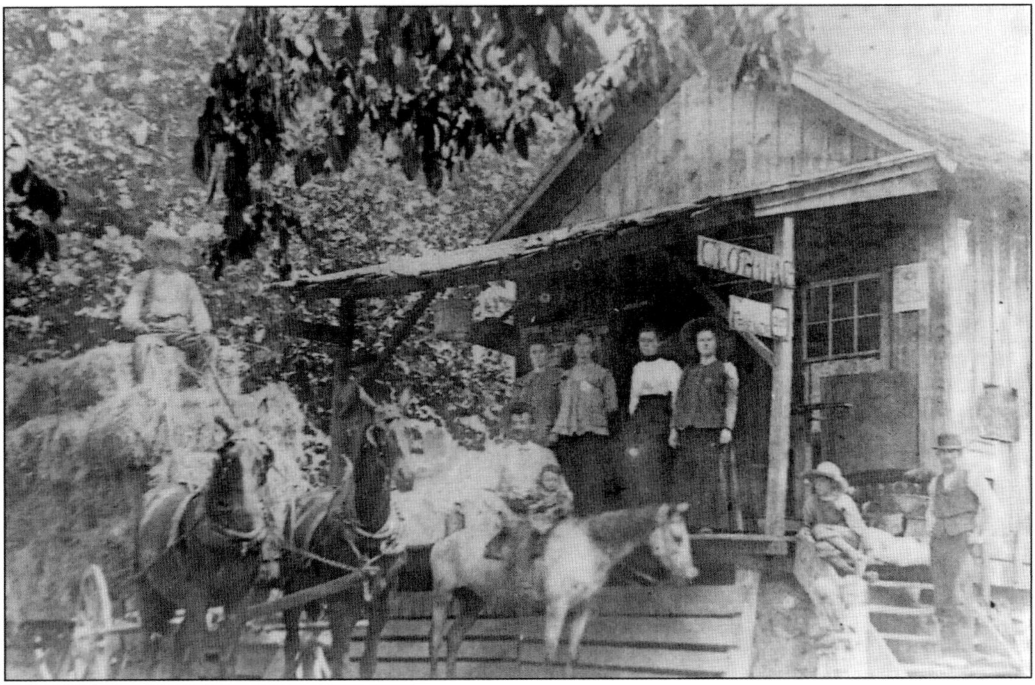

Amerine Store, run by George Amerine and his family, was located close to Peery's Mill. Items for sale included produce, nuts, beans, and nails. They were placed in old wooden barrels for storage. Items such as fabric and sewing notions, household items, soaps, medicines, spices, crockery and dishes, cartridges, and shells were also sold. When customers walked into the store, it was very dark, as the early country stores had no side windows. Sometimes the post office, if there was one, was tucked into a corner or in the back of the store. The cash register would be on the counter, maybe a coffee mill, scales for weighing grocery items and nails, and a wrapping paper unit with string attachment. Most every country store would have a pot-bellied stove surrounded by a couple of chairs, a coal bucket, a spittoon, and a checkerboard sitting atop an empty nail keg. This was the central location to visit with neighbors and enjoy a good game of checkers. (Courtesy of Missy Tipton Green.)

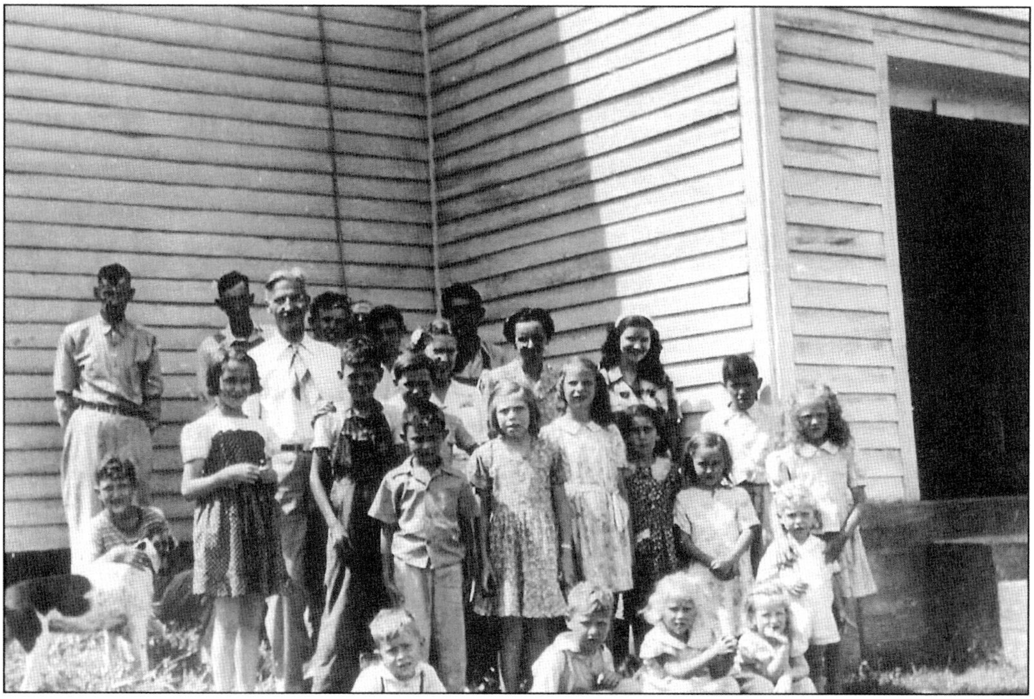

Keebles Chapel Mission, sponsored by Cold Springs Baptist Church, was organized on December 25, 1960, and began services on January 8, 1961. It was organized as a church on August 13, 1967. This church is in the small but beautiful cove of Cold Springs. The original building was old and been used at different times by Presbyterians, Methodists, and Baptists. In 1965, a new building was erected, and by the time the church was organized and the building finished in 1967, it was debt free. (Both, courtesy of Linda Christopher Baker.)

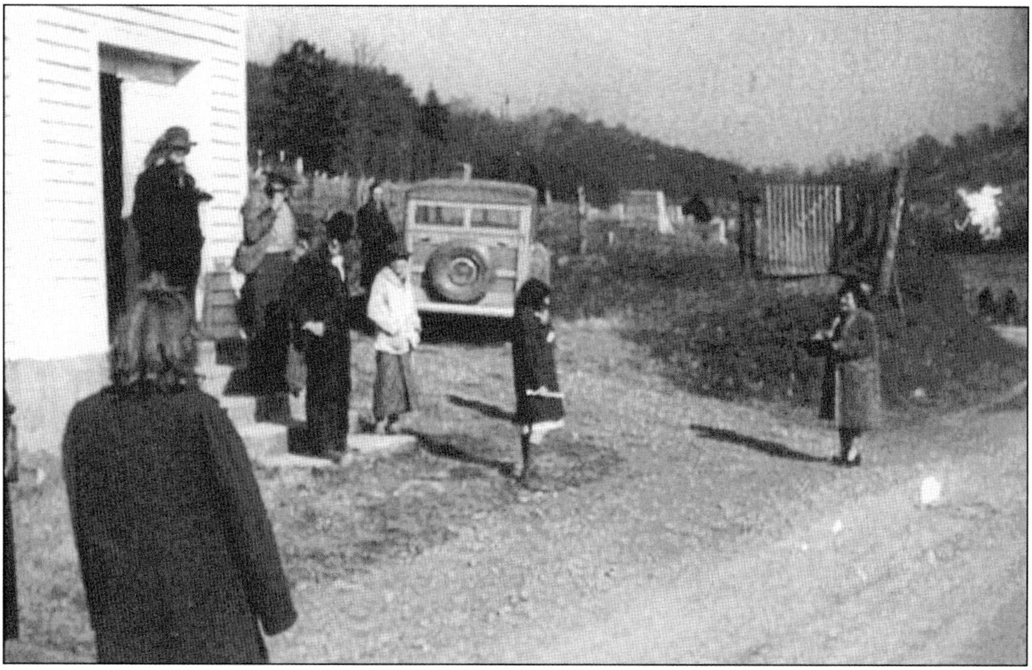

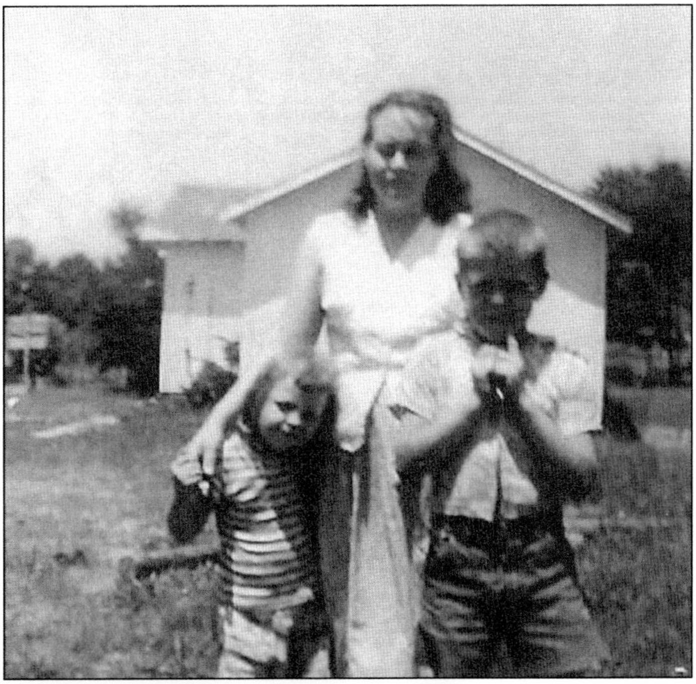

Linda, Ruth, and David Christopher are pictured standing in front of Cold Springs School. This was a two-room school, with a "Big" room and a "Little" room. The "Little" room was for grades one through four, and the "Big" room was for grades five through eight. School started at 8:00 a.m., lunch lasted for one hour, and school dismissed at 3:00 p.m. Students that attended Cold Springs School all lived in walking distance to the school, so they would walk home for their lunch. There were two outhouses: one for the boys and one for the girls. (Courtesy of Linda Christopher Baker.)

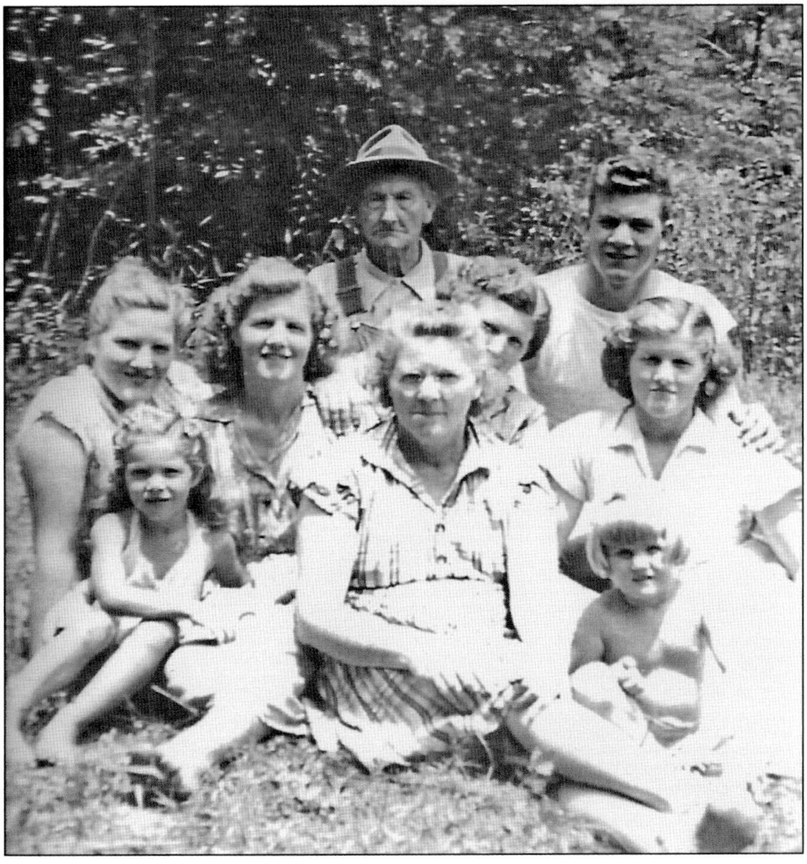

Pictured is the family of William "Huse" Houston Whitehead and Cora Blanche McClanahan Whitehead of Cold Springs. From left to right are (first row) Louise Franklin, Cora Whitehead, and Olette Davis; (second row) Selva Lou, unidentified, Gladys Davis, and Curtistine Whitehead; (third row) Jim McClanahan and Doyle Whitehead. (Courtesy of Mable Compton Whitehead.)

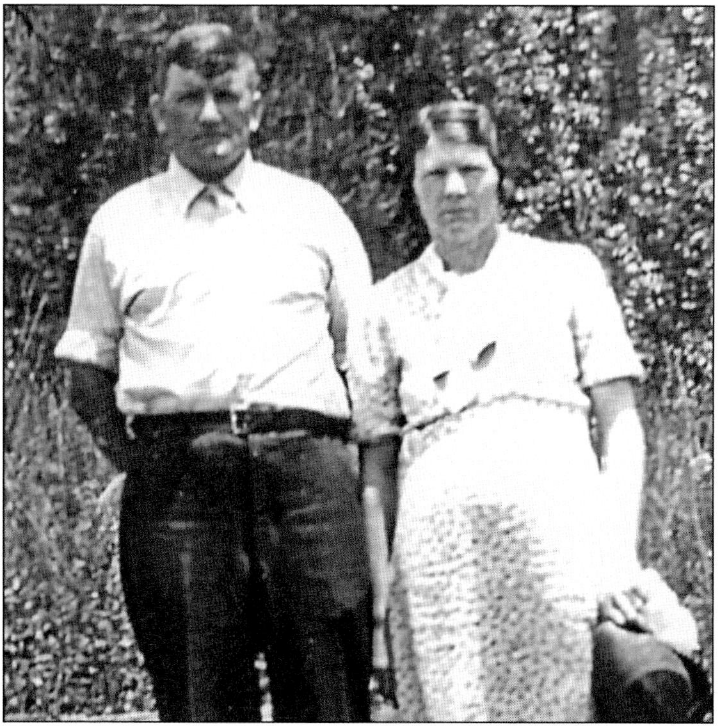

William Houston "Huse" Whitehead and Cora Blanche McClanahan were married on April 20, 1919, and made their home in Cold Springs. Huse was the son of Samuel Wilson Whitehead and Nancy Elvira Donaldson Whitehead. Cora's parents were James D. McClanahan and Margaret Louisa Davis McClanahan. (Courtesy of Mable Compton Whitehead.)

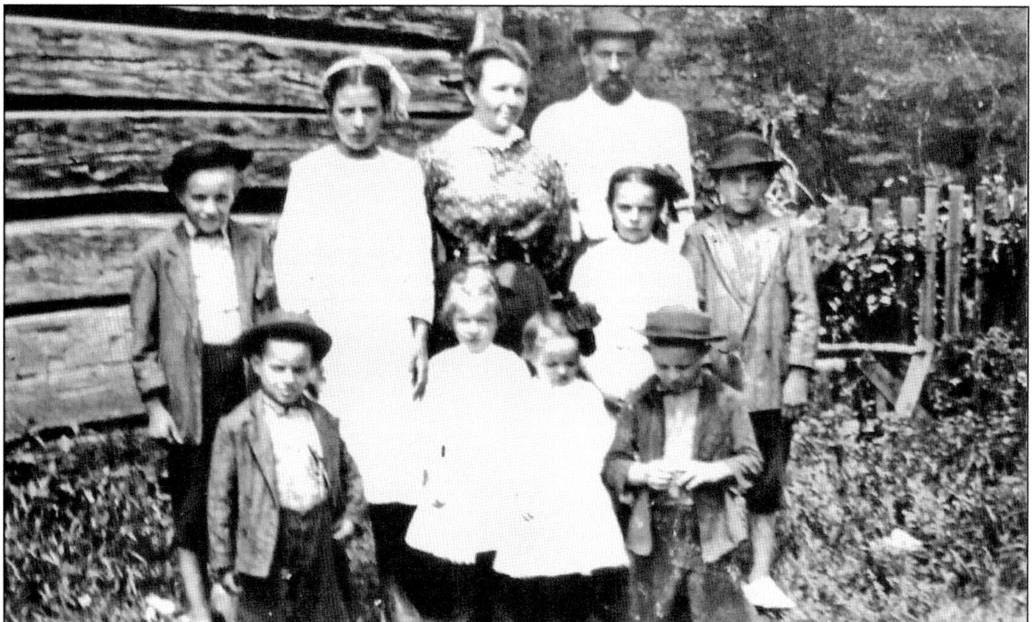

The family of John Houston and Sarah Jane Burns Whitehead of Cold Springs is pictured about 1913. From left to right are (first row) Alice and Fred; (second row) George, Ethel, Lucy, and Dock; (third row) Tom, Pearl, Sarah, and John. John and Sarah were married on December 21, 1899. John Houston Whitehead was born on June 16, 1876, to Johan Jacob Whitehead and Mary Jane Sherrill Whitehead. Sarah Jane was born on December 22, 1879, to William Thomas Burns and Mary Stillwell Burns. (Courtesy of Missy Tipton Green.)

Linda Christopher is ready to enjoy time with family and friends on Christmas morning. Linda's parents are Austin Christopher Jr. and Ruth Hatcher Christopher. (Courtesy of Linda Christopher Baker.)

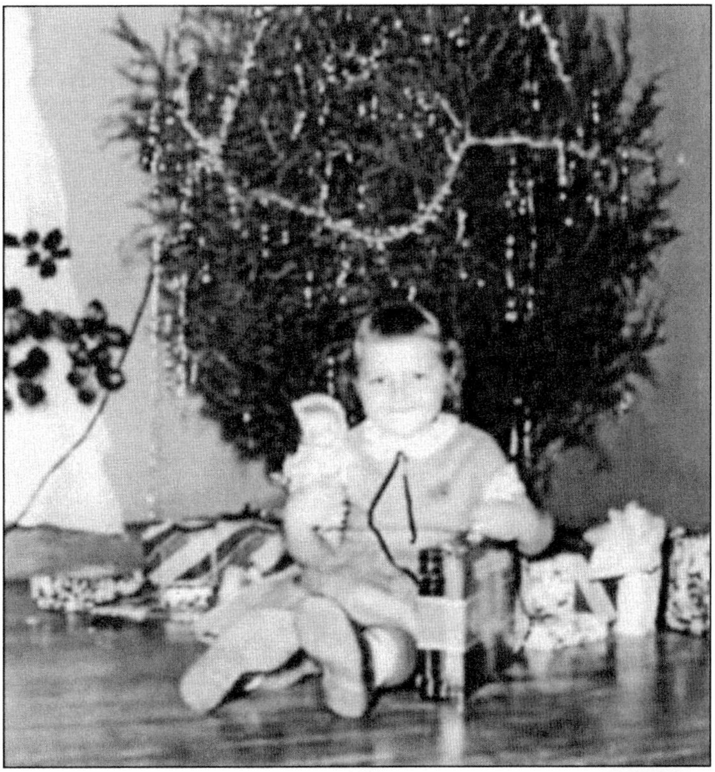

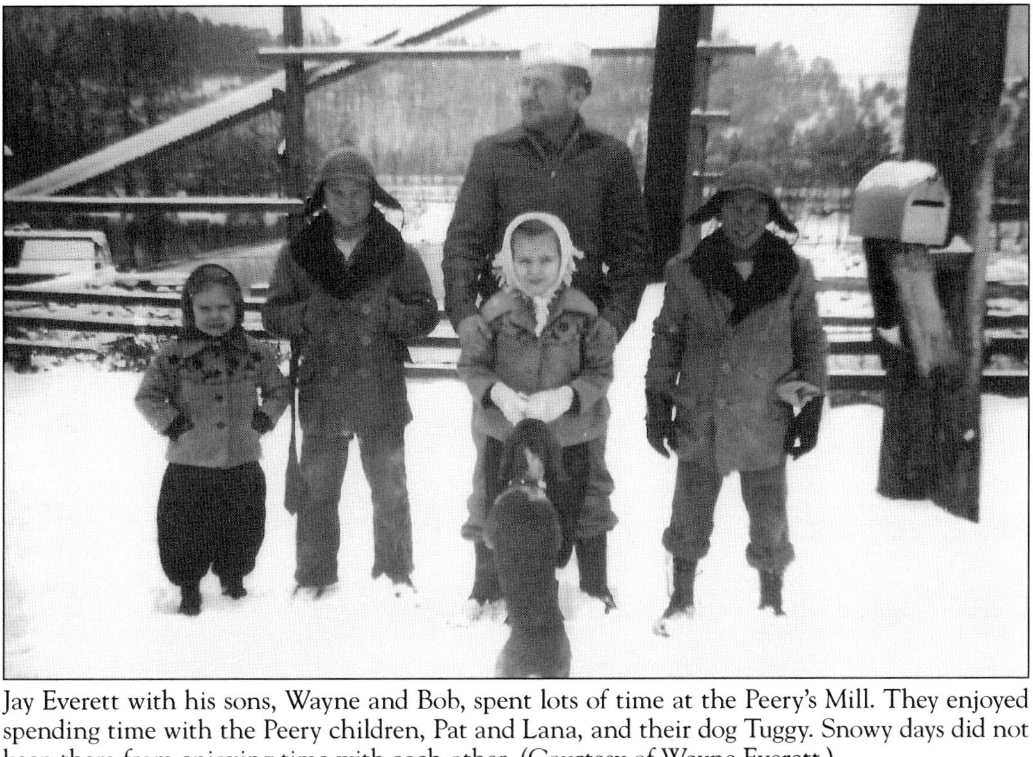

Jay Everett with his sons, Wayne and Bob, spent lots of time at the Peery's Mill. They enjoyed spending time with the Peery children, Pat and Lana, and their dog Tuggy. Snowy days did not keep them from enjoying time with each other. (Courtesy of Wayne Everett.)